LONGING FOR JUSTICE

Higher Education and Democracy's Agenda

M000101440

A timely and persuasive discussion of higher education's obligations to our democratic society, *Longing for Justice* combines personal narrative with critical analysis to make the case for educational practices that connect to questions of democracy, justice, and the common good. Jennifer S. Simpson begins with three questions. First, what is the nature of the social contract that universities have in regard to public life? Second, how might this social contract shape undergraduate education? And third, how do specific approaches to knowledge and undergraduate education inform how students understand society?

Simpson argues that today's neoliberal educational norms foreground abstract concepts and leave the complications of real life, especially the intricacies of power, unexamined. Analysing modern teaching techniques, including service learning and civic engagement, Simpson concludes that for higher education to serve democracy it must strengthen students' abilities to critically analyse social issues, recognize and challenge social inequities, and pursue justice.

JENNIFER S. SIMPSON is an associate professor and Chair of the Department of Drama and Speech Communication at the University of Waterloo.

JENNIFER S. SIMPSON

Longing for Justice

*Higher Education and
Democracy's Agenda*

UNIVERSITY OF TORONTO PRESS
Toronto Buffalo London

© University of Toronto Press 2014
Toronto Buffalo London
www.utppublishing.com
Printed in the U.S.A.

ISBN 978-0-8020-9978-5 (cloth)
ISBN 978-0-8020-9670-8 (paper)

Printed on acid-free, 100% post-consumer recycled paper with
vegetable-based inks.

Library and Archives Canada Cataloguing in Publication

Simpson, Jennifer S., author
Longing for justice : higher education and democracy's agenda /
Jennifer S. Simpson.

Includes bibliographical references and index.
ISBN 978-0-8020-9978-5 (bound). – ISBN 978-0-8020-9670-8 (pbk.)

1. Education, Higher – Social aspects.   2. Education, Higher – Political
aspects.   3. Democracy and education.   4. Higher education
and state.   5. Political participation.   I. Title.

LB2322.2.S54 2014   378'.0.15   C2014-905011-9

University of Toronto Press acknowledges the financial assistance to its
publishing program of the Canada Council for the Arts and the Ontario
Arts Council.

University of Toronto Press acknowledges the financial support of the
Government of Canada through the Canada Book Fund for its publishing
activities.

Contents

Acknowledgments

Over the past several years, the support, insights, and commitments of numerous individuals have contributed to the content and completion of this book. I have been extremely fortunate to have been in conversation with these colleagues.

Tony Chambers, Elizabeth Minnich, Alma Clayton-Pedersen, and John Saltmarsh, often in the context of meetings hosted by the Association of American Colleges and Universities, have kept me attuned to the challenges and priorities of a liberal arts education. Elizabeth Minnich helped me sort out central ideas and questions in the very early stages of my thinking about the manuscript. Through dialogue and suggestions regarding chapter 3, John Saltmarsh has sharpened my understanding of civic engagement and service learning. Gust A. Yep and John P. Elias offered important feedback to the ideas and content in chapter 6, related to queer theory and neoliberalism. Portions of chapter 6 draw on an article entitled "'I Thought This Course Was Going to Be Streamlined!': The Limits of Normal and the Possibilities of Transgression," published in 2012 in volume 59 (no. 7) of the *Journal of Homosexuality*, and are used with the permission of Taylor and Francis Group, LLC.

I am grateful for the work of several research assistants over the past few years, including Jennifer Guo, Leahjane Robinson, and Erin Yun. They all assisted in important ways with specific areas of content. Ongoing dialogue with Erin has also been a source of encouragement and hopefulness in the context of addressing numerous challenges related to higher education and justice.

Dwight Conquergood, Toinette Eugene, and Sandra Richards were for me both superb teachers and exceptional intellectual mentors during my graduate work, and their early and substantive commitments to my education continue to ground my current intellectual pursuits. I value as well the ongoing friendship and conversation with Toinette Eugene and Sandra Richards.

Over the past few years, I have had the privilege of directing the Anti-Colonial Project, a research and knowledge mobilization effort addressing ongoing forms of racism and colonialism in Canada. Collaboration with members of this project has been invaluable. This work has kept in the foreground the importance of moving content and dialogue about the costs and consequences of systemic inequity to the centre of educational institutions. Conversations with members of this project, and in particular Martin Cannon, Alison Duke, Eve Haque, Tasha Hubbard, Carl James, Yasmin Jiwani, Shelina Kassam, Johnny Mack, Minelle Mahtani, Mona Oikawa, Liss Platt, Gordon Pon, Anthony Stewart, and Verna St. Denis, have been insightful and instructive. I appreciate the conversations with Rinaldo Walcott about "structures of believability" and education more generally. Exchanges with Minelle Mahtani, as we worked on books at the same time, were instructive, and I value Minelle's consistent encouragement. Sherene Razack read and offered useful feedback on chapters 1 and 4.

I am also fortunate to work in a department at my home institution that offers an engaging intellectual environment in which to do the work of teaching, research, and service. Conversations I have had and continue to have with my departmental colleagues about program and curricular objectives have allowed me the opportunity to work at the ideas in this book in an immediate and concrete way. Rob Danisch, a faculty colleague, read the entire manuscript and offered crucial feedback. I greatly appreciate the financial support offered through the Faculty of Arts and the Office of Research at the University of Waterloo, which contributed to preliminary research and pre-publication requirements.

It has been a pleasure to work with the University of Toronto Press. Doug Hildebrand has been unfailingly professional and insightful in his role as editor. I appreciate the comments of three anonymous reviewers, as well as the feedback offered by the book's copyeditor.

Anna-Maria Schultheis has, when and as I needed, listened, supported, and encouraged my work on this book over the past several years. In my experience, completion of a book requires both specific intellectual capacities and the knowledge, in moments of confidence and especially of doubt, that I have something worth saying, and the ability to say it. Anna-Maria helped me hold on to this knowledge, and I deeply appreciate her caring and companionship.

LONGING FOR JUSTICE

Higher Education and Democracy's Agenda

1 Higher Education and Democracy's Agenda: Resisting "Streamlined" Education

In the winter term of 2008, I taught a Gender, Communication, and Culture course. A common offering in communication departments, the course broadly addresses the influence of gender and communication on each other. Syllabi for classes on gender and communication note the importance of "understanding various perspectives of communication as they relate to the social construction of gender" (Blewett), refer to coverage of "the range of perspectives available on the relationship between gender and communication" (Foss, 2009), and prioritize increased "aware[ness] of gender hierarchies" (Earnheardt, "Gender Communication Syllabus"). Ideally, in such courses, students will learn to better understand and respond to the ways in which gender norms act to limit the contributions that individuals make in a range of settings, including the workplace, family, and leisure contexts. Following such a course, students might be better able to recognize and address gender stereotypes at work or to talk about how sexism is operative in their own lives and relationships.

Three weeks into the course I taught in 2008, the students had read a chapter from a book that examined the idea that gendered communication practices are learned. This chapter outlined the ways in which behaviours associated with a particular gender, such as nurturing as typically feminine or assertiveness as generally masculine, are connected to both conventions and ideologies. The authors discussed the ways in which many of these behaviours become "common sense" over time through a process of "naturalization," even as they are not, in fact, "natural" but constructed and chosen (Eckert & McConnell-Ginet, 2003, p. 43). I planned to begin class by asking students to identify what they had learned from this chapter. In pairs, the class of about 25 students would answer two questions: What is one idea from this reading that will stay with you? What is one question that you have after completing this reading? I asked each group to write their responses to these questions on the board. In the classroom, the students moved quickly into conversations. Within a few minutes, they are up and writing. When each pair has finished responding to the two questions, I encourage the students to read what is on the board. Then I ask: "Where do you want to begin the conversation?"

One student draws our attention to the following response: "What about masculine women and feminine men?" The student who wrote this on the board explains: "I've been thinking about this. If how we communicate in relation to our gender is naturalized, then why is it that sometimes women do what is considered masculine, and men do what is considered feminine?" Students are nodding; they are interested. They talk as a whole class, disagree with each other, ask questions. The discussion focuses on gender roles and stereotypes, on how the students act in correspondence or not with what is expected of them in relation to their gender, and on dating, always the opposite sex, per their examples: "he" paired with "she." This information is familiar – students date; they know the complexities of masculine and feminine behaviour; they think routinely about gender-related norms at the gym, at work, with their parents and friends; and they are consciously aware of when they act in accordance with and in opposition to role expectations. A few of their comments are relatively mundane, clearly not achieving the complexity I hope we will reach in terms of conceptual understanding. Yet, the students are all here, present. My hope is that starting here, where they are engaged, will encourage deeper levels of investment as we move to a more complex discussion.

When they momentarily pause, I say: "You are doing a great job with these issues. You have clearly understood central concepts in the reading. I wonder, where is sexuality in your ideas? Most of you have talked about gender and heterosexuality. Are you assuming that all people are straight? Is what you have said true only for straight people? The course objectives clearly state that the concept of sexuality is important in this class. Do you think about gender and communication and the differences of being straight, gay, lesbian? What is going on for you here?" I am intentionally raising these questions, as a kind of notice for them. I am letting them know, "We will address sexuality in this class." I do not expect a thorough response to my questions during this class meeting.

I hope the fact that the questions are on the table, and early in the term, will lend support to future attention to these issues.

There is a moment or two of silence. Then, the students offer an abundance of explanations: "Related to gender, sexuality is not really relevant." "Sexual identity shouldn't matter." "You know, gays and lesbians are really exceptions." "I want people to come to me as a clean slate." "Categories do not matter – ultimately we are all people."

A few students have a different perspective. "It seems like you [said to another student] are being defensive. Don't you think sexuality matters?" "Whoa, what's going on? Jennifer did not accuse us. She asked a question." "Jennifer is challenging us to think about the connection of gender and sexuality. Why shouldn't we do this?"

In the pause, I remind them: "In this class, we will consider sexuality. Queer individuals and communities – they are an intentional part of the course, not a topic we will cover by chance."[1] I continue to respond to their comments: "You just spoke in very sophisticated ways about how gender matters, about how categories for what is considered masculine and feminine are important in your own lives. Why is it that when I asked about sexuality, categories do not matter? What does it mean to say about a person, about a group of people – they are an exception? What is going on here? We will come back to this – what we do with difference, where we put it, how we talk about it."

I am ready to call for a break. The atmosphere is still slightly charged. Too many questions remain among us, unanswered. The students did a great deal of work in the first part of the discussion. I sense that they initially felt that they had a strong grasp of the material. Indeed, I affirmed this. I have tipped this grasp over, said "yes" to their discussion, and then asked: "What about ..." They know we will take a 10-minute break soon, and they seem eager for the easy familiarity of checking voice mail, getting coffee, talking with friends. As I open my mouth to say it is time for the break, Cindy, a young woman in her fourth year of university, states with a mixture of intensity, surprise, and concern: "I thought this course was going to be streamlined!"

"Streamlined?" I ask myself. Even as her comment is firm, an undeniable claim, it also seems wholly detached from my pedagogical goals. Immediately, with the reference to "streamlined" education, Cindy has dropped a clear challenge into the room: What are we doing here? What do you want? Cindy's assertion seems spontaneous on her part. It also succinctly names a kind of epistemological fault line on which we are already standing: What exactly is knowledge? Will it contain or crack open, simplify or unsettle? Simplify whose lives? Unsettle whose take on how gender works?

Cindy's comment momentarily jars. I also feel an amused irony. Streamlined? This has not entered my mind in relation to any course I teach. What are we up to, each of us, all of us? What has this student learned to expect? How do educators negotiate that epistemological fault line? What is the subject, and how do we decide? Cindy was asking an important question about the content of a course on gender, communication, and culture. When it comes to queer lives and communities, are they in or out? Are they part of the subject or not?

In a broader sense, as educators, we routinely consider the shape of our courses, the content that we will foreground, and the ideas with which we want students to be familiar by the end of the term. In ensuring that the course I was teaching offered attention to gender and sexuality, I was perhaps representing the social in ways that were problematic for Cindy. Education is in part the construction of a "we," of how faculty members and instructors envision course subject matter in relation to how such subject matter acts on bodies, and the ways in which that subject matter has consequences for how people live. The discord between Cindy's comment and my pedagogical priorities points to central questions in the context of undergraduate education. What is the subject? Who is the "we"? How do we, as faculty members, understand and act on our obligations to the social?

This book centrally explores the interrelationship of three broad questions. First, what is the nature of the social contract that universities have with public life?[2] For those in post-secondary institutions who acknowledge the existence of such a contract, what does it demand? Second, what is the "subject" of any given course or discipline? In a course addressing, for example, communication and gender, are queer lives and communities part of the subject, content worth knowing, or not? Finally, in what ways do specific epistemological frameworks inform constructions of the social? How do epistemologies lead, for instance, to a notion of a "we" that boldly denies the relevance, for example, of queer lives? I assume that responses to such questions are inevitable. In all of our teaching, faculty members "talk back" to these three concerns. Our primary starting points and assumptions, and the ways in which we conceptualize and present course content, profoundly shape what students learn, as well as students' capacities and desires in regard to imagining the relationship of self and other.

Scholars generally agree that education and knowledge production constitute the two primary tasks of higher education (Daniels & Trebilcock, 2005). Less discussion exists as to the ends to which these tasks might be directed. Education has profound implications for public life. The years that students engage in completing a degree reach far beyond the confines of the classroom. At a minimum, students graduate with a stronger grasp of a particular subject area. At best, they improve their abilities to think through issues and across concepts and to consider a range of often-conflicting viewpoints. Students develop ideas about what is important, expected, and possible. What students learn shapes the ways in which they understand the intricacies of relationships, the workings of communities, the demands of social issues, and the glare of individual and institutional inequities. This book grapples with the ways in which undergraduate education bears on all aspects of social life.

Universities are undeniably implicated outside of the institution: research results inform policy, contribute to advances in a range of fields, and speak to difficult social questions. Graduates take up positions of relevance and influence across the public and private sectors. University education – deciding what counts as the subject in any given course, which knowledge will be included and which left out, and how students will learn and be evaluated – is always a way of marking what matters and how. Education is a way of asserting these concepts matter, and others do not; these ways of understanding the subject are valid, and others are not. As instructors, we have a range of expectations of our students. We ask that they analyse, memorize concepts, think independently, question their own beliefs, challenge each other, consider their responsibilities to life outside of the classroom, accept the legitimacy of textbook knowledge and the assumptions within a discipline, and bring their own ideas to the classroom or leave those ideas at home. Students learn to use knowledge so that they can simplify, complicate, generalize, specify, mimic, maintain, and resist. Particularly in relation to undergraduate education, higher education is an institution that shapes habits of knowing and doing, constructs the ways in which graduates see the world in which they live, and contributes to social norms in terms of understanding self and other. What kinds of habits, ways of seeing the world, and social norms do universities affirm? Within the profound and complex educative role higher education inhabits, universities have a responsibility to consider how the work of undergraduate education considers or not the public good and related social issues.

A careful rationale for the components and reach of this responsibility might provide a great deal of clarity at a time when universities are facing several challenges. Scholarship has addressed the importance of educators articulating the relevance of universities to the broader public (National Task Force on Civic Learning and Democratic Engagement, 2012; Axelrod, 2002; Bok, 2006; Chambers, 2005; Dzur, 2008; London, 2003). Institutions of higher education in North America are struggling simultaneously with reduced public funding and with pressures to commercialize (Polster, 2002, 2006; Tudiver, 1999; Turk, 2008). Scholars have offered attention to student engagement and grade inflation and to appropriate and desirable educational outcomes and the kind of knowledge that will support such outcomes (Axelrod, 2002; Bok, 2006; Côté & Allahar, 2007; Fallis, 2007; Giroux, 2007b; Nussbaum, 1997; Pocklington & Tupper, 2002).

Questions about knowledge persist. Should students leave higher education with breadth or depth in a certain subject area, or both? Is knowledge a resource separate from the values one has, or is knowledge always "interested," with priorities? Many scholars assert that knowledge has failed to adequately recognize and account for existing forms of oppression. Do representations of knowledge continue to harm those the dominant group has defined as "Other" (Collins, 1998; Dunne, 2009; Hokowhitu, 2009; Mbembe, 2001; Mignolo, 2009; Mohanty, 2003; Razack, 1998; Smith, 2001)? Further, what are higher education's responsibilities to the material conditions of how people live, and what is the role of knowledge in relation to these responsibilities?

While scholars have paid considerable attention to undergraduate education and its connection to democratic life (Boyte, 2008; Colby et al., 2007; Côté & Allahar, 2007; Hansen, 2006; Kezar, Chambers, & Burkhardt, 2005; Lund & Carr, 2008b; Westheimer & Kahne, 2004), many questions remain unanswered or call for additional clarity. What kinds of knowledge do students need in a democratic society? What ethical framework might best ground the work of higher education? To whom and to what are universities primarily accountable, and what does this mean for curriculum and pedagogy? Much of the literature that addresses broad questions about democracy and higher education does so at abstract and primarily conceptual levels (Côté & Allahar, 2007; Fallis, 2007; Hansen, 2006), leaving largely unexamined the complications of real life, the tangle of social relationships, and the intricacies and reach of power.[3] When scholars do explicitly take power into account, and substantively consider the existence of injustice (Collins,

2000; Giroux, 2007b; Razack, 1998), critics charge that these scholars lack objectivity, that they are inappropriately taking sides, and/or that they have an agenda (see, e.g., Fallis, 2007, pp. 136–137). What does consideration of democratic practices and the public good demand of undergraduate education and of knowledge? When instructors teach, what is it that we want to offer to our students? As educators, what conceptual framework informs our intellectual and pedagogical work? In what ways do we consider democracy, the public good, and justice?

Situating democratic practices, the public good, and justice as ethical priorities for universities does not necessitate the imposition of a particular radical, liberal, or conservative political agenda. Rather, it affirms that democratic societies do endorse a set of values and that universities have an obligation to consider and support these values. Democratic societies demand of those of us involved in higher education that we pursue the work we do with our eyes open to the material conditions of how people live. Broadly understood, democratic practices allow individuals and groups to construct the communities we want to inhabit (Dallmayr, 2011; Darder, 2011; Dryzek, 2000). They include the means by which we might engage each other, address conflict, consider the uses and consequences of power, and respond to long-standing social problems (Della Porta & Rucht, 2013a, 2013b). In a strong democracy, the public good is not an empty notion. Rather, people have a language and an imagination for what the public good is and looks like. As healthy democracies rest, to at least some extent, on the presence of justice and the absence of injustice, democratic practices also call for consideration of and attention to equity. While insisting on one "correct" way to link higher education with democratic practices, the public good, and justice is profoundly problematic, I will assert in this book that the socio-ethical framework that grounds the work of universities ought to thoughtfully attend to all three.

Practising democracy, longing for justice: this book starts with a set of investments in higher education, investments that are simultaneously my own and that are grounded in a broader intellectual framework. All education and knowledge production are meticulously constructed statements about what matters. The material we teach and the knowledge we pursue represent the complicated maps of our own commitments, our stake not simply in knowledge itself, but in knowledge that has significance in specific ways. Practising democracy, longing for justice: one way to set down the weight and shape of my own allegiances, to name an intellectual and affective loyalty to teaching and knowledge production that matter to how people live together. The work of education – shaping curriculum within a discipline, articulating learning objectives, making decisions about course content, and forming judgments about disciplinary assumptions and norms – is always a response. Such work is a way of taking up and talking back to what and how we see, to our understandings of our subject areas, and to what we imagine we can contribute. Where do your own loyalties reside? What about your own teaching and knowledge practices has weight and significance? What draws your attention and commitment? Our teaching and our representations of knowledge are always forms of investment, of setting priorities, and of marking our own beliefs and agendas. They are, at their core, the ways we demonstrate the intricate patterns of our own caring.

Practising democracy and longing for justice make claims on the work of higher education, demand a responsiveness to specific priorities and values, and ask those in higher education to consider the consequences of our intellectual investments. Democratic societies depend on certain habits and rely on the individuals that live in them to participate in social life in very particular ways. What are higher education's responsibilities towards these habits, and how can it best fulfil them? Asserting that higher education has responsibilities in a democratic society is an act of profound hopefulness and one that requires a deliberate and thoughtful response. This chapter provides a brief overview of the scholarly, social, and ethical contexts in which this book sits; articulates the book's primary contributions; and provides an overview of the book's contents.

Education and Knowledge: Questions of Practice

This book explores the demands that democratic societies place on universities, particularly in the context of undergraduate education. It asserts that knowledge and education are not neutral, but that they serve concrete interests and lead to specific ends. One can readily affirm the general benefits of a university degree, such as increased grasp of a subject matter, improved thinking skills, and a broadened perspective. These benefits do not, in and of themselves, ensure any particular set of consequences or practices, nor do they explicitly point to any specific ethical orientation or set of ethical priorities. Improved thinking can be used to increase a business's profits, charge that same business with unfair hiring practices, or both. Improved simply means better. It does not give us clues about improvements for whom and better in what ways. Knowledge and education cannot be neutral, suspended in a kind of academic and acontextual holding zone. Students will act on what they have learned. Even as some scholars claim that a fixed, impermeable boundary between what we know and what we do can be established, such a boundary is non-existent (see, e.g., Gray, Braver, & Raichle, 2002; Hill & Morf, 2000; Meshulam, Winter, Ben-Shakhar, & Aharon, 2012). How anyone uses what she or he knows will bear on individuals and communities in ways that do both good and harm.

In what ways do democratic societies place demands on knowledge and require us, as educators, to offer a more nuanced response to the question of educational objectives, one that goes beyond, for example, "improved thinking"? As stated previously, this book begins with three interrelated questions in the context of undergraduate education and the representation of knowledge. First, what is higher education's social contract with the material conditions of how people live? Second, what is the subject in any given course and discipline? Finally, how does knowledge construct the social?

Ideally, our responses to these questions will be closely intertwined: higher education's obligations to the social will inform what students learn, which will inform and be informed by how we construct the subject and knowledge itself. Within the context of scholarly discourse on higher education, liberal and critical scholarship represent two intellectual traditions whose authors continue to centrally examine these questions and to offer important attention to these concerns.[4] Particularly among those writing about higher education from a liberal perspective, primary educational objectives have included critical thinking, effective communication, appreciation for diversity, and the development of students as rational individuals (Axelrod, 2002; Bok, 2006; Nussbaum, 1997; Rothblatt, 1993). As one scholar states, the central starting point of a "liberally educated person" is the "idea of the wholeness of the individual" (Rothblatt, 1993, p. 22). Liberal scholars have asserted that these objectives have served and will continue to serve society well in a variety of ways. Within this body of work, scholars focus more on the capacities themselves than on an in-depth analysis of how they matter, in concrete terms, to public life.

In contrast, work among critical scholars endorses a more explicit stance on education and public life. This scholarship makes clear demands on universities: "it remains the task of educators to make sure that the future points the way to a more socially just world" (Giroux, 2007a, p. 2). Critical work insists on the existence of oppression and on the importance of education that "disrupt[s] the hegemonic ways of seeing through which subjects make themselves dominant" (Razack, 1998, p. 10). This body of scholarship asserts that all theoretical and pedagogical work must begin with the realities in which people live; claims that a relationship exists between location, how one sees, knowledge, and power; and points out the failings and obligations of social theory (Darder, 2011; Grande, 2004; Kincheloe, 2008). Both liberal and critical bodies of work make substantive contributions to the ways in which higher education has responded to questions central to this book.

For the most part, these two bodies of work speak past each other. Each is read largely by its own followers. Important differences in the two fields related to undergraduate education can be difficult to access, particularly if one is not familiar with the literature. At the same time, the questions that these scholars pursue have relevance to all aspects of education, in ways both routine and profound. Related to this, perspectives on education and pedagogy, and particularly the ways in which approaches to knowledge play out in the classroom and have significance, are narrowly discussed and broadly relevant.

This book sets critical and liberal work, two bodies of scholarship that each employ a different set of ontological and epistemological assumptions, and that pursue parallel concerns, in conversation with each other. It provides a broad and systematic rationale for the role of higher education in public life and the implications of this role, particularly for undergraduate education. I offer a socio-ethical framework that relies in part on critical scholarship and that grapples with liberal thought; that does not shy away from complex and difficult questions, especially those related to the growing attention in higher education to market-based priorities and decreased consideration for the public good; and that might be useful to anyone grappling with the role of higher education in public life. As a way of grounding theoretical analysis in educational practice, I rely throughout the book on stories from the classroom and other settings to illustrate central questions and concerns.

"I thought this course was going to be streamlined!" – Cindy's statement, public and bold, feels like a demand. In my mind, her assertion harbours several questions. These questions are about the social contract, the subject, and my construction of the social, or the "we," in my course. Cindy clearly believes that such a claim is permissible and appropriate. Her statement reminds me that my students' expectations for their learning are real and pressing, perhaps most obviously so when I contradict those expectations. Back in the classroom, following Cindy's insertion, I pause. How had my priorities disturbed Cindy's? Who is the "we," and who is the "they"? What is worth learning, and for whom? I state to the class as a whole that I wonder what this assertion means and how others feel. I offer the students a chance to talk about their ideas. They choose not to comment. None of us, myself included, seems to know exactly how to respond. The moment passes, and we take our 10-minute break.

During the break, I consider my priorities for this class, what I hope students will grapple with and learn. Cindy's comment signals more than a minor detour for our discussion. It seems much more rooted, with far-reaching significance. It represents a set of sharply drawn lines that set the possibilities and constraints for Cindy's learning. She is letting me know that she did not come here for that. My own objectives for the course, stated in the syllabus, include: "To further your ability to make links between gender, sexuality, communication, and power in your day-to-day lives" and "to sharpen your sense of yourself as a communicative agent related to gender, sexuality, and the public good." Regarding my objectives, I hope that students will leave with a deeper understanding of the complexities of gender and sexuality in their own lives and in the contexts in which they live. I want them to gain an awareness of gendered communication norms and of their contribution to maintaining or resisting these norms related to their own communicative practices. I hope that they might increase their attentiveness to the ways in which communication can both open up and restrict what it means to be a man or a woman, a boy or a girl, straight or queer. When I ask students about their own expectations for the course, they often state that they want to learn more about how men and women communicate, and about the ways in which particular communication styles are linked to being a man or a woman.

When I consider the pedagogical context in which the "streamlined" comment sits, I interpret it as a call for simplification. The students in Cindy's class had had an extended conversation addressing how gender works in their own lives. I had both affirmed and challenged this conversation: "Great work" and "Are you assuming everyone is straight?" Many students defended their right to leave out the reality of being queer, the possibility that gender is also, always and everywhere, about sexuality. In this context, the call for a streamlined course seems to be, at least in part, a demand to reduce course content to what that particular student determines is a manageable, perhaps predictable, set of concepts. This desire to "fix" the subject eliminates any space for disagreement, questions, and ambiguity. It hints at an understanding of education as leading to "mastery" of the subject. Such "fixing" supports an understanding of education as an ability to contain the subject, to achieve a kind of ease with what is contained, and then call this combination of ease and containment knowledge. All of these moves are both social and epistemological. They are about who and what are worth knowing, and on whose terms.

epistemology

A year later, I am again teaching the Gender, Communication, and Culture course. Near the end of the term, students read an article on the ways in which the media represent white women and Indigenous women, particularly in relation to coverage of violence against women (Jiwani & Young, 2006). The article points out that, in many ways, white women are represented as "law-abiding [and] rational," and Indigenous women are portrayed as "unreasonable" and "deserving of violence" (Jiwani & Young, 2006, pp. 898–899). The previous week, we had discussed the concept of intersectionality, the idea that gender identity overlaps with, for example, one's race and ethnicity. Several of the racial minority students have addressed this concept in their own experience and spoken in class about how race and gender mark their lives at home, at school, and with friends. The reading for today demonstrates that the media treat white women as qualitatively different from Indigenous women in Canada, and that this treatment finds its way into "common sense" understandings. of white and Indigenous women. I hope that this reading will encourage students to think carefully about how the media communicate about specific groups of women and men and how the students rely on these messages or not.

The students are required to submit a one-page synthesis and a one-page reflection of each week's reading. Allison, one of the students in the class, has written a response to the Jiwani and Young reading that causes me to stop, to pause before I continue marking other students' assignments. Allison is an Asian Canadian woman who has taken one other class with me besides this one and who has been to my office a couple of times to discuss how to raise her mark on these assignments. After these visits to my office, I see a different quality in her work, a deeper level of grappling with course concepts. She has spoken with humour, sincerity, and insight, to the class and in her responses, about her own struggle to navigate, within the context of family and white and non-white peers, expectations in relation to her gender, sexuality, and race. Along with many if not all students, she feels acutely pressures to conform and to play into established scripts about being a (straight) woman.

In the reflection part of her response to the Jiwani and Young reading, Allison has described recent experiences in which people made destructive assumptions about her based on her brown skin and her gender. To Allison, these experiences demonstrated that race and gender matter in her life, and also marked the impossibility of separating these facets of her identity. She is thinking through not only the readings for today and the previous week, but also what the idea of intersectionality means for her as a racialized woman. The last two sentences in her response read: "All of these factors and occasions are leading me to believe that the notion of Canada as a multicultural hub is crap. As awful as it may sound to a lot of my classmates, I really feel no connection or loyalty to this country because they clearly feel none towards me." The class will be over in two weeks. As far as I am aware, Allison has at no point shared these ideas with other students, at least in the formal classroom setting. These ideas both reflect Allison's understanding of the subject matter in the reading and assert that for Allison, "These concepts matter to me. My experiences as a racialized woman are part of what I know."

As I take in Allison's words, they seem a kind of secret, privately uttered, yet also demanding to be heard. I think of Allison – working at her assignments, her ease with other students, the fact of her, at least in my perception, "fitting in" yet thinking apart: "As awful as it may sound ..." This knowledge is relevant to this class, to our understanding of gender, communication, and culture. I want this knowledge to be public. I hope that these privately uttered words, both hesitant and bold, and so obviously problematizing the possibility of "streamlined" knowledge, might make their way into the classroom. Allison has, for me, "unfixed" Cindy's desire to contain knowledge. She has unpinned Cindy's knowledge, refused any attempt to obliterate her experience of gender and race and her knowledge of the subject. I am standing again, always, on that epistemological fault line. Streamlined education, mastery of ideas, fixing the subject: such knowledge is haunted and troubled. In the hands of educators like myself, it does harm. Any kind of knowing that simplifies the lives of some to make the lives of others easier, is a problem (see Simpson, 2008).

Cindy's comment anticipating Allison's. Cindy hoping for simplicity. Allison refusing. The comments are a year apart, seemingly separate. Yet, where does Allison's knowledge have a place in educational environments that are streamlined? How does "streamlined" education reduce or eliminate space for Allison's experience of gender? In what ways does knowledge, and its representation in the classroom, discourage or encourage a range of realities and of ideas of what it means to be human? As teachers, what are our educational priorities? What are the experiences, realities, habits, and content that we seek to normalize, to make familiar, to invite? What, as educators, do we do with Cindy's surprise, with Allison's insistence? What are they each asking, asserting? How do ideas about what is possible and impossible shape our own pedagogical choices?

Cindy's comment points to central issues within disciplinary knowledge, one of which is the tension between generalizations and specificity. In a course on gender, for example, Cindy has identified, if indirectly, the issues one might raise in addressing concerns beyond narrow understandings of gender. Addressing sexuality in a course on gender may, for some, unnecessarily and excessively complicate the subject. A faculty person can certainly teach a gender course without addressing in any depth sexuality or the ways in which gender and racial identity intersect. In lower division undergraduate courses, generalization is often the norm. The organization and content of textbooks, the press of being realistic about what one can cover in a term or semester, the newness for students of disciplinary concepts and language, and large class sizes that make discussion difficult all encourage and often reward teaching that is streamlined and affirm education that presents knowledge, at least to some extent, as fixed and categorical.

Cindy made her statement after I had asked students to consider sexuality in relation to their discussion. The students had just had a conversation that, for me, implied that being straight was worth considering and that being gay and lesbian were, plainly stated, irrelevant to course content and subject matter. Streamlined knowledge might include knowledge that is categorical, predictable, manageable, measurable, and containable. For some, it might refer to knowledge that exists separately from lived reality and that has a kind of fixed conceptual relevance. In this sense, I was perhaps "breaking the rules" on which Cindy had come to rely. In her mind, this course was on the topic of gender, which was, implicitly or explicitly for Cindy, not about sexuality. Further, Cindy apparently had no interest in combining knowledge about sexuality with knowledge about gender. Even as this overlap does occur in real life, extending the discussion on gender in such a way was, for Cindy, inappropriate. Cindy's comment, however much her own, also has its roots in ongoing educational discourse. Cindy's claim was in part about the type of content with which she was familiar. Her comment, in far-reaching and profound ways, was also about what higher education teaches all students to expect. It was an assertion about knowledge, education, and the question of what counts as the subject in any given course.

Allison's statement seemed to be informed by the reading itself, the preceding two months of class, and an understanding of the concept of intersectionality, an idea we had not covered when Cindy called for streamlined education. Allison made a choice to pursue knowledge and ideas that refused simplification and that potentially pushed against her perception of what her classmates might believe about multiculturalism and gender in Canada. Allison was insisting on knowledge that had a fit with her own life, on knowledge that, by definition, could encompass her experience, her reality, and her naming of the subject. At first glance, an instructor might read Allison's comments as off-topic and unrelated to the reading's content. If an instructor's understanding of gender does not necessarily incorporate race, that instructor might wonder what Allison's comment has to do with gender at all. Yet, for Allison, the intersections of race and gender are part of the subject.

Streamlined education; the interplay of gender, sexuality, and race; questions of loyalty and belonging: how do we as faculty members approach our work as educators and understand our obligations to particular priorities and publics? Cindy's and Allison's assertions rearticulate the three questions I identified earlier as central to this book. What does it mean to say that higher education has a social contract with public life? When it comes to a course on Gender and Communication, or other courses and different disciplines, what is the subject? How do epistemological frameworks shape ways of seeing and knowing, and how do they define and demarcate practices of sociality? This book explores, from a variety of angles, the inseparability of the social contract, the subject, and epistemology. Further, it assumes that all teaching is a reflection of these three concerns and that all education is in part a response to what we as faculty members believe is the central work of higher education. "What is the subject" is in many ways an intentionally concrete question, one carrying frank, immediate, and practical demands. As educators who design and teach courses, we must decide, again and again, what content these courses will examine. We will choose, many of us four or five times in an academic year, with which areas of knowledge we want students to develop a familiarity.

From another angle, the question of what is the subject refuses the limits of one course or a single discipline and seeps beyond the clear beginning and end of a term. "What is the subject?" is an ontological question, a query that brushes up against understandings of what it means to be human. In responding to deliberations of course content, of the body of knowledge or material we opt to foreground, faculty members are also inevitably engaging questions of epistemological legitimacy, questions of how certain content comes to be central or not to a discipline and course objectives. "What is the subject?" is a question about conditions for subjecthood; about power and agency in relation to subjects in various positions and locations; about professional, intellectual, and ethical loyalties; and about the parameters of our own cognitive and affective longings.

Claims concerning the inherent separateness of a distinct subject and object, or a mutually exclusive subjectivity and objectivity, rely on and embrace a limited individualism (Collins, 2000). Indeed, drawing a firm line between the two is an intellectually unsound move, based on a dichotomy that in no way parallels lived reality. I am interested in engaging language and a set of practices that assume implication, relationality, power, and ethical agency. Stated simply: as educators, if we assume that higher education has a social contract with public life, and that ways of knowing inform ways of seeing and doing, then we must also turn towards the question of what is the subject, at both immediate and abstract levels. Faculty members cannot step outside of the press of such questions; we cannot extricate ourselves from their challenges and possibilities.

Cindy and Allison turned towards exactly these concerns with their comments. They seemed to be asking: what are we learning, and what does it mean? Education is a response to what we assume, to what takes us by surprise, and to what confronts our expectations. Education can be and often is streamlined, categorical, and neat. Yet, life is complicated. To what extent must education meet the demands of real life? Whose lives have significance, and in what ways? How does education respond to lives that do not fit existing categories, including categories that refuse queer lives and communities, or Allison's understanding of her own life as one that in part has "no connection" to nation? How does education act to shrink the space for whose lives are worth considering, for how we decide who and what matters? Education can serve to illuminate complexity or to reduce complexity to a false simplicity. I am wary of streamlined education, especially as it has the power to shrink the space for what it means to be human, and to limit the range of experiences that are considered part of the subject. Ideally, education is the work of our collective imagination. Education is a way of understanding reality and naming the subject, of locating self in relation to other, and of imagining what kind of world is possible.

Socio-ethical Starting Points and the Work of Undergraduate Education

As demonstrated by the previous two examples from the classroom, education is consequential and has implications, often influencing what students understand as falling within and outside of the boundaries of what is worth learning. Obviously, these implications will influence how students like Cindy and Allison see and live in the world beyond the classroom. Gays and lesbians can be part of the subject or not; gender-related communication behaviours are wrapped up with race or not. As instructors, we offer our understandings of knowledge, understandings that set up parameters for identifying and addressing the subject. Allison was interested in knowledge that mirrored the complexity she saw in her own life. Cindy seemed focused on a different kind of knowing, perhaps one that also mirrored her understanding of herself. These examples point to a second set of questions, all grounded in notions of the subject and the social, and also pedagogically relevant.

First, what are the ends or aims of undergraduate education?[5] What does undergraduate education want to achieve? As instructors, what do we hope for as students like Cindy and Allison complete our classes and a degree? Second, what are the links between the representation of knowledge and what students learn? How do frameworks for knowledge, for notions of "the subject," represent patterns of relationality, power, and agency? How do such frameworks and notions set up possibilities for how students understand the content of any given course, and for what they believe is appropriate within the boundaries of that subject matter? Finally, how does undergraduate education support and limit consideration of democratic practices, the public good, and justice? Inasmuch as education is a response, a way of engaging specific areas of concern, what are the obligations of undergraduate education to life outside of the classroom, to the public good, and specifically to equity issues?

Cindy's statement felt as if it were both question and demand. It was a question: "Where do you think you're going with this?" It was also a demand: "If we're going to talk about sexuality in this course, you must defend your choice to do this." Allison insisted on expanding the subject that Cindy, a year earlier, had wanted to narrow. As I consider Cindy and Allison's learning, their take on their own education, their concerns remain a set of questions that refuse to disappear. They call for conceptual clarity and challenge me to respond: "Here is what we are doing. This is what I hope for." I want to offer all students an understanding of education that takes their questions and concerns seriously; that gives them room to question, doubt, and assert; and that draws a connection between education and the material realities of how people live. I strive to offer educational content that will encourage my students to see the complexities of the world in which they live. Communication is a discipline that defines itself as "the shared process of making meaning." I will always, as much as I am able, opt to pursue meanings that open up, rather than restrict and narrow, what it means to be human and to live together well.

In the interests of living together well, of valuing the public good and justice, how do we learn to define the subject? How does education shape our understandings of what is and is not relevant and what matters in the context of any given course? What is the relationship of that subject to the material realities of how people live? These are epistemological questions. Should knowledge, as Cindy was suggesting, be streamlined, categorical, and neat? How can instructors best represent knowledge to students, particularly in the interests of democratic practices? Finally, what do instructors do with complexity and difference? How do we consider and represent lives and experiences that challenge, that fall outside narrowly defined disciplinary boundaries, and that boldly reject the possibility, desirability, and legitimacy of streamlined knowledge? These concerns have direct ties to questions of democracy, the public good, and justice. If education shapes habits, and is a process of making sense, how does it encourage a "way of being in the world" (Alexander, 1987, p. 143)? How do the objectives of undergraduate education, the consequences of learning, shape our understanding of self and other and of what it means to live as "associated individuals" (Dewey, 1993, p. 46)?

As faculty members, through our teaching, research, and creative work, we inevitably assert our ideas about "associated individuals," about the "we" of the communities in which we live. The ways in which we understand the world around us shapes what we do in the classroom, how we approach knowledge itself. While many faculty members opt to ignore or deny the presence of ethical priorities in our teaching and research, these ethical starting points and desires are, in fact, always present and significant. Our own ways of knowing, as well as the ways in which we define the subject, are necessarily weighted with particular ways of seeing the world. All teaching and research is a response to the question: How do I see my life in relation to others? While some faculty members opt for transparency regarding our response, and others vocally deny the presence of such concerns, all of us inevitably answer this question. Scholarly research and writing always begin with a certain understanding of how things work, our own take on what constitutes a problem or an issue worth pursuing.

What are my own ethical starting points and desires? The title of this book is a lament and a hope, a statement of what is possible yet lacking. It signals a way of seeing and knowing that goes beyond rationality, that expresses a longing and acknowledges desire. The title makes explicit reference to educational work as longing. It also plainly notes the existence of an "agenda" in societies with democratic aspirations, even as the word "agenda" continues to make large numbers of educators uncomfortable. In the context of intellectual work, of knowledge production and representation, one's socio-ethical framework is intimately connected with how one sees the world in which one lives. Ethics is a way of asserting: I see this, care about this. Ethics is also a way of understanding: this is why things work this way. Finally, one's ethics indicate loyalties and allegiances: this way of seeing, of understanding, has more legitimacy than that way. All ethical frameworks engage the social and concern how we choose to live with others. My own socio-ethical frame of reference, especially with regard to democracy, the public good, and justice, acts as an inescapable set of norms and commitments, a way of seeing, thinking, feeling, and doing. Again, a set of stories helps to illuminate the socio-ethical starting points for this book.

I moved to Kitchener, Ontario, a city of 200,000 located about an hour's drive west of Toronto, in August 2007. I moved to Canada after accepting a faculty position at the University of Waterloo. The city of Waterloo has a population of about 100,000, and borders Kitchener. Waterloo is home to my institution, a university with nearly 35,000 students, and to Wilfrid Laurier University and its 17,000 students. I was exhausted and hopeful on my arrival in Kitchener, attentive to the usual demands of moving, and glad for many certainties: I knew that I had an income, a secure job, a safe and comfortable place to live, and the benefit of movers who would carry furniture and boxes up the stairs.

On a Friday, the movers unloaded their truck and carried everything up two-and-half flights to my apartment. I spent some time unpacking a few necessities, and then made a trip to the grocery store. The next day, I went to the main branch of the public library in Kitchener. I planned to find the public use computers and read my email. In visiting the library, I was also looking forward to getting a sense of where I now lived.

The public computer space at the library was in a room of about 15 by 20 feet. Ten to 12 computers were lined up along the walls around the room, with the people using them facing outward. There were also a few computers in a small area in the centre of the room – a configuration of a smaller square of tables and computers within a larger square. I waited a few minutes for my turn, and then sat down for my allotted 60-minute session. The computers were all occupied with library patrons – women, men, girls, and boys, old, middle-aged, and young – reading email, surfing the Web, playing games, and watching videos. There was a low level of noise, not bothersome but present. To my right, a couple of boys sat at the same computer, talking; nearby sat an older white man, laughing frequently. To my immediate left were two boys, dark-skinned and about 13 years old, sitting at one computer and quietly enjoying the game they were playing. To their left, two computer stations down from me, was a white man, about 35, who had several sheets of paper on both sides of his computer. Two boys who were dark skinned and seemed to be about 11, sitting directly behind me, came over every now and then to talk quietly with the two boys to my left.

After about 15 minutes, I hear an insistent kind of hissing, like a cat might make, from the white man sitting two computers to my left. I look in his direction. All four of the boys are at the computer next to me, and are now silent. The white man is visibly angry. He continues to make the hissing sound, glaring at the boys. He points to his papers, some of which are clearly in the boys' computer space, and says tightly, "Be quiet. Don't touch." He continues to glower at the boys. The two younger ones quietly said, "Sorry," and quickly return to their computer behind me. They do not talk further. One of the two older boys at the computer directly to my left holds the man's gaze. After several seconds, he and the other boy go back to their game. The man continues to stare angrily at them.

Perhaps sensing the man's eyes on him, one of the two older boys returns to look at the white man, and says: "You shouldn't stare at us like that. I don't like you. I hate when you do that. I hate you right now." I hear a quiet fury in the boy's voice. The white man and the boy who spoke are still looking at each other. I look at the white man, and then say loudly enough for all in the room to hear: "You have no reason to hiss at them, to communicate that way. You could have simply asked them to be quiet."

The white man finally drops his gaze and goes back to his computer. The boys go back to their game. Others in the room return to their work. I sit for a few minutes, staring at the computer. No one speaks of what happened. After a couple of minutes, the white man to my right contin-ues laughing, quite loudly.

On one of the days during which I am working on this chapter and thinking about what happened in the library, I walk to a yoga class. I enjoy the feel of the sun, warm in early June. Halfway down the block from where I live, I say hello to a white, middle-aged man sitting on his porch. I am nearly past his house when he starts talking to me. I stop walking and turn to face him as he says: "The Jays, they were up seven to two, now it's seven to six. I wonder who's going to win. The pitcher … same thing happened the last game. Overall, you know, they've been doing well … Just these last two games." He goes on, recounting parts of today's game and the game from yesterday for me. I struggle to keep up. I listen and wait, trying to hold onto the details he is handing over. He asks, "Do you follow the Jays?" I reply, "No. Now that you've filled me in, maybe I'll have to pay more attention." I laugh. He smiles as well. He says a little more about the team, their playing. When I raise my hand goodbye, he smiles again, and says, "Well, thanks for listening to my story." His voice is light, slightly amused. He also sounds glad I stopped.

"Thanks for listening to my story." All morning, I have been think-ing about the library, a white man's anger, a brown boy's indignation. "Thanks for listening to my story." Listening to stories is one part of the work of democracy. Listening to some stories is easier than listening to others. On my way to yoga, in the act of listening, my only other con-cern was that I not be late to my yoga class. In the library, I wondered what stories we all took home. Did others leave with a distinct memory of the events from that day? Have they, like me, held onto that story, let it live under their skin, not ready to let it go? Listening to stories most often begins with a certain way of seeing. How and what we see gives us clues, leads us in one direction and not in another. My neighbour on the porch: here was a man looking for easy conversation, sharing his interest in the Jays. From another angle, might he be someone going on about a topic in which I have no interest, rudely taking up my time?

Friendly or badgering? I suppose many if not most of us would be generous enough, regardless of our interest in the Jays or sports at all, to offer this man a few minutes. He is our neighbour. The subject of the Jays, while provoking excitement for some, rarely offends. What I see is still my choice, but one I make within certain parameters including the topic itself, getting to a class, and/or the facts that this man is a neighbour and I am enjoying the warm weather.

The story of what happened at the library on my second day in Kitchener continues to challenge me. At that point in time, I had, as a student and faculty person, studied race for over 15 years. I had taught in the field of communication for 10 years. I try to stay close to how race matters to how people live. Perhaps I was especially attuned to the interaction in the computer room. I know that how we talk to each other is an ethical act, not everything, but certainly something. Always a beginning, and the place we start to make meaning, together. How we see is played out in seconds, and constructed over years. Did others see a man who was appropriate in his request, if a little harsh? Perhaps some in that computer room saw four boys acting out of order? Did they see tensions between a middle-aged man and four youths? Or a racist level of complacency among the adults in the room? When I told a group of advanced undergraduates this story during my first year of teaching in Waterloo, they laughed, possibly out of discomfort. They said little, except to express surprise at the boy's statement, his assertion: "I hate when you do that. I hate you right now." One white student said this seemed a little "over the top." At this, a few of the other white and Asian Canadian students in the classroom nodded.

I was upset that day in the library, furious with the white man. His hissing, especially, and then the sharp comments: he shredded the space we were all sharing. After that, nothing was the same. What was there – several people getting along, at least on the surface; the ability to sit, work, and play with relative ease; my hope, not named until it was gone, that all of us would act well; a public space that offered a façade of mutual respect; the ability to come to a public institution without the experience of at best disregard and at worst racism – was gone. In its place, for me, was a rush of anger, a keen stab of loss. I felt a kind of despair mixed with disbelief. I am caught, sorting through the apparent swiftness of change in public spaces; the unadorned arrogance, a form of violence, of the white man; and the silence of nearly everyone in the room. Certainly, disrespect happens. We can all communicate badly, and do. Yet, these are boys, enjoying their time at the computer. They are talking with each other, and producing a level of noise that is equal to if not less than what I hear from the man to my right.

What is learned, and by whom? Who in that library room has those boys' backs, is even slightly concerned with their well-being, with the possibility of the adults in the room demonstrating even a minimal level of concern with what is occurring? When I do opt to question the white man, I am nervous. I participate in a kind of social vanity when I wonder to myself: "If I say this, criticize the white man, what will the others in the room think about me?" My actual comments are burdened with my own hesitation, my concern for what others will think. After I say what I can, I look blankly at the computer screen, and sit with a mix-ture of ideas and emotions. I feel a stone of disgust in my gut, mostly directed at the white man, and some directed at myself. Alongside that stone is a wide sadness, a general anger at the mess we are in, the mess we have made, the behaviours we seem to find acceptable, even desir-able. I feel overwhelmed by the weight of too much wrong. My knowl-edge that what is wrong will persist, and lives everywhere, fills spaces beyond the walls of this small room in my public library. Here I am, I think. Here we are.

There is so much broken for me in that computer room. The damage done is at once a weight, solid, and on the move. I sit in the midst of shards, flying. The practices of inequity and oppression, like pieces of broken glass, are sharp-edged and inflict bodily harm. These practices move among us, persistent and inescapable. Who will experience harm, and how? What will stick? What will we let loose? Nothing is finished. I want to insist to the white man, "Leave them alone!" When I do speak to him, my tone is calm and angry. He has treated the boys like animals, less than human, or at least less human than him. What do his actions mean for the boys? Where has this man learned that his actions are per-missible, appropriate? Where have other adults in that room learned to be quiet, to ignore, to pretend? I sit, staring at the computer. I remind myself: I came to read my email. This now feels irrelevant, a ridicu-lous distraction. My anger grows. I resent the silence, the pretense. All this politeness, acquiescence. We embrace the work of not noticing, of forgetting, of leaving behind. What are the costs of such work? What sticks? What will we let loose? What remains, under whose skin?

Such stories exist within larger societal frameworks. A seemingly brief exchange in a public library sits alongside stories that are more widely known. In Toronto, parents and educators have articulated the importance of Black schools, particularly in relation to the dropout rate for Black students of 42% compared with 31% for white students (Dei, 2008). Carl James has stated in an article in the *Toronto Star* that what is needed is "'a curriculum and a school program that responds to the needs and expectations of students who are black'" (James, 2007). When I talk with students about this issue, often at their initiative, the conversations routinely focus on what might be wrong with the idea of Black schools – the lack of a need for such schools; the apparently problematic possibility that other groups might also want such schools; the adequacy of existing schools, with the implicit assumption that as existing schools are adequate, it must be the (Black) students who are at fault; the difficulty of offering a curriculum that acknowledges many perspectives and experiences.

Because so much attention, and perhaps fear, is focused on the above concerns, many people who address this issue seem unable to ask: What if we begin with the assumption that most kids should complete high school, that differential graduation rates by race are not acceptable, and that all kids should be able to go to school and have those educational institutions attuned to and engaged with their realities and perspectives? If we begin with these assumptions, we need to acknowledge the concerns voiced by primarily Black parents, and to develop a more in-depth understanding of their ideas, as well as the broader context for schools in Toronto. Knowledge of the broader context would ensure that my students and others are aware of the fact that the Toronto school board already supports 33 alternative schools that serve 4,852 students. These schools have been "created for all kinds of reasons – some pressing, like fear of physical attacks on gay, lesbian, bisexual and transgender students; others merely philosophical, such as parents wanting a looser, less formal and structured school environment for their kids" (James, 2007). Further, little to no public discourse has considered the possibility of especially white students, and presumably their parents, taking for granted that schools will normalize, solidify, and elevate their perspectives and experiences. Again, as in the library, whose lives are valued, and how? What do we see?

What stories stick to our skin, make claims on our attention? Sherene Razack, a scholar who has long addressed issues of racism in Canada and other countries, spoke about Frank Paul at a conference I attended in November 2008. Frank Paul, an Indigenous man, died in Vancouver on 5 December 1998. Members of the police services in Vancouver brought Paul into custody and put him into a drunk tank and then released him. Later the same day, the police took Paul into custody again. The second time, the police decided not to put Paul into jail. A video shows police officers dragging Paul in and out of the police station, in wet clothes and apparently unable to walk. Police left Paul in an alleyway that led to the Vancouver Detox Centre. Paul died a few hours later from hypothermia and acute intoxication. A month later, police told Paul's family that he had died from a hit-and-run accident. There was no formal investigation into Paul's death until 2007. Razack's research demonstrates that what happened to Paul happens to homeless people as well (RACE Conference, 14 Nov. 2008). Documentation of other "freezing deaths" across Canada exists (see, e.g., Hubbard, 2004). What do we do with stories that surprise, offend, and reveal? How do we understand the world in which we live? As Cindy and Allison seemed to ask: How do we see our lives in relation to others?

Ethical issues – how we choose to live together – are not only present in exchanges like the one in the library of which I was a part. Rather, as in the case of Black schools and the death of Frank Paul, they live and breathe in numerous issues about which we may or may not be aware. They are not only the conflict between a few boys of colour laughing and talking together and a white man responding, but are bound up with institutions and systems that many of us take for granted, such as police services and education. They are issues both intimate, written on bodies – issues such as a boy's reasoned fury, the choice of the police to leave Paul in an alleyway in weather that could and did kill, the ways in which educational institutions and those in them affirm the lives of their students or not – and large and systemic, with a multitude of interests at stake. They invoke questions of what it means to be human, of the process of dehumanizing, and of habits and dispositions, learned, maintained, and defended, that can and do result in great harm.

Longing for democracy is a way of being human, of seeing self and other, of holding onto stories, whether they reassure or disturb. A white man's disrespect, a boy's clarity of mind and heart, a range of witnesses: the particular components of one of millions of interactions that go on every day. The interaction in the library is one held by larger forces, including media that naturalize racist ideologies, over and over; government policies that make judgments about people depending on their appearance; the myth that "real Canadians" are white, and thus have some higher claim on public space. Another component is the belief, systematically constructed and then issued without thought, that those boys in the library were worth less than even basic levels of regard. In most ways, the adults in that library space accepted the white man's behaviour. I made a comment that indicated that I had a problem:, "You did not have to communicate that way." I also managed to ignore certain aspects of the behavior I found problematic. Why did I not ask, "Why don't you complain about this man who is laughing – he is louder than the boys?" or "The boys have been speaking quietly. What's your problem?"

I begin this book with the assumption that questions of democracy and justice, of how to live well together, persist. I taught for 10 years in the United States, and now live and work in Canada. What I felt in the library computer room – that there was too much wrong – is a belief I hold about both countries. While certainly both offer opportunity and the possibility of a meaningful life to some, they do not offer these in an equitable way. In both the United States and Canada, there is evidence of ongoing systemic discrimination (Armaline, Glasberg, & Purkay-astha, 2011; Bonilla-Silva, 2010; Henry & Tator, 2009; Cannon & Sun-seri, 2011; Parenti, 2008). At very broad levels, inequitable pay based on one's gender (Drolet & Mumford, 2012; Lips, 2013; Monsebraaten, 2013), schools' failure to support students equitably across racial lines (Dei, 2008; Rocque & Paternoster, 2011; St Denis, 2011), and the dispro-portionate number of Black and Indigenous adults and youth in deten-tion and criminal justice facilities (Gomberg-Muñoz, 2012; Murakawa & Beckett, 2010; Owusu-Bempah, 2013; Pedwell, 2013) are only three areas that begin to document the variety and significance of different forms of inequity. Situated globally, especially those in privileged communi-ties in the United States and Canada deplete far more than our share of the earth's resources, do more harm to the environment, and enjoy a significantly higher quality of life, on the whole, than those living in countries in the southern hemisphere (Bauman, 2011; Roberts & Parks, 2007). How do we, as a society, live well together?

Inequities exist. By most measures, individualism and material-ism are increasing. One is hard-pressed to find, in universities and more broadly, a robust language and imagination for the public good. Responding to these concerns is, at least in part, the work of higher education – to consider what is wrong; to imagine, at a minimum, how it can be less wrong; and ideally, to consider how we can move together from what is wrong to what is just. While I certainly acknowledge that, as a society, we have got certain things right, I choose to turn towards the reality of too much wrong. The reality of too much wrong – this is where democracy and justice are most necessary; this is where we demonstrate, individually and collectively, our understanding of what matters, of what we think it means to be human, and of how we will work at what it means to live well together.

Theoretical and Methodological Starting Points

This book is situated in a specific set of theoretical and methodological frameworks. Theoretically, I draw heavily on understandings of democracy, the public good, and justice that foreground relational practices, as well as on critical theory and critical race theory. Methodologically, I rely on a combination of auto-ethnography and socio-ethical analysis.

Theoretical Starting Points

In this section, I examine democracy, broadly understood, and its relationship to the public good and to justice, as well as critical theory and critical race theory.

Democracy, the Public Good, and Justice

Democracy concerns the "just harmonization of individual and social interests" (Dewey, 1993, xvii), and is centrally "about the body's interaction with the social and material world" (Darder, 2011, p. 354). When we consider questions of democracy, we are invoking questions of power (Della Porta & Rucht, 2013b). Democratic practices offer us a way to be human, to live together well, to witness that which is ugly, damaging, and violent, notice, and to hope for and work at something different. Understood in this book as far more than a set of political institutions or forms of deliberation,[6] democracy engages shared interests and stays in conversation when those interests clash. It is concerned with questions of meaning and power and requires ongoing participation. Ideally, attentiveness to democracy will ensure routine consideration of the possibilities for and realization of justice.

Democracy has also been a political and social mode of doing great violence and harm, often carried out by prominent religious, educational, and governmental institutions. North American institutions have "wielded" democracy as a "virulent weapon of mass destruction" (Grande, 2004, p. 32). In particular, "it has never been against US law to commit genocide against Indigenous peoples" (Smith, 2006, p. 70). In North America, public officials work within institutions that claim or aspire to democratic processes and outcomes and that threaten, harm, and take the lives of, for example, Black and Indigenous men and boys such as Frank Paul, Amadou Diallo, and more recently, Trayvon Martin. As Indigenous scholars have pointed out, given such uses of "democracy" by formal political institutions, "indigenous peoples have not ... been fighting for inclusion in the democratic imaginary" (Grande, 2004, p. 98; see also Alfred & Corntassel, 2005). Grande's reference to inclusion is significant in regard to the issues I address in this book.

When confronted with challenges to a supposedly democratic and equitable state, such as calls for streamlined education and for the erasure of queer communities from the subject, and with the fact of a disconnect from nation, liberal thought frequently responds with calls for "inclusion" or "recognition" (Coulthard, 2007; Macdonald, 2008). In this logic, the "exclusion" of queers or racial minorities can be remedied by "including" them into existing political and social networks. What liberal scholars rarely address is the possibility that the "current discourse of social inclusion does not sufficiently accept responsibility for causing the situation [related to 'exclusion'] in the first place" (Preece, 2001, p. 3). Indeed, the language of inclusion and recognition necessarily imposes normalizing technologies, an expectation of "sameness," and a "common social standard" (Macdonald, 2008, p. 352; see also Dunne, 2009). The "dominant group or entity" is the grantor of inclusion or recognition, even as neither dominant nor subordinate groups "can significantly modify, let alone transcend, the breadth of power at play in colonial relationships" (Coulthard, 2007, p. 443). Thus, while the rhetoric of "inclusion" might be convenient for those who possess institutional forms of power, inclusion's logic, in effect, requires a repudiation of forms of self-determination and personhood that in any way "deny [the state's] legitimacy" (Macdonald, 2008, p. 348).

As I articulate further in chapter 4, when it includes a critique of power and of "the historic, economic, and material conditions of 'difference'" (Grande, 2004, p. 34), understanding democracy as a form of sociality can offer a way to name injustice and imagine justice. Democracy, broadly understood, offers the possibility of constructing stories that give us pleasure, that offer meaning, and that move us towards justice. Democracy, and the values it carries – democracy's agenda – can act to hold those of us in higher education to account and remind all educators that we have public responsibilities. Democracy offers a way of seeing what is wrong, what dehumanizes, and what shrinks the space for our well-being. It can offer us hope, hard-earned and always a labour, not only concerning the public use of computer space in the library, but in a range of other situations as well, such as when communities disagree about the existence and role of Black-focused schools, or in relation to the ways in which individuals in institutions like the police services interact with Indigenous communities. Democracy offers us ways of pursuing an identification of injustice and the possibilities for justice. It offers us ways to disagree, address that disagreement, and move towards a deeper understanding of how power works and of creating the communities, at the local, national, and international levels, in which we want to live.

How do we see our lives in relation to others? According to John Dewey, education is about making sense, about habits and dispositions. He writes that "democracy is an educative process" and that education "constitutes a firm and continuous reminder that the process of living together" is necessarily tied to the "understanding of our relations to one another" (1993, 248). Or, as one scholar states, "My own political project involves trying to connect educational discourse to questions of social justice and the creation of citizens who are able to conceive of a democracy which is not the same as 'the free market'" (Mohanty, 2003, p. 205). This book begins with commitments to democracy, the public good, and justice. It asserts that these concepts are of value and require our attention and consideration. In this book, I assume that, as both Cindy and Allison seemed to understand, education is at least in part about how we see both self and other, and how that seeing becomes a part of what we know, and ultimately, what we do. I am interested in democratic practices as forms of sociality and of ethical relationality. The practices of democracy in North America have been and continue to be unjust. How might democracy represent a "form of desire and endeavor" (Dewey, 1993, 42) that insists on all life as social and offers possibilities for justice?

The public good refers to practices through which institutions place a higher value on citizen engagement; on quality of life indicators such as health care, education, a living wage, and meaningful work; and on the well-being of and reduction of suffering among social groups than on privatized, market-based profit and individual gain. The public good depends in part on the existence of "noncommodified public spheres," which provide a space for individuals and institutions to "address the relationship of the self to public life, social responsibility to the broader demands of citizenship, and provide[s] a robust vehicle for public participation and democratic citizenship" (Giroux, 2002b, pp. 427–428). Further, I am using the term public good within a critical rather than liberal framework. Within the latter perspective, "the current picture of liberal society gives us an autonomous individual and then tries to construct a social order that would best preserve and allow that autonomy to flourish" (Bell, 1998, p. 36). In this sense, public goods might be seen as "extrinsic or external to the relationships that exist among those who form the community or society in question" (Hollenbach, 2002, p. 8). Such a view foregrounds the well-being of individuals and dilutes attention to the workings of power and to the sociality of all existence.

When the public good and parallel notions of justice are reduced to rights, or what autonomous individuals can attain, have, or possess, this can lead to a "moral mediocrity" (Bell, 1998, p. 42). Foregrounding individuals often leads to a devaluing of the relational. In contrast, in an understanding of the public good that at a minimum questions liberalism's emphasis on the individual, "the quality of ... relationships among society's members is itself part of the good" (Hollenbach, 2002, p. 8). That is, the shared work and pleasures of relationships, more than any individual experience of or benefit resulting from those relationships, constitute the public good. In understandings of the public good that foreground relationships, we must grapple with how communities are brought "into being," and with the ongoing practices of constituting social relationships, structures of power, and forms of public life that will lead to justice.

Finally, I agree with Iris Marion Young when she states that "social justice concerns the degree to which a society contains and supports the institutional conditions necessary for the realization of these values ... (1) developing and exercising one's capacities and expressing one's experience ... and (2) participating in determining one's action and the conditions of one's action" (1990, 37). Justice concerns issues of access and power, and requires attention to questions of privilege and oppression, as well as to the realization of equity. As Patricia Hill Collins points out in a discussion of Young's work, social justice concerns "the degree to which society maintains social institutions necessary to oppose oppression and domination" (1998, p. 273n8). In relation to higher education's social contract with public life, to the constitution of the subject, and to epistemological concerns, these understandings of democracy, the public good, and justice act throughout this book as a set of ethical referent points for an analysis of undergraduate education and its obligations to the social.

Critical Theory and Critical Race Theory

Critical theory and critical race theory are both grounded in analyses of power that will ideally lead to the reduction of human suffering and the increase of equity in a range of interactions and institutions. Critical theory has roots in the Frankfurt School, a group of theorists working in the mid-twentieth century who believed "that injustice and subjugation shape the lived world" (Kincheloe, 2008, p. 46). As an "intellectual tradition ... that center[s] social analysis on advancing democratic possibilities" (Torres & Rhoads, 2006, p. 5), critical social science generally asserts that all research and knowledge are political and consequential and that injustice exists at systemic levels (Collins, 1998; Grande, 2004; Torres & Rhoads, 2006). Critical theory encourages rigorous attention to the connections between knowledge and power and to concrete possibilities for social change and for justice.

Critical race theory has important parallels with critical theory. For critical race theorists, racism is routine and systemic in North America; social analyses must draw on the knowledge and realities of racialized individuals and communities; and intellectual work should invest in the "eliminat[ion of] racial oppression as part of the broader goal of ending all forms of oppression" (Matsuda et al., 1993, p. 6; see also Delgado & Stefancic, 2005). Critical race theorists also espouse interdisciplinarity, challenge the idea of neutrality (in relation to law and academic work), and insist on the importance of context. The study of whiteness, or examinations of how structures of race privilege work, has been a focus of many critical race theorists. Critical race theory "claims that there are racialized patterns to which whites subscribe" (Simpson, 2010a, p. 368) which must be interrogated in any effort to end racism (Crenshaw, 1995; Delgado & Stefancic, 2013; Razack, Smith, & Thobani, 2010; Zamudio, Russell, Rios, & Bridgeman, 2010).

In relation to critical theory, recent literature has grappled with the pressures of an increasingly market-based society on higher education at multiple levels. Growing numbers of scholars are examining the effects of commercialization on higher education, particularly in relation to the ability of critical scholars to pursue the public good within institutions that affirm corporate priorities. Both liberal and critical scholars have asserted that commercialization is fundamentally at odds with the values and goals of higher education and that commercialization has harmful effects on teaching and the production and dissemination of knowledge (Bok, 2003; Magnusson, 2000; Polster, 2002, 2006;

Schugurensky, 2006; Turk, 2000, 2008). In sum, in the world of higher education today, "new priorities, funding arrangements, and market-oriented values" often take priority over attention to "equity, accessibility, autonomy, and the contribution of higher education to social transformation" (Schugurensky, 2006, p. 317). As a result, "institutions for hire that are reactive to the market are incompatible with autonomous public institutions in pursuit of ... the common good (ibid.). As I note in chapter 6, market orientations and economic and discursive forms of neoliberalism have significant effects on the possibilities for considering justice in higher education.

Methodological Frameworks

Methodologically, I primarily rely on auto-ethnography and socio-ethical analysis. Auto-ethnography is "an approach to research and writing that seeks to describe and systematically analyze (*graphy*) personal experience (*auto*) in order to understand cultural experience" (Ellis, Adams, & Bochner, 2011, n.p.; emphasis in original). It is especially useful when one critiques a set of practices in which one is implicated, as auto-ethnography directly challenges "the traditional denial of the authorial presence of the self" favoured in much academic research and writing (Dauphinee, 2010, p. 799). Throughout this book, I address higher education and race. I am a faculty member with deep affective and intellectual investments in educational practices. As a white scholar, I am critiquing a set of practices (racism) from which white people, including myself, routinely benefit. Auto-ethnography allows for high levels of complexity, ambiguity, and contradiction. It offers a way to lay bare the intricacies, messiness, and possibilities of the social, and to centre intellectual analysis in the practices of bodies and their relationships to institutions, particularly in terms of how those institutions structure harm, advantage, and agency (Alexander, 1999; Alanís, 2006; Ellis, Adams, & Bochner, 2011).

I rely on critical socio-ethical analysis in order to offer insistent and rigorous attention to questions of history, ideologies, social norms, lived experience, power, and change. Grounded in critical theory, and alongside a commitment to moving towards justice, socio-ethical analysis offers a way to name what is wrong, to identify the intricate and ongoing construction of injustice, and to consider possibilities for different practices of relationality. It assumes that all of life is both social and ethical (Collins, 1998, 2000). Further, it asserts that social locations, or the ways in which power structures experience, "have real material effects and that their effects are systemic rather than accidental" (Moya, 2002, p. 45). Critical theory requires a "moral vocabulary" that has "practical significance" (Strydom, 2011, p. 118). Paired with auto-ethnography, critical theory offers a way to investigate the routine and profound in located interactions and to then situate such interactions in broader systems of meaning and power. In methodological terms, critical theory is "marked by a suspicion that all is not well in capitalist society and its liberal democratic institutional arrangements" (Strydom, 2011, p. 115), and encourages a "critique of the relevant structural developments of a society that systematically have a detrimental effect on intersubjective social relations" (p. 117). I am interested in moving theoretically and methodologically between agency and structure, investigating broad social norms, and exploring possibilities for resisting those norms.

Chapter Overview

The chapters in this book do the interrelated work of naming and imagining. That is, they identify and expand on issues central to the aims of undergraduate education and the social contract higher education has with public life. In regard to these two areas, chapters 2 and 3, in particular, assess existing scholarship and analyse its limits. Naming in these chapters is a way of exploring where scholars stand on these issues, articulating what has been normalized, and pointing out the reach and significance of this normalization. Such naming can expose the intellectual and practical underpinnings of what is taken for granted, and provide a clear sense of the parameters within which nearly all work in higher education takes place. Naming what is serves as a precursor to imagining what might be different. Chapters 4 through 7 continue with the work of naming. They also begin to imagine or to move out of mainstream and liberal educational frameworks and into possibilities for undergraduate education that take the public good and justice into account.

Chapters 2 and 3 both serve as a kind of intellectual and practical inventory of existing work concerned with undergraduate education, democratic practices, the public good, and justice. Scholars continue to offer attention to all of these concerns. However, in mainstream educational discourse, one is hard-pressed to find work that carefully considers the connections among higher education's social contract, the aims or ends of undergraduate education, democratic practices, and justice. Further, many faculty members routinely demonstrate our acceptance of mainstream educational scholarship, often with little awareness or consideration of the ways in which it potentially obscures consideration of the public good and equity.

Chapter 2 focuses on the responsibilities that higher education has to public life and on the ends of undergraduate education. I am especially concerned with the ways in which existing scholarship, particularly that within a liberal framework, lacks a robust theoretical consideration of the links among the social contract higher education has with public life, the ends of undergraduate education, and democratic practices. I delineate four frameworks that scholars have asserted in relation to the social contract and offer a brief analysis of these frameworks. In chapter 2, I also discuss the existing literature on the ends of undergraduate education, including intellectual, civic, and vocational.

In chapter 3, I am centrally concerned with scholarly, institutional, and faculty members' commitments to civic engagement and service learning. Over the past two decades, even as there continues to be resistance, service-learning programs have made significant inroads into a range of settings in higher education. How do the theoretical and practical aspects of both civic engagement and service learning offer possibilities for justice? In addition to addressing the use of terms including engagement, civic engagement, and service learning, I offer a critique of the shortcomings of these areas of scholarship in relation to consideration of democratic practices and institutional injustice. I examine the assertions that civic engagement literature has not sufficiently addressed the interest-driven nature of all scholarly work and that its acceptance of liberal norms acts against possibilities for justice.

Chapters 4 through 7 continue to assess the limits of existing scholarship and also start to imagine the shape of intellectual and educational work that might be explicitly responsive to democratic values. In chapter 4, I identify four parameters of public life, or assumptions about the social. In brief, I assert the following: (1) public life is insistently relational, (2) injustice exists, (3) power matters, and (4) democratic societies require attention to the public good and to justice. I also carefully examine basic assumptions in liberal and critical scholarship and discuss how these bear on considerations of justice in educational settings. In chapter 5, I address work by two liberal scholars, Derek Bok and Martha Nussbaum; consider the problematic presence of dualisms in higher education; and examine what might be required to "change the *terms* of the conversation" (Mignolo, 2009, p. 162; emphasis in original).

Chapter 6 offers an analysis of the ways in which epistemological frameworks set up possibilities for understanding the subject. I am in this chapter especially concerned with what had led my student Cindy to believe that she could expect and demand "streamlined" education. As a student nearing graduation, how had her education so far made it sensible to dismiss queer lives from a course on gender and communication? After addressing the significance of pedagogical expectations in relation to what and how students learn, I examine traditional epistemologies and epistemological approaches to difference. The latter half of chapter 6 expands on the idea that undergraduate education often teaches students to value generalizable, acontextual concepts at the expense of the materiality of lived experience. I examine the role of textbooks in ensuring such valuing, and I also make explicit links between neoliberal ideologies and neoliberal epistemology. I examine the rise of neoliberalism, and its congruence with educational practices, particularly those that normalize "streamlined" education. I assert that what I call "neoliberal epistemology" justifies the elimination of lives that transgress dominant norms. The increasing prevalence of individualism and market-based logics in nearly all aspects of social life, including the ways in which these logics might have informed Cindy's demand for streamlined education, urge a grappling with the ways in which such logics infuse pedagogical settings and with how educators opt to reproduce such logics.

Finally, in chapter 7, I consider the possibilities for faculty members to rigorously pursue educational outcomes that include the capacity to consider democratic practices, justice, ethical agency, and power. Returning to the questions asked in chapter 2 about the obligations of higher education to the social and the related aims of undergraduate education, I offer a rationale for those aims that is grounded in the reality of too much wrong and in the press of implication and interests. In presenting a way to approach the "work of the we" in pedagogical settings, I address how faculty members might consider democratic practices, the public good, and justice. I am interested in this chapter in the role of the disciplines, the constitution of the subject, and the curricular and pedagogical constructions of living together well. Ultimately, I am invested in imagining a different logic for considering the social and the subject, one that can shift the landscape of educational work so that implication and interests are where we begin.

I hope that this book might contribute to possibilities for change in higher education related to the ways in which undergraduate education supports attention to democratic practices, the public good, and justice. My interest in such change, as I have communicated in this chapter, is centrally linked to my belief that in North America, with regard to inequity and justice, there continues to be "too much wrong." I am interested in normalizing, in a range of educational settings, considerations of injustice and possibilities for equity. At a broad level, this book might be useful to anyone with an interest in higher education, and to those concerned with how higher education bears on public life and with what higher education might offer to an engagement with entrenched social issues. At more specific levels within discourses on higher education, I hope that this book is instructive to scholars who in any way pursue questions regarding the role of higher education in public life. The book will likely be relevant to anyone who believes that the work of scholars and educators might benefit from increased clarity and analysis with respect to the purposes and aims of undergraduate education and higher education's obligations to the social. I identify as a critical scholar, and I hope that this book might be of use to liberal scholars. As I state later in the book, faculty members with liberal understandings of education and public life will, on the whole, shape the vast majority of what and how students learn in colleges and universities across North America.

Universities are not monolithic institutions. Differences across institutions of higher learning exist at multiple levels. Objectives and priorities (evidenced by mission statements, etc.); forms of governance; historical developments, current obligations, and primary identities and allegiances; disciplinary structures and norms; and faculty members' priorities, areas of expertise, and training, are only a few of the factors that distinguish universities from each other. At the same time, all universities, regardless of the ways in which they differ from each other, are institutions of power and influence. Faculty members and administrators, those most involved in curricular and pedagogical decisions and activities, have a high degree of agency, even as all of us work within specific institutional, budgetary, and practical constraints that vary from institution to institution. This book explores the ways in which faculty members and institutions take up that agency in relation to a range of questions regarding undergraduate education and the public good. Rather than offering a set of prescriptions or generalizations about how those in university settings pursue such questions, this book is an exploration of the possibilities and ways in which educational institutions and those in them engage with particular understandings of the social and of higher education's obligations to the public good.

The specificity of the location from which I pursue these questions – that of a faculty member working in the social science and humanities disciplines – offers depth to the analyses I present rather than a fixed set of limits or prescriptions. One might work in a faculty or college of liberal arts or math or computer science; a professional school such as law, social work, or education; or at a large, research-intensive university or a small institution focused on teaching. Whatever the contextual factors, all faculty members enact a certain ethical and intellectual orientation to the three questions articulated at the start of this chapter concerning higher education's contract with public life, the constitution of the subject, and how epistemological frameworks construct the social. Even as these questions might be more readily taken up by faculty members in the humanities, social sciences, or the professional schools, they are questions with which we all engage. Likewise, this book might be useful to anyone concerned with the construction and negotiation of curricular and pedagogical work in relation to the broad aims and investments of universities.

At another level, this book brings together a critique of liberal scholarship and an engagement with the materiality of systemic racism in North America. As a white scholar who has been attentive to issues of racism, public life, and higher education over the past decade and a half, I believe that we live with the daily costs and violent consequences of racism. As an educator, I choose to direct my intellectual and affective investments to the significance of those costs and consequences, both in and beyond the professional setting in which I am the most implicated, that of higher education. As I wrote a decade ago, "I critique a cultural practice, racism, from which I benefit and in which I participate. I am a part of the subjects I address" (Simpson, 2003, p. 7). In regard to issues of race in higher education, again, my audience at a broad level is anyone interested in "participat[ing] in [racism's] undoing" (p. x) and in grappling with the ways in which educational practices prevent and hinder us from living together well.

The ways in which different racial groups take up the discourses and material practices of racism are never essentialized. We can all, regardless of our racial group, opt to resist and act against ongoing racial injustice. At the same time, positionality matters. In the library computer room, of the adults in the room, all of whom appeared to me to be white, only one raised an objection to the white man and how he communicated with the boys. In regard to Black-focused schools or state-sanctioned violence against Indigenous men, those who take up these concerns are usually those in racial minority communities. I hope that this book is of value for those who may not have deeply considered the ways in which routine educational practices have racial significance, which may be primarily and not only white people. I also hope that for those who come to the book with an in-depth belief in and understanding of the existence of systemic racism in North America, which may be primarily and not exclusively racial minorities, this book might offer support for a parallel pursuit of change, equity, and justice.

Finally, I want to state plainly that my commitments to racial equity, in particular, and to justice, broadly, come firmly out of an interest in engaging what I understand as an ethical relationality. I might occasionally slip into the long-standing and always accessible routine of exploring issues of race, in order to, as a white person, "do good," fix what is broken for "others," take the moral high ground because "that is what good white people do," or offer a well-meaning charity to "disadvantaged" groups. Despite these possibilities and well-travelled routes, my interest in and commitment to understanding race and racism emerge out of the realization that my complicity in racism harms the relationships in which I participate, and ensures my support for the continuation of an inequitable world. By ignoring racism and other forms of injustice, I participate in constructing a future I do not want to inhabit. Even as the costs of racism are the most burdensome, violent, and consequential for racial minority communities, racism dehumanizes all of us. Racism, and my participation in it, dehumanizes me. Racism and other forms of oppression have significance for the communities in which all of us live. A white man's disrespect, police violence, disproportionate graduation rates by race, broad and significant injustices in North America and globally: none of these inequities are inevitable. We can choose otherwise. We can live differently.

What is wrong persists. To stop looking, to stop seeing, is one place where injustice begins. Hope emerges out of the belief that we can look fully at what is wrong, take in a white man's arrogance, a brown boy's righteous fury, our own response, and choose to imagine, and then practise, a route to a different outcome. Democracy begins with the labour of hope, with a belief in what is possible. Cornel West (2001) has articulated that while "optimism" exists when there is evidence "that things are going to be better," hope acknowledges that "it doesn't look good at all," and "go[es] beyond the evidence and attempt[s] to create new possibilities." Hope, then, can reckon with the fullness of what is wrong and find ways to move forward. Anything less than working at the labour of hope is indulging in a kind of "culture of cynicism" rather than a "language of critique and possibility" (Giroux, 2003, pp. 1, 28). "Thank you for listening to my story." "I hate when you do that. I hate you right now." What did you see in the library? As a teacher, researcher, student, staff person, administrator: what stories do you see, hear, and tell? What hopes live under your skin? The promise of moving from too much wrong to less wrong to justice. This is where my heart lives. This is where this book begins.

This book draws on understandings of democracy, the public good, and justice; critical theory and critical race theory; and auto-ethnography and socio-ethical analysis to question the underlying assumptions of educational practices, as well as to consider how educational spaces might be places of critique and movement towards justice. Through specific and broad stories and analyses, I ask: How do we see? What do we know? How do we act, together? How are we living together well, or not? It demands witnesses. It demands that we keep our eyes open and that we attend to the material realities of how people live. It asks that we listen, especially to the stories of those with whom we disagree. It requires us to question power. Higher education offers an opportunity to consider the work of democracy and our practices of seeing and habits of sociality, to listen to a range of stories, and to question power. Universities provide a place to learn, disagree, contest, doubt, hope, and hold onto our own caring. Universities offer a place to think not only about what and how, but about why and in whose interests. The process of learning, of working at knowledge, can become a story that gets under our skin, that pulls at our commitments, that reminds us that our choices matter.

2 Higher Education and the Social Contract: Considering the "We" of Public Life

On 15 February 2012, I attended the first annual Indigeneity Lecture sponsored by the Centre for Indigenous Governance at Ryerson University in Toronto. Taiaiake Alfred, a professor of Indigenous Governance and Political Science at the University of Victoria, spoke about the construction of Indigeneity in Canada, and he asserted that "who we are in Canada today is still" grounded in colonial frameworks. Alfred focused on ongoing expressions of that colonialism, linking such expressions to the Indian Act, assimilation policies in Canada, and the 1969 White Paper, all government policies and practices that have made it impossible for Indigenous communities to maintain any level of sovereignty or self-determination. As Alfred pointed out, no evidence demonstrates that assimilation alleviates any of the suffering that is a result of colonialism. Challenging those "satisfied with an artifice of comfort," Alfred made clear in his lecture his position that Canada has not achieved justice in relation to Indigenous communities.

Alfred is certainly not alone in his assessment of the ongoing existence of colonialism in Canada (Coulthard, 2007; Mack, 2010; St Denis, 2011; Thobani, 2007). Scholars across disciplines have been highly critical of ongoing manifestations of colonialism in Canada, addressing, for example, the high rates of Indigenous peoples in prison in Canada and the destruction of Indigenous land and communities (La Prairie, 2002; Mack, 2010; see also Carleton, 2011; Edmonds, 2010; Freeman, 2010; Krebs, 2011; Lee, 2011; Moore, Walker, & Skelton, 2011). As these scholars have pointed out, Canada has generated and continues to generate much of its wealth through the plunder of natural resources. At the same time, for many of those living in Canada, "creating devastation is termed progress" (Lawrence, 2008).

Scholars who offer this critique, through publications and public lectures, in classrooms, and in other venues, ensure that such knowledge remains part of public and intellectual discourse. At the same time, it is possible to live in North America and, indeed, to teach and conduct research as if the existence of racism and colonialism are non-existent and/or irrelevant to public life. Such issues again invoke questions of how and what we see, of what holds our attention and makes claims on our priorities. The challenges these intellectuals pose to the nation-states of Canada and the United States, to institutions, and to those of us living here are critical to understanding both the failures of democracy and the difficulties of justice. These scholars directly raise questions of the public good and of the social. As Alfred said during his presentation, referring to Canada at a broad level, "Our idea about our self is a contention." How do faculty members regard and respond to such knowledge? Do we seek it out? Dismiss it? Offer it to our students?

On the morning of 16 February 2012, the day after Alfred's presentation, I turned on my computer and went online. At that time, the template for my university's homepage consisted of a large photograph depicting students, faculty members, or others from the university; the text "Everything you discover at Waterloo belongs to you," in all capital letters, and superimposed in large script over the photograph; and links across the top and bottom, and in a small area on the right of the screen. The photograph, which changed every four or five days, and the superimposed script, took up about 80% of the screen. On 16 February, the photograph was different from the day before. On the 16th, I opened up the homepage to see a photograph of Chris Lok, a University of Waterloo student, standing in front of pump jacks in Cold Lake, Alberta. According to the photo caption on the website, "4B Mechanical Engineering student, Chris Lok, poses on a co-op work term in Cold Lake, Alberta. Cold Lake is the second largest oil sand deposit in Canada next to Fort McMurray. This photo is taken on a worksite called a pad and the left-hand side are pump jacks pumping oil off the ground."

According to a news release addressing oil sand licences in Cold Lake, Alberta, "Although tar sands occur in more than 70 countries, the bulk is found in Canada in four regions: Athabasca, Wabasca, Cold Lake, and Peace River" (Marketwired). In February 2012, Imperial Oil Ltd, owned by Exxon Mobil Corp., confirmed that it would "go ahead with a C$2 billion expansion of its Cold Lake oil sands project, adding 40,000 barrels per day of new production to Canada's largest thermal oil sands development" (Haggett, 2012).

As I looked at the picture on my university's website, with the pump jacks dominating in the foreground, Chris Lok in a work helmet and uniform, a few fir trees in the background, and the proclamation that "everything" one "discovers" at Waterloo is theirs to have, I thought back to Alfred's presentation. How can universities not be socially implicated, part of the complicated sets of relationships in which people live and work? If, as critics charge, "the ethics of tar sands development are highly questionable ... com[ing] with a heavy price in terms of [Indigenous] health, cultural traditions, and ways of life" (Vasey, 2011), how do university practices represent alignment with or resistance to such projects?

The University of Waterloo boasts "the largest postsecondary school co-op program in the world with almost 16,000 students enrolled over three semesters" (University of Waterloo, 2012). Chris Lok most likely gained experience that may well be useful in oil sands production. Yet, how does such experience and use of that experience become "devastation" that is "termed progress"? Universities communicate their investments in routine and far-reaching ways. A large number of students participate in the co-op program in my department. Those involved with co-op programs, across departments, faculties, and universities, interact with multiple settings and organizations. As faculty members and students, we are enmeshed in a variety of relationships beyond the university.

How do those in universities consider the range of conflicting interests in which they are implicated? As I started my day on the 16th, sitting with Alfred's critique that I had heard the night before, looking at the picture of Chris Lok standing next to huge pump jacks, I wondered: how can we not be implicated, as faculty members and as universities? What is the significance of denying our sociality, of turning away from difficult yet persistent ethical questions, of claiming that neutrality is possible and desirable? What do students learn when they read, every time they see the university's homepage, about making "discover[ies]" that they then own?[1] Where is the "we"? Where is a notion of the public, the possibility and value of equitable conditions for everyone living in Canada and the United States?

As I asked in chapter 1, how do we move from too much wrong to less wrong to justice? How do we see, identify, and approach the interpersonal intricacies, as well as the broad social relationships and norms, that constitute our day-to-day lives? What is required in order to name injustice and to imagine justice? What is the role of undergraduate education in this process? Interactions in a library computer room, differential graduation rates by race, public officials leaving Indigenous men in the cold to die, students completing their co-op terms in industry settings that have consequences for how we live together: all undeniably have a presence in public life. What do these and other issues have to do with knowledge production and teaching, the central work of universities? How is the work of faculty members a response to these concerns?

As researchers and teachers, we inevitably locate ourselves in regard to our disciplines and the subject matter we pursue. All of our teaching and research in some way considers, prioritizes, challenges, ignores, examines, and is otherwise implicated in relation to the undeniable sociality of public life. As educators, we are social actors with both agency and responsibility. What we choose to teach and study is in part an indication of our ways of seeing, of how we make sense of self in relation to other. This chapter begins with the assumption that, at their best, colleges and universities in North America will encourage in students a willingness to consider the material conditions of people's lives, an active sense of their own agency in relation to effecting change, an ability to link knowledge with power and practice, and an imagination for the public good. All four of these capacities are centrally connected to strengthening democratic life.

In this chapter, I am concerned with the first of three questions I articulated in chapter 1: What does higher education's social contract with public life require? What are the obligations undergraduate education has to the public good and to the material conditions of how people live? When I communicated my hope that students would consider sexuality, Cindy responded with an expectation of her own. Allison asserted her sense of un-belonging in the nation-state of Canada. Both of these students articulated their sense of the world around them and their relationship to it. Likewise, Alfred's lecture, his assertion that in Canada, "our idea of our self is a contention," stands in direct relationship to that photograph of Chris Lok on my university's homepage. In some ways, all of these scenarios pose a very basic question about teaching, a question I began to discuss in chapter 1: What is the subject? They also pose a fundamental question of higher education generally: How does higher education negotiate its relationship with a range of communities, and with interests that can and do conflict? This chapter centrally examines two issues. First, how does higher education, at a broad level, understand its obligations to the communities in which we live? Second, given these obligations, what are the ends of undergraduate education? This chapter offers an overview and analysis of existing literature on these questions.

Education and Public Life: The Expectations of the Social

This book examines the relationship of undergraduate education and public life. Many scholars assert that clarity about the world into which students will graduate can inform how we approach undergraduate education (Biesta, 2006; Kezar, 2005; London, 2003; Lynd, 1939; Mills, 1959). While scholars widely acknowledge that the particulars of that world are complex, changing, multilayered, and with numerous and conflicting interests (Axelrod, Anisef, & Lin, 2001; Nussbaum, 1997; Schneider, 2000; Tudiver, 1999), these scholars, especially those working within a liberal framework, have simultaneously authored very little work that succinctly and plainly addresses how one might evaluate and choose among these interests. Scholars note the value of teaching discernment (Nussbaum, 1997; Rothblatt, 1993), yet do not specify what ends such discernment ought to serve. Thus there remains in the literature a persistent open-endedness as to where such discernment might lead individuals and communities, even as scholars have acknowledged that "universities have an important responsibility to address social needs" (Bok, 1982, p. 302).

At first glance, such acknowledgment might seem to be a useful starting point. As "the list of democracy's discontents grows lengthier with each passing year" (Schneider, 2000, p. 107), "social needs" are not lacking. "Social needs" might include individuals repeatedly removing the banner of the queer student group at my university and the lack of any institutional response, public service employees leaving Indigenous men in the cold to die, and growing income inequities across North America. Yet, "social needs" might also be perceived to include ensuring that local businesses stay competitive through supporting pay rates that drop below a living wage; maintaining public trust in police services, even as these services might harm and kill individuals in Black and Indigenous communities; and continued extraction of oil across Canada. The vast majority of higher education scholarship offers few clues as to how educators might negotiate these needs. The term "social needs" is all-encompassing. Stating that universities should consider social needs does not necessarily point to any particular kind of future. In the context of much of higher education scholarship, when it comes to discerning among competing interests, the most logical conclusion one might draw is that all choices, or at least most, are equally valid.

When Cindy raised the charge of "streamlined," this came after we had briefly discussed the repeated removal of the queer student group's banner on my campus. Is the removal of this banner potentially a "subject" in undergraduate education? How do institutions respond to the press of public concerns that play out in various ways on campuses? In conversations with Adam Garcia, the student Coordinator of the queer student group at the University of Waterloo from September 2009 through December 2011,[2] I learned that prior to 2010, students typically raised the large banner of the queer student group in a kind of informal yet very public event during Coming Out Week every October. The raising of the banner was a form of community building and affirmation for queer students. The banner was removed twice before the end of Coming Out Week in October 2007 and once in October 2008. In 2008, the banner was found in a garbage can on campus.

At the start of Coming Out Week in October 2009, in response to the banner's removal in 2007 and 2008, students in GLOW set up an overnight watch staffed by student volunteers to hopefully prevent removal of the banner and contacted campus police to assist with this. A year later, in 2010, GLOW decided to put up a smaller banner in a different location. Because the new location offered a more permanent home, and because of the height of the new location, Plant Operations staff rather than students raised the banner in 2010. The new banner is approximately one-quarter the size of the larger banner that was removed in 2007 and 2008.

Garcia was not aware if any formal complaint had been registered with campus police in the three instances of the banner's removal in 2007 and 2008. To my knowledge, the student newspaper did not cover the removal of the large banner and the adoption of the new, much smaller banner.[3] In the class in which Cindy called for "streamlined" education, very few students were aware of the banner's removal. Indeed, streamlined forms of education might deem such subject matter irrelevant to a course on communication. This is a clear example of how educational institutions engage with the social, respond to, in this case, the "we" of institutions, and their relationship to queer students. How do we publicly engage these issues? What stays behind the scenes, removed from view? How do individuals and institutions invest in public spaces, and what do these spaces affirm and normalize? For Cindy, the issue of the banner's removal apparently had little if anything to do with her education, even as this issue was close at hand and had significance in relation to the university at which she and her peers were students.

When considering the deaths of Indigenous men, differential graduation rates by race, and violence against queer communities, many might consider these priorities highly problematic. For such individuals, these issues might have nothing at all to do with "the subject" in undergraduate education. For faculty members and students, how do various social needs inhabit different levels of urgency and locate themselves within the landscape of what takes priority? How do we understand the expectations of the social? What is our relationship to interactions that disturb, upset, and unsettle? Are institutions of higher education responsible for considering "what is going on in the general struggle for power in modern society" (Mills, 1959, p. 99)? Education is always a response to these questions. Whether we adopt a stance of indifference or of investment, or a combination of both, we are "talking back" to these concerns (Pagano, 1999; Rooke, 2003).

Students earning a social work degree learn about the complications of poverty and the dynamics of family systems. Those in a business program become familiar with management techniques or the possible responses to organizational conflict. Philosophy students better understand our desire for meaning and our sense of good and of evil. The social work graduate, employed in a community health care centre, will offer financial resources, recommend counselling, encourage job training, and pursue removing a child from or returning a child to his or her family. The philosophy major, for example, works as a customer service officer for the Conservative Party of Canada and responds to inquiries and requests in ways that endorse a particular vision of Canada and its politicians. Particularly concerning what students learn, higher education is an institution that contributes to practices of thinking, feeling, and doing; informs the worldview that students hold; and bears on social norms in regard to the relationship of self and other (Bok, 2006; Bowen, 1977; Colby et al., 2000; Nussbaum, 1997; Pascarella & Terenzini, 2005; Rothblatt, 1993).

Scholars continue to grapple with higher education's responsibilities to life outside of the classroom and with the primary aims of undergraduate education (Aronowitz, 2008; Axelrod, 2002; Bok, 2006; Coté & Allahar, 2007; Schön, 1995). As I noted in chapter 1, all faculty members exercise agency within a complex set of possibilities and constraints. For many scholars, the "shift from a public good knowledge/learning regime to an academic capitalist knowledge/learning regime" represents a significant constraint (Slaughter & Rhoades, 2004, p. 8); see also Polster, 2006; Readings, 1997; Rhoads & Torres, 2006; Turk, 2008; Woodhouse, 2009). In many ways, this shift, and the emphasis in universities on "faculty, students, administrators, and academic professionals … using a variety of state resources to create new circuits of knowledge that link higher education institutions to the new economy" (Slaughter & Rhoades 2004, p. 1) sets up a far-reaching and powerful set of institutional norms and priorities. All faculty members work within these norms and priorities, regardless of the extent to which they agree with this shift or not. Particularly in relation to considering the obligations higher education has to the social, the ways in which institutions of higher education and those in them orient themselves to these obligations (in terms of institutional structure, governance, policies, reward systems, etc.) are crucial.

In a public good knowledge/learning regime, knowledge is a "public good to which the citizenry has claims" (Slaughter & Rhoades 2004, p. 28). In this framework, which exists alongside the academic capitalist knowledge/learning regime, the pursuit of knowledge has a direct relationship to public benefits. Knowledge and related goods offer benefits to society as a whole. In contrast, in a model based on academic capitalism, universities pursue "privatization and profit taking in which institutions, inventor faculty, and corporations have claims that come before those of the public" (Slaughter & Rhoades 2004, p. 29; see also Woodhouse, 2009). This basic shift and university allegiances with various forms of academic capitalism do actively bear on the ways in which faculty members consider higher education's obligations to public life.

In considering what these obligations entail, scholarship variously claims (1) that a social contract exists between higher education and public life (Aronowitz, 2005; Bok, 1982; Kezar, 2005; London, 2003; Schneider, 2000) and (2) that civic outcomes constitute one of the aims of undergraduate education (Aronowitz, 2008; Axelrod, Anisef & Lin, 2001; Biesta, 2006; Côté & Allahar, 2007; Dzur, 2008; Giroux & Searls Giroux, 2004; Saltmarsh, 2011a). At the same time, beyond these two broad assertions, important issues persist. What does this social contract include? Does it require an allegiance to specific interests? How do democratic societies bring certain ethical priorities to bear on individuals and communities? What is the most appropriate way for faculty members to attend to these priorities in our teaching?

This chapter examines two assertions: (1) higher education has a social contract with public life and (2) undergraduate education ought to be attentive to the significance of the public good. What as educators do we understand our responsibilities to be, not only to the business, philosophy, or social work student, but also to the communities in which these students will live and work? Issues persist not only among scholars located in the field of higher education, but among faculty members teaching across a range of courses. Again, most broadly, what are the ends of undergraduate education? Should faculty members be centrally concerned with offering content, communicating disciplinary knowledge, preparing students to consider "ever-changing social ends" (Martínez Alemán & Salkever, 2001, p. 106; see also Bok, 2006; Fallis, 2007; Lynd, 1939), developing students' ability to negotiate among competing interests, or all of these objectives? How do we as faculty members construct our own sense of the social, of the aims of knowledge, and of our relationship to the worlds in which we and our students live? Which and whose interests have priority in democratic societies, and what do these interests and priorities have to do with undergraduate education?

Higher Education, Public Life, and the Purposes of Undergraduate Education: An Overview

In considering the relationship of democratic practices to undergraduate education, this chapter considers two areas of scholarship: (1) the responsibilities that higher education has to public life and (2) the aims of undergraduate education. In the next chapter, I examine the literature on the scholarship of engagement, civic engagement, and service learning. Throughout the book, I will draw on theories of democratic practices as they relate to both education and public life. The term democratic practices broadly refers to the habits of "associated living" (Dewey, 1998, p. 390) that individuals, institutions, and communities pursue and to the "process of discovering the means by which a scattered, mobile, and manifold public may so recognize itself as to identify and define its interests" (Dewey, 2008, p. 327; see also chapter 1). Democracies require substantive and ongoing attention to the "hard-won idea of a public good: a good that, being more than the aggregate of individual interests, denotes a common commitment to social justice and equality" (Nixon, 2011, p. 1). The notion of "democratic practices," situated within a discussion of the responsibilities of undergraduate education to the social, is an explicit acknowledgment of my assumption that democratic modes of living have a necessary connection to higher education in North America.

There has long been attention in higher education to the basic aims of colleges and universities and to the ends they might serve, especially in connection with public life (Bok, 2006; Daniels & Trebilcock, 2005; Engell & Dangerfield, 2005; Fallis, 2007; Lynd, 1939). While most scholars agree that the purposes that undergraduate education serves generally include professional/vocational, civic, and intellectual (Engell & Dangerfield, 2005; Nussbaum, 1997), there is less agreement concerning the specifics of each of these purposes and their consequences for both higher education and public life. One set of scholars orients their discussion of purposes to capacities with which students should graduate, grounds their theoretical orientation in the individual rather than the social, and advocates caution in terms of making commitments to concrete needs and priorities (Axelrod, 2002; Côté & Allahar, 2007; Fallis, 2007; Nussbaum, 2010). Another group of scholars explicitly addresses purposes as related to the material realities of how people live, individual capacities in the context of relationships of power, and ethical investments in the interests of justice (Aronowitz, 2008; Freire, 1998; Grande, 2004; Mohanty, 2003; Razack, 1998).[4] In the conclusion to this chapter, I will assert that, to a large degree, work by liberal scholars that addresses the aims of undergraduate education simultaneously (1) maintains a high degree of currency with faculty members and other educational stakeholders and (2) often obscures and harms possibilities for justice and for what one scholar has identified as the "modification of the institutional framework as a whole" (Mills, 1959, p. 90).

The Relationship of Higher Education and Public Life

In 1939, Lynd asserted that the basic question of what educational institutions should do was rarely asked. More than three-quarters of a century later, few faculty members have an opportunity to consider this question in a sustained manner, yet the question of purpose is obviously a crucial point of departure. One way in which scholars have responded to this question is through articulating higher education's responsibilities to life beyond the institution. Four frameworks for understanding the "social contract" higher education has with public life include (1) a basic acknowledgment that a social contract exists (Bok, 1982; Côté & Allahar, 2007; Fallis, 2007; Nussbaum, 1997; Pocklington & Tupper, 2002), (2) a more specific recognition of the public

Table 2.1. Higher Education and Its Social Contract with Public Life: An Overview of Four
Frameworks

Framework	Central idea	Key components
Social contract exists	Offers basic attention to "needs of society"; universities have "ethical responsibilities"	• Consideration of social needs and of ethical responsibilities, abstract and unspecified • Urges scholars to remain "neutral" regarding prioritization of needs
Attention to public interest	Clear references to universities having obligations to "public interest"	• "Public interest" generally contrasted with private interests • Scholars address university as a public good, and importance of students learning about public good • Some attention to pressures to "train" students as a dilution of education as public good • Little consistency in regard to meaning of "public good"
Consideration of moral and ethical dimensions	Social contract requires scholars to consider concrete values in relation to university work	• Commonly referenced values include truth, justice, community, and academic freedom • Critique of market-based values and individualism
Analysis of competing interests and justice	Universities are obligated to pursue justice through teaching and research	• Assumption that injustice exists, at individual and institutional levels • Research and teaching are not neutral activities; always have specific interests • Universities have obligation to convey to students a robust understanding of and imagination for public good

interest (Grant, 2002; Piper, 2003; Rooke, 2003; Sossin, 2004; Turk, 2000),
(3) attention to the moral and ethical dimensions of the social contract
(Chambers, 2005; Kezar, 2005; London, 2003; Minnich, 1997; Walzer,
2006), and (4) an insistence on grappling with competing interests
and the importance of power in connection with concrete social issues
(Giroux & Searls Giroux, 2004; Lynd, 1939; Mills, 1959; Mohanty, 2003;
Razack, 1998; Torres & Rhoads, 2006; Simpson, 2003). Broadly speaking,
the first three levels of attention primarily address concepts detached
from practice, and the fourth area of work explicitly considers ethical
priorities and competing interests in regard to questions such as differential high school graduation rates by race or state-sanctioned violence
against Indigenous communities (see Table 2.1).

The first type of commitment primarily affirms that a "social contract" exists, with a largely unspecified understanding of what this contract involves. Scholars assert that "universities must constantly address … ethical responsibilities in all their relations with the outside world" (Bok, 1982, p. 299); that "universities have an obligation to use their academic resources to respond to public needs" (p. 78); that universities ought to "articulate, explore, and affirm the social contract … listening and responding to the concerns of the society" (Fallis, 2007, p. 115); and that universities "should render thoughtful service to society … teaching must be relevant to societal needs" (Pocklington & Tupper, 2002, p. 9). All of these scholars generally affirm that (1) the world beyond the university exists and (2) those in the university ought to consider this world. At the same time, these scholars leave unarticulated both the focus of that consideration (i.e., which or whose issues and priorities) and the desired outcomes of that consideration, particularly in relation to competing interests.

Alongside references to "concerns" or "public needs," one finds almost no in-depth identification of what these needs are or might be in concrete terms. Further, these scholars critique those who do opt to openly indicate allegiances to specific priorities. Fallis (2007) expresses his support for "disinterested research" and notes that "it might be that social criticism … spoils the habits of good scholarship" (2007, p. 137). Pocklington and Tupper (2002) refer to "independent universities" (p. 9), implying some form of separation from society. Schneider (2000), addressing liberal education in the second half of the twentieth century, sums up this approach well:

> In a complex world, the academy prepared citizens, not by teaching them about any particular set of issues, but rather by developing minds that would become, as an outcome of higher learning, capable of engaging many issues … This is the primary outcome of your liberal education … a capacity for disciplined inquiry in any and every endeavor you choose … The academy … does not presume to provide judgments on fundamental questions of public values – whether of the good society or the good life. (pp. 105–106)

As Schneider's analysis suggests, scholars who endorse this viewpoint posit that students should be prepared to think about concrete issues once they leave the university, and that consideration of "public values" is not to be part of their education. Beyond asserting that higher education must consider social needs, this group of scholars offers very little specificity on the content of these needs.

This approach to higher education is deeply rooted. The social contract, often referred to as a charter, has been in place since Harvard College was founded in 1636. Since this time, the development of higher education has included ongoing commitments to serving society, through various structural measures including land grant colleges, statewide extension services, and outreach programs at urban universities (Chambers, 2005).[5] In a discussion of historical debates regarding the obligations universities have to the public, Bok (1982) argues that "everyone involved – traditionalists, multiversity enthusiasts, activist reformers – believed that universities ought to serve society" (p. 66). In sum, nearly all scholars would likely agree that "higher education's role has been considered critical to society's well-being" (Newman & Couturier, 2002, p. 6). At the same time, despite the widespread commitment to this role, most scholars have not offered in-depth attention to what this means in concrete terms, with regard to "society's well-being" or to undergraduate education.

A second framework for considering the role of universities in public life can be found among scholars who make specific reference to the public interest (Grant, 2002; Piper, 2003; Rooke, 2003; Sossin, 2004; Turk, 2000). While their attention to the term "public" is minimal, these scholars sufficiently contrast the term public to a set of "private" interests so as to constitute a more specific conceptual framework than that of "social needs" articulated by the first body of literature. Scholars who both acknowledge the existence of a public good, and assert that universities should consider it, primarily make reference to the public good in relation to higher education in three ways: (1) the university as a public good that makes a positive contribution to social life (Aronowitz, 2006; Daniels & Trebilcock, 2005; Nixon, 2011; Sossin, 2004), (2) the ways in which universities ought to encourage in students an awareness of the public good (Nixon, 2011; Rooke, 2003), and (3) discussion of the meaning of the term public good (Giroux, 2005a; Nixon, 2011; Sossin, 2004).

In broad discussions of the relationship between the state and higher education, Daniels and Trebilcock (2005) state that, in part based on public funding for universities, "the activities of the institution [ought to be] congruent with the public interest" (Daniels & Trebilcock, 2005, p. 87). According to Sossin (2004), "public universities exist in order to advance the public interest" (p. 1). The public good is also a concept with which students ought to be familiar (Nixon, 2011; Rooke, 2003). In response to social challenges, for example, "To be able to reason together ... is a necessary public good," and a good worth teaching (Nixon, 2011, p. 90). Further, scholars have asserted that the process of discerning the public good, which involves "helping students to move beyond the self as presently constituted to an appreciation of the perspectives of others," will not necessarily "develop 'naturally.'" Rather, this process must be taught (Rooke, 2003, p. 230).

With regard to the meaning of the term public good, identifying consensus or extensive detail in the higher education literature is difficult. A review essay that covers three prominent books on higher education published in the mid-2000s concludes that, even as all three books address the threat of commercialization of higher education to the public good, "each of the authors says little about the notion of the public good" (Kezar 2005, p. 473). As a result, readers must "develop their own understanding" of what public good means" (Kezar (2008, p. 481n1)). A few scholars do offer some attention to the meaning of the public good generally and in higher education contexts. Contrasting the public good with the public interest, Nixon (2011) asserts that the "public interest is the aggregate of individual interests or preferences" (p. x), while the public good "involves complex moral and political judgements regarding what constitutes the good for the polity as a whole" (ibid.). Linked to "cultural, economic, personal and social well-being," higher education "offers a dedicated space" to address the public good and "supports the development of an educated public" who might be actively involved in articulating the public good (ibid.). In this sense, higher education is a public good, and it contributes to the public good. Further, higher education remains one of the few institutional settings in which individuals can work at defining and realizing the public good.

The contrast Nixon makes between "individual interests" and the "polity as a whole" is taken a step further by those who distinguish between increasing privatization and inequity and the erosion of the public good (Aronowitz, 2006). Concerning the mission of universities, scholars have pointed out the role of higher education in "training" students: "The new mantra of higher education is that by training technically competent labor, but also by providing income to a large number of blue-collar, clerical, and professional workers, post-secondary schooling makes significant contributions to local and regional economies" (Aronowitz, 2005, pp. 116–117). For these scholars, contrasting the public good with privatized, economic gain clearly points to the public good as requiring attention to understandings of social well-being that go beyond market norms and priorities.

An additional aspect of the definition of the public good in the higher education literature is connected to values and to the public good as a framework or process. For Sossin (2004), "public interest values" include "citizenship and civic virtues, pursuit of knowledge, [and] accessibility of social mobility" (p. 1). Further, the public good is more a framework than a fixed "set of directives," and involves a "participatory claim on whose voices will be considered legitimate … and whose vested interests must be considered" (p. 2). In sum, references to the public good make bolder claims on the substance of higher education's social contract with public life than do discussions of higher education's obligations to respond to "social needs."

A third level of regard for the social contract is evidenced among scholars who make reference to the public good, and go further to suggest a particular set of values that institutions of higher education ought to recognize and pursue through teaching, research, and service (Kezar, 2005; London, 2003; Minnich, 1997). These scholars link values including "equality, service, truth, justice, community, academic freedom, and autonomy" to democratic practices (Kezar, 2005, p. 23). In a framework of aspirational democracy, these values also encompass a commitment to supporting human rights, to undoing social hierarchies and divisions, and to pursuing an "egalitarian, relational pluralism" (Minnich, 1997, p. 199). Less specific language that nevertheless invokes a sense of values notes higher education's obligation to consider "conscience and community" (Thomas, 2005, p. 31) and "civic change and renewal" (London, 2003, p. 23). While the above-mentioned work does not necessarily offer exhaustive discussions on the significance of these values for higher education, their attention to values does potentially make demands of faculty members to consider the ethical components of specific social needs.

Scholarship that is broadly defined as "critical theory" constitutes a fourth body of work that addresses the social contract and directly challenges much of the literature addressed above. Critical theorists generally support the idea "that injustice and subjugation shape … the lived world" (Kincheloe, 2008, p. 46).[6] They are interested in understanding "the social construction of experience" in the interests of a "more egalitarian and democratic social order" (pp. 47–48). On the whole, critical theorists agree that institutional injustice exists, that unchecked capitalism harms democratic forms of living, and that "research ought to serve an emancipatory goal" (Torres & Rhoads, 2006, p. 6). This work centrally and explicitly addresses questions concerning the social contract that higher education has with public life.

For critical scholars, the obligations that higher education has to public life must be explicitly and rigorously connected to democratic life and the reduction of human suffering. Building on critical theory, which has long (1) acknowledged the importance of "fight[ing] domination and exploitation" (Kellner, 2000, p. 308) and (2) asserted that "schools are 'sites of struggle' where the broader relations of power, domination, and authority are played out" (Grande, 2004, p. 6), these authors are concerned with issues that include widening income gaps; disproportionately high numbers of individuals from Black, Latino, and Indigenous communities in the criminal justice system; homophobia in schools; and a host of additional social concerns that bear on the material conditions of how people live. For critical scholars, faculty members ought to be centrally concerned with institutional transformation and social change that lead to justice and equity. The work that higher education does through knowledge production and teaching is not neutral, and it goes far beyond "transmitting" information. Rather, especially teaching ought to instil in students the importance of "shap[ing] a better world [and] ... creating a world without exploitation and oppression – a world without poverty, ignorance, and disease" (Aronowitz, 2008, p. xiii). In response to the question of "education for whom, and for what" (p. 72), critical scholars believe that ignoring injustice puts democracy itself at risk.

In addition to the social contract requiring attention to capacities for social change and institutional transformation that will lead to justice, a second component of the social contract that higher education has with public life for critical scholars is the necessity of imparting to students an awareness of and imagination for the public good. This awareness requires the ability to rigorously critique and question the relationship of knowledge, power, and the conditions in which people live. Further, faculty members and students alike must become familiar with the requirements and dimensions of the public good. This familiarity begins with a language and sensibility that can discern among competing interests, particularly as these interests will align in various ways with democratic possibilities and with market-based outcomes. In this sense, democratic societies have commitments to particular ethical priorities such as equity, reducing all forms of oppression, the possibility of wide participation among individuals and communities in shaping the policies and practices that will affect the conditions in which they live, and support for representational and material practices that do not do violence. Part of the social contract involves ensuring that students can articulate and enact such practices, particularly in the context of increasing levels of greed, individualism, and economic efficiency, which actively reduce the possibilities for being human and for living in a just world.

In sum, for critical scholars, educators must not only acknowledge questions of social justice and the existence of the public good, but also have an obligation to pursue "democratic possibilities" that include "people actively engaging in meaningful social relations and participating in decisions that affect their lives" (Torres & Rhoads, 2006, pp. 5, 6). These scholars are firm about the existence of injustice at individual and institutional levels, and they assert that education should "draw out and examine links between the practices of everyday life and wider structures of domination" (Coté, Day, & de Peuter, 2007, p. 7). Critical scholars make strong links between the existence of injustice, democratic values, and the public good, and claim that the task of higher education is to explicitly consider these links.

These four areas of commitment offer overlapping yet distinct perspectives on higher education's commitment to public life and point to how these commitments might inform undergraduate education. The first three bodies of work, largely authored by liberal scholars, offer almost no specificity or concreteness regarding (1) what the social contract includes, (2) how the social contract has necessary connections with democratic ends, and (3) what its ethical priorities are. Likewise, many of the same scholars object to the ways in which critical theorists "have an agenda" and maintain too little distance from the subjects they pursue (see, e.g., Fallis, 2007, p. 137).

On the whole, in the first three bodies of work, abstract formulations prevail, and can be interpreted in a variety of ways. One cannot be certain, for example, whether or not the social contract requires, encourages, or leaves entirely optional attention to questions of justice. In terms of ethical content, a faculty person might ask if contributing to an increase in profits for a high tech company and decreasing disproportionate graduation rates by race are equally of value. While the second and third bodies of work do name specific value-related terms, they offer little discussion addressing how these values might be applied, particularly when one must navigate competing interests. The fourth body of work avoids these areas of ambiguity. Critical scholarship is transparent and specific about its ethical commitments. Following a discussion of the ends of undergraduate education, I will further examine these tensions.

The Ends of Undergraduate Education   — *start*

Scholars broadly affirm three ends to which students ought to be educated, including (1) intellectual, (2) professional/vocational, and (3) civic/social. Intellectual capacities have long been central to the aims of undergraduate education. Although preparation for "the normal obligations of citizenship" (Kimball, 1995, p. 21) held sway in higher education until the early fifth century, by the early 1800s, there had been a shift to a focus on the "proper exercise of mental faculties" (p. 151). The intellectual ends of higher education have often included the acquisition of knowledge, which can encompass "a broad understanding of human nature, society, and institutions, accompanied by a critical capacity to make choices and distinctions, and to exercise, where necessary, a responsible independence of mind" (Rothblatt, 1993, p. 63). These scholars generally affirm the value of knowledge as an end in itself (see, e.g., Hauerwas, 2007; Newman, 1888). Intellectual ends also include a respect for and encouragement of what is commonly termed "the life of the mind" – the routine exercising of intellectual curiosity, the examination of different perspectives, the ability and willingness to consider inconsistencies in one's own ideas, and a rigorous pursuit of concepts and theories and the ways in which they shape how we understand the world around us (Axelrod, 2000; Nussbaum, 1997; Rothblatt, 1993).

At a minimum, most would agree that undergraduate education should have some role in preparing students for the workforce and employment (Brint, Riddle, Turk-Bicakci, & Levy, 2005; Endres, 2002). Indeed, little to no scholarship calls for a complete disregard of vocational ends. Rather, scholarship has examined the ways in which higher education, including the education of undergraduates, has been overly attentive to the demands of the economy. While ideally, "knowledge for its own sake and knowledge for the sake of power and economic usefulness cohabit and reinforce one another" (Engell & Dangerfield, 2005, p. 209), many scholars share the concern that economic ends are too heavily shaping university education (Turk, 2000; Tudiver, 1999). In sum, even as nearly all scholars would agree that education ought to consider how higher education prepares students for workforce demands, finding attention to the question of how vocational and intellectual ends might coexist is more difficult. While many scholars might agree that the intellectual ends have priority over vocational ends, consideration of how faculty members might prioritize the intellectual ends and simultaneously give appropriate attention to vocational ends is much rarer.

Scholars have clearly addressed the civic-related outcomes of higher education (Colby, Beaumont, Ehrlich, & Corngold, 2007). According to Fallis (2007), "the democratic aims of universities should be made more explicit" (p. x). Engell and Dangerfield (2005) assert, "Higher education acts as an *instrumental social good* when it promotes awareness of, and derives benefit from, the lives of all participants" (p. 26; emphasis in original). Other claims related to the role of undergraduate education in terms of its civic function include the importance of a social purpose rather than an individualistic aim (Johnston, 2000), a liberal education in the interests of an "effective, pluralistic, community" (Martínez Alemán & Salkever, 2001, p. 134), the "development of citizens able to participate in key decisions affecting the polity" (Aronowitz, 2001, p. 98), and liberal education as a "cultivation of the whole human being for the functions of citizenship and life generally" (Nussbaum, 1997, p. 9). The significant increase of scholarship on civic education and service learning also attests to a focused consideration of the civic ends of undergraduate education. (I further address this body of work in chapter 3). For the most part, this scholarship articulates the components of civic ends without connecting these components, for example, to Cindy's query about where queer lives fit in a course on gender or how government employees engage in violence against Indigenous communities.

Most would agree that scholars must consider intellectual, civic, and professional/vocational purposes when addressing the aims and ends of undergraduate education. On the whole, these ends have been examined as distinct and often discrete priorities. Fundamental questions remain as to the relationship of these ends to each other and, even more importantly, regarding the connection of these ends to life outside of the classroom. Indeed, the latter concern, regarding how graduates will put their education to use, ought to ideally shape questions of the former, or the relationship of civic, intellectual, and professional ends. Engell and Dangerfield (2005) assert that the "instrumental functions" of higher education include economic, social, and civic. These functions rest on the ethical application of knowledge and on an intellectual goal. The "intellectual goal or end is the definitive one. It is the final cause of the ethical goal, as well as the economic, social, and civic functions" (p. 24). Likewise, Bok criticizes those who believe that "there must be a *single* overarching purpose" (2006, p. 58; emphasis in original) for undergraduate education, and emphasizes the mutually reinforcing nature of intellectual and civic ends, in particular. Despite these initial forays into considering how the three ends relate to each other and which, if any, takes priority, a vagueness about the relationship among all three, and a lack of robust discussion of how these ends relate to the social contract persist.

Ideally, the ends of undergraduate education will have a conceptual and practical fit with the social contract that universities have with public life. In this way, the work of undergraduate education might be explicitly integrated with the role that universities play in society more generally. As noted earlier in this chapter, among liberal scholars, the social contract is not thoroughly defined. Understandings remain largely in the abstract. Further, scholars who carefully consider the relevance, requirements, and implementation of civic, professional, and intellectual ends, most often do so without providing conceptual or theoretical attention to how the social contract informs these ends. Further, even as a few scholars do situate the purposes of undergraduate education within a broader social mandate that includes attention to the public good, this scholarship often leaves un- or underaddressed crucial questions, particularly questions that relate to specific ethical frameworks, the demands of democratic societies, and the prevalence of competing interests.

With regard to the ends of undergraduate education, the work of critical scholars coalesces around three broad themes: the socio-ethical context in which all education occurs, what might most appropriately shape the content or subject of education, and the desired outcomes of education. Critical scholars clearly articulate crucial parameters of educational contexts, and they are transparent about how they see the institutions in which they work. Two components of this context include the belief that all educational work, including teaching, research, and service, is political and value-laden and that democratic practices and market logics are fundamentally at odds with one another. Scholars have long claimed that institutions of higher learning are "disinterested," or distinct from the complexities and investments of life outside of the institution (Simpson, 2003; Smith, 2001; Stanley & Wise, 1993). In this sense, scholars have claimed that higher education institutions are apolitical or beyond the reach of specific interests and priorities that make up the everyday of public life.[7]

In contrast, critical scholars have asserted that "theory is a deepening of the political, not a moving away from it" (Mohanty, 2003, p. 191). Put another way, "the issue is not about whether public or higher education has become contaminated with politics. It is, more importantly, about recognizing that education is already a space of politics" (Giroux, 2007b, p. 37). Further, the choice of research area or course content is also a matter of politics: "values are always present in the initial selection of a problem. If they are not overt and announced, they are nonetheless latent and tacitly accepted" (Lynd, 1939, p. 184). Stated simply, all scholars pursue specific values: "the central issue is ... which values" (Allen, 1993, p. 207).

A second component of critical scholars' assessment of the current context for higher education is their rigorous insistence on the opposing logics of democratic and market-based priorities. For these scholars, the relevance and reach of privatized, market-based discourse and commitments throughout higher education and social life more broadly are not peripheral or occasional. Rather, they directly impinge on possibilities for critique and for democratic futures. In addition to examining the ways in which corporate influence prohibits institutions of higher education from fulfilling their social contract, these scholars assert the importance of "challenging corporate ideology" and discerning between "identities founded on democratic principles and identities steeped in forms of competitive, atomistic individualism that celebrates self-interest, profit making, and greed" (Giroux & Searls Giroux, 2004, p. 237). Educators cannot afford to simply ignore or downplay market ideologies and priorities. As one scholar states, "If a key mission is to serve the public and to improve the communities and regions in which they operate, it is not self-evident that by serving business interests they are automatically serving the community" (Schugurensky, 2006, p. 315).

In sum, critical scholars consistently draw attention to the political nature of all learning and knowledge and to the necessity for higher education to oppose market-based logics and encourage consideration of democratic practices and possibilities for justice. Even as faculty members may (1) deny that education is political and (2) reject their role in creating democratic futures, critical scholars assert that such denial and rejection are in themselves forms of support for existing social practices and institutional norms. Faculty members cannot opt out of expressing political and ethical allegiances. In this sense, "political" is a question of commitments to both broad ethical priorities and to the uses of knowledge in achieving those priorities, rather than a matter of strict adherence to the political descriptors of "conservative," "liberal," "progressive," or "radical," or to positions that are commonly attached to any of these descriptors. Faculty members who understand their work as disinterested are, in fact, most often furthering existing social conditions, which in itself constitutes a particular agenda. Questions about the ends of undergraduate education cannot escape questions of politics. All education in some way engages with dominant patterns of social interactions and practices and seeks to maintain or resist such patterns. Whether or not faculty members address the material conditions of how people live and consider justice, they are, ultimately, playing a role in either furthering or interrupting existing material conditions and relationships of power.

Critical scholars also address the ends of undergraduate education through their attention to what is most suitable for educational content or what might most appropriately constitute "the subject" in democratic societies. At a minimum, education that attends to "the conditions at hand" and that connects knowledge "to everyday issues rooted in material relations of power" (Giroux, 2007b, p. 29) will make it more likely that higher education will fulfil its social contract with public life, which is to strengthen democratic practices and reduce human suffering. Inasmuch as higher education ought to pursue democratic possibilities, identify and work towards the public good, and reduce suffering, educational content must enliven students' abilities to do this work. Likewise, the ability to consider and grapple with the complexities of the communities in which one lives is essential. One must turn towards white men and racism in library computer rooms, Canadian institutions leaving Indigenous men in the cold to die, and differential high school graduation rates by race. Knowledge must be linked to "operations of power" (Giroux & Searls Giroux, 2004, p. 125), and power must be linked with institutional change.

Finally, in addition to addressing the context of and content for undergraduate education, critical scholars clearly articulate what they see as the preferred outcomes of undergraduate education, which include ensuring that students leave the university with a sense of their own agency, capacities for "social citizenship," and a sensibility for "deepen[ing] and expand[ing] the possibilities of collective agency and democratic life" (Giroux, 2007b, p. 35). As stated earlier in this chapter, all students will have a presence in particular contexts, and all will make choices that will in a variety of ways bear on public life and on the conditions in which people live. Likewise, ideally, the ends of undergraduate education will prepare students to live in those contexts and actively demonstrate a regard for and commitment to democratic values. As one scholar claims, referring to the role of the social sciences, students will learn to "be troublesome [and] to disconcert the habitual arrangements by which we manage to live" (Lynd, 1939, p. 181).

Even as many scholars have challenged their work, critical scholars have made the most explicit links between the social contract that higher education has with public life and the aims of undergraduate education. Further, critical scholars demonstrate little ambivalence about their educational priorities. When it comes to the aims of undergraduate education, liberal scholars, at a minimum, leave too many issues insufficiently explored. In this chapter, I have offered a rationale for this assertion and drawn attention to the ways in which most scholarly considerations of the social contract and the aims of undergraduate education offer little to hold onto when it comes to pressing yet also routine social concerns. We will, in our teaching and research, indicate our understandings of both the social contract and the aims of undergraduate education. We might opt for a seemingly benign yet profoundly consequential endorsement of the status quo. We might also opt for a rigorous engagement with the complexities of that social contract in relation to ongoing practices of injustice and inequity.

Conclusion

What responsibilities does higher education have to public life? How might undergraduate education engage with these obligations? As I sit with students, consider my educational and course-related expectations, remember a white man and his inhumane treatment of a few boys of colour, and deepen my knowledge of how the state continues to do violence to men like Frank Paul, it feels profoundly inadequate to return to the classroom with my hands empty of a thoughtful response, with ineffectual rhetorical promises, or with a list of democratic values with no parallel attention to the violence of inequity and the labour that justice requires. The demands of public life are complex, persistent, and too often ugly. Injustice has deep roots. It destroys and kills. A white man blatantly disrespects boys of colour and the adults in the room silently affirm this disrespect. My student Allison claims no connection to nation. The media construct images of especially men and boys of African and Middle Eastern descent as violent, dangerous, uncivilized, and less than human. The state, through the workings of powerful institutions, kills those in Black and Indigenous communities.

Where are the possibilities for democracy and for justice, what Iris Marion Young defines as creating a society in which the good life includes "participating in determining one's action and the conditions of one's action" (1990, p. 37)? How does higher education open up spaces to consider the ugliness and complexities of injustice, rather than shut such spaces down? In constructing the subject, what are educators communicating to students like Cindy and Allison about the world in which we live? How do we construct educational settings in which students and faculty members can listen to scholars such as Alfred and others who critique widely accepted norms and practices in North America, turn towards university co-op programs in the tar sands, and consider the role of universities?

Put simply, as long as injustice exists, higher education has an obligation to consider the necessity of and possibilities for justice. Inasmuch as education is, in part, a process of shaping what will become habitual for students once they graduate, in terms of their thinking and their doing, I hope that objections to a white man's disregard for four boys of colour, support for consideration of queer lives, and condemnation of state violence against racialized individuals and communities might be routine. Such objections, support, and condemnation will require clear and concrete commitments on the part of educators. They will not be sustained by polite and cautious calls for the development of the "whole individual" or loose references to "social needs." When I turn towards a white man's disrespect and four boys laughing in a computer room, when I face my student Cindy and her request for "streamlined" education, when I consider Alfred's assessment of ongoing colonialism, I do not want to waver. Commitments to development of "the whole individual" and "social needs," in the end, have little if anything to do with naming the inhumanity of a white man towards four boys of colour or with offering support to queer lives. In practice, commitments to "the whole individual" and to "social needs" have not spoken and will in no way speak to the press of injustice or to the failures of democratic practices. When considering the obligations of higher education to the social and to the ends of undergraduate education, I am interested in practices of thinking and doing that can rigorously and repeatedly respond to the fact of too much wrong.

Through attention to the social contract and the aims of undergraduate education, scholars have considered the contours of such thinking and doing. Indeed, this scholarship, even as it disappoints with its lack of depth, has informed most of Cindy's, Allison's, and other students' educational experience. A substantive conversation concerning the social contract and the aims of undergraduate education that grapples with the challenges of tar sands, colonialism, and a host of other social concerns is crucial. The work and consequences of education are too important for scholars to avoid such conversations, to primarily speak to those in their own circles, or to quickly dismiss the components of others' scholarship that critique their own conceptual assertions. Primarily with regard to its focus on the individual and its insistence on disinterested scholarship, liberal approaches to higher education not only fall short of imagining democratic futures, but actively obscure possibilities for justice. I will address these issues at length in chapters 4 and 5. In the next chapter, I examine the growing attention in the scholarly literature and in educational settings to civic engagement and service learning, efforts that have, in large part, attempted to strengthen higher education's ability to support democratic practices. Even as these initiatives have frequently been housed outside of disciplinary and departmental structures, they have offered the most concentrated institutional response to questions of the social contract and the ends of undergraduate education in democratic contexts.

3 Civic Engagement and Service Learning: The Burden of Liberal Norms

In the fall of 2011, I was one of two respondents on a panel entitled "Speaking with the Voices of Marginalized Communities through Communication Activism Education: Exemplars in Experiential Service-Learning to Promote Social Justice" at the National Communication Association's annual meeting. The organizers of the panel were at the time working on a book on communication activism pedagogy and service learning, for which I was writing a chapter. As in many disciplines, the presence of service-learning panels at the largest meeting of communication educators in North America has increased in the past decade, despite resistance to courses that integrate some form of service learning. Many faculty members who pursue service-learning courses do so working against institutional norms and without obvious support for this work. At the same time, service learning has attained a high enough level of academic legitimacy to generate its own formal set of awards. Indeed, two of the senior faculty members on the panel to which I responded had been recognized for their service-learning work.

The panel offered explicit attention to service learning's connection to both activism and social justice. I appreciated that I would have an opportunity to act as a respondent. All three papers discussed typical examples of service-learning efforts. Two presenters discussed their work with graduate and undergraduate students addressing hateful/hurtful speech in public high schools, reducing levels of indifference among students, and analysing expressions of bullying in schools (Cox & Geiger, 2011). Another pair of presenters talked about their efforts with communities in Belize to articulate community priorities in the area of health communication (Walker & Hart, 2011). A final presenter addressed a course in which students produced a video in collaboration with a non-profit organization serving migrant farm workers for the purposes of community education. This video represented the struggles of Latino/as, their aspirations, and the economic role they played at local and broader levels (Kennerly, 2011).

In their presentations, these educators considered the pedagogical and programmatic components of service learning, as well as social justice. They addressed social justice primarily in relation to individual priorities, rather than at institutional levels. In regard to course outcomes, the most substantive attention was given to student empowerment. Presenters also addressed the enjoyment they experienced in seeing students encounter new subcultures, have conversations with people from backgrounds different from their own, increase their awareness of social issues, and engage in dialogue with individuals they might have previously avoided.

I felt a kind of awkward and uneasy pleasure as a respondent to this panel. On the one hand, my own work was squarely related to the title of the panel. Even as I do not practise service learning in my courses, I do have a strong interest in how pedagogy connects to social justice. I had been in conversation with the panel chair and my co-respondent over the past couple of years about these issues. At the same time, I planned to offer challenges to the papers to which I would respond. I wanted to raise concerns with not only the work of the educators to whose papers I would respond, but with service learning as a body of work. I wanted to know: Where was an analysis or even mention of power and how it works? Why did all of the papers offer a clear focus on individual behaviour and change and no attention to institutions or structures? The faculty members who presented seemed to be quite comfortable with students' ability to gain access to a variety of settings and experiences, possibly leading to an increased sense of entitlement. I wondered: How can such understandings of service learning have any connection at all to social justice?

This chapter examines the concepts referenced in the title of the panel on which I was a respondent. As articulated in chapter 2, scholars have considered in various ways the question of higher education's social contract, and they have also attended to what might constitute the central aims of undergraduate education. A third substantive area of scholarship in relation to higher education's connection with democratic life is that of the scholarship of engagement. This body of work, with origins in community service efforts at the turn of the century, includes literature addressing service learning, civic engagement, civic education, and democratic outcomes. In addition to a wide and deep literature (Barker, 2004; Brabant & Braid, 2009; Colby, Beaumount, Ehrlich, & Corngold, 2007; Hartley, 2009; Kezar & Rhoads, 2001; Morton & Saltmarsh, 1997; National Task Force on Civic Learning and Democratic Engagement, 2012; Peters, 2004; Ruitenberg, 2009; Varlotta 1997; Wang & Jackson 2005), civic engagement and service-learning efforts have enjoyed concrete and ongoing support from colleges and universities in North America. From mission statements to university centres to disciplinary initiatives, one can track institutional commitments to service learning and civic engagement across the landscape of research, teaching, and service in higher education settings. Service-learning and civic engagement efforts constitute one of the most sustained and systematic responses to the question of higher education's relationship with public life.

This chapter offers an overview of this work, with careful attention to the ways in which service learning scholarship considers ethical commitments related to justice and power. How have service-learning and civic engagement priorities supported careful attention to the entrenched nature of injustice and to possibilities for justice? In what ways have the same programs made it more likely that students and faculty members will consider the deaths of men like Frank Paul, routine homophobia in schools, or high levels of incarceration of Black and Indigenous men, and the avenues to systemic change that will reduce inequity and oppression? Are faculty members who offer service-learning courses primarily concerned with what students will gain or with the practices of justice in concrete institutional settings? Even as both objectives may seem attainable by faculty members, which priorities are foundational and enduring? Does attention to civic engagement establish clear ethical allegiances in democratic contexts, or does this work leave largely unaddressed possibilities for considering power and negotiating competing social interests? These questions set the framework for this chapter.

An extensive body of work on the scholarship of engagement, civic engagement, and service learning exists (Bjarnason & Coldstream, 2003; Brabant & Braid, 2009; Calderón, 2007; Colby, Beaumont, Ehrlich, & Corngold, 2007; Kezar & Rhoads, 2001; Morton & Saltmarsh, 1997; Saltmarsh & Zlotkowski, 2011b; Sandmann, 2008; Singh, 2003; Speck & Hoppe, 2004). My objective in this chapter is not to offer an exhaustive review or analysis of the history, implementation, or curricular and pedagogical aspects of this work. Rather, I am centrally concerned with the ways in which service-learning and civic engagement efforts make it possible and even desirable to rigorously consider Cindy and Allison's ontological and epistemological assertions, the question of what is the subject in democratic contexts, and the material and discursive practices of injustice and possibilities for justice. Inasmuch as civic engagement and service-learning efforts continue to garner institutional and faculty members' support, how are both able to sustain a set of democratic priorities that habitualize rigorous consideration of power, justice, and systemic change?

I will focus my discussion on the broad term "scholarship of engagement" and two closely aligned areas of work, including civic engagement and service learning. Given the multiple and at times varying uses of terms such as the scholarship of engagement, civic engagement, service learning, civic education, political education, and democratic outcomes, a clear conceptual framework regarding these concepts will be useful. The terms the "engaged university" (or the "engaged academy") and "scholarship of engagement" provide a primary point of entry into the discussion, and foreground the ways in which the work of teaching, research, and service might orient itself towards social needs. Faculty members often use the terms civic engagement and service learning interchangeably. This can be misleading, as the two are not the same. Service learning, very basically, refers to university study that connects course content with structured experiences outside of the classroom. Civic engagement refers to the ways in which universities and faculty members might practise investments in public concerns, with "civic" implying "a set of public, democratic, and political (though not necessarily partisan) dimensions" (Saltmarsh & Zlotkowski, 2011a, p. 7).

The concept of engagement carries its own ambiguities. For some scholars, the term civic engagement "as it is currently used … includes the entire 'kitchen sink' of public and private goods" (Berger, 2009, p. 335), in some cases constituting a significant dilution of the concept of civic priorities. Others have asserted that "mere activity in a community does not constitute civic engagement" (Saltmarsh & Hartley, 2011b, p. 17). To a large extent, civic engagement efforts affirm long-standing epistemological assumptions and institutional norms, thus offering few challenges to those in colleges and universities. This acceptance can act to constrain robust critiques of power and justice.)

Service learning broadly refers to instructional efforts that "connect … students' academic study with public problem-solving experiences in local community settings" (Saltmarsh & Zlotkowski, 2011c, p. 287). Components of service learning include "service-related activities," interactions in which students will "encounter community members actively immersed in issues related directly to the course content" and intentional reflection by students "on their service-related observations and experiences" (Hironimus-Wendt & Lovell-Troy, 1999, p. 361). While faculty members that pursue service learning often embrace civic engagement's concern with public and democratic priorities, one can also practice service learning with little or no attention to civic outcomes. Likewise, faculty members can pursue civic engagement objectives and in no way link concepts with experiences outside of the classroom. As one scholar states, "not all service-learning involves civic engagement, and not all civic engagement involves service-learning" (Exley, 2004, p. 85). In relation to (1) the "scholarship of engagement," (2) civic engagement, and (3) service learning, I will offer an overview of these concepts and a discussion of the ways in which they are positioned to respond to questions of injustice and possibilities for justice. Before examining these concepts, however, I return to my own investments in civic engagement and service learning, as articulated in my participation on the panel on service-learning initiatives.

Civic Engagement and Service Learning: The Challenges of Practice

What would I do with the uneasy pleasure I felt in acting as a respondent? Where were the gaps between the presenters' articulations of service learning and a pedagogical commitment to justice? In my role as respondent, when considering the presentations on bullying in schools and the class that produced a video on Latinos, the two papers to which I would most explicitly respond, I was especially interested in how service-learning efforts might support robust consideration of the public good and of moving from too much wrong to less wrong to justice. The papers I read left me with several questions about the primary philosophical and conceptual assumptions on which the courses were based, which I raised in my response. First, attention to power, particularly at systemic and structural levels, was minimal. Beyond references to "empowerment," none of the three presentations carefully analysed power relationships related to the service-learning work and community settings. On the whole, presenters did not address power generally, raise questions about positionality or access, consider the institutional components of power, or address how power is connected to both injustice and to justice.

Second, all three service-learning courses the presenters addressed were primarily directed at providing information about and reflecting on individual behaviours rather than effecting change at institutional levels. As noted above, course outcomes were overwhelmingly articulated as related to changed student behaviours. There was little to no in-depth attention to more just relationships or practices in community settings, either among students and community members or in relation to specific institutions in which injustice was present. Again, I understand injustice to be in part connected to institutional practice. Likewise, movement towards justice requires consideration of institutional contributions to injustice. As with many service-learning courses, the institutional component seemed to be left to chance or simply not part of moving towards justice. Presentations implied that as long as the interventions increased awareness of the existence of an issue, or shifted students' understanding related primarily to individual attitudes, this would be sufficient. None of the presentations offered attention to the existence of structural power dynamics. While increasing awareness may certainly lead to justice, on its own, increased awareness will not reduce or eliminate injustice.

At a third level, attention to outcomes was primarily directed at how, in most cases, already privileged students could gain access to information and experiences that they would not otherwise have (i.e., how students with significant levels of privilege could further exercise that privilege and gain increased levels of access to communities other than their own). Attention offered to outcomes for community partners was primarily framed as hoped-for possibilities and secondary to student outcomes. Presentations did make reference to what might be understood as "civic" learning outcomes (as opposed to both "personal" or "social justice" outcomes), and referred to an increased sense of involvement, a stronger sense of empowerment among students, a more complex understanding of the self, and a deepened awareness of social issues. I understand the difficulty of addressing institutional injustice and change within the constraints of a semester-long course. Yet leaving institutional considerations out entirely can give students the impression that justice will be achieved when attitudes change or simply by virtue of students expanding their experiences with those culturally different from themselves.

Finally, even as all three courses explicitly made reference to race or to communities of colour, there was no careful consideration of race scholarship and the ways in which racism plays out through multiple avenues of privilege, power, and discrimination in routine contexts. At a very basic level, references in one presentation to "students" and "members of the Latino/a community," implying that these groups are mutually exclusive, is problematic, in that such references imply that students are not Latino/a (Kennerly, 2011). Such constructions themselves obscure the importance of one's location in relation to structures of power when moving towards justice. Service-learning faculty members who do not consider the existing scholarship on race and racism in an intellectually rigorous manner communicate the idea that racism is non-existent and/or irrelevant. Whether or not such oversight is intentional, the lack of such intellectual examination is problematic, given the extensive body of work on racism as pervasive and systemic (Bonilla-Silva, 2010). I am not aware of any systematic study of how service-learning scholarship addresses the racism present within institutions of higher education and among its students and faculty members, and the service-learning literature offers little consideration of these issues.[1]

As I stated in my formal response to the panel, one working assumption I have is that "in as much as social injustice exists at individual and institutional levels, efforts at social justice must be articulated and practiced at individual and institutional levels. Efforts focusing only on the individual level will not be sufficient for justice" (Simpson, 2011). I suggested that "change efforts that do not explicitly attend to unjust systems will generally align with a liberal focus on attitudes and beliefs, and will serve to recenter and privilege those already in power." If power and competing interests are a given, which was the case in all three contexts, what is lost when faculty members fail to ask students to consider these components of the contexts they are examining? Efforts directed towards change that overlook power may offer surface-level alterations to a specific issue, but will fail to bring about lasting transformation. With regard to the significance of race and the prevalence of racism, and given the profound lack of any race analysis in the papers, did these faculty members see themselves and their students as beyond the complications of race? Finally, will social justice be achieved when our students feel better about themselves, as this seemed to be a central priority? Is an enlarged sense of empathy, with little to no knowledge of or concern for the structural conditions that underlie injustice, a useful outcome for service-learning courses and, if yes, for whom and to what ends?

The presentation offered by the senior faculty members on their work with students in Belize demonstrated all of the above concerns. I was particularly struck by two references that the presenters made to student outcomes, and I point to these with a sense of urgency related to what is at stake in regard to undergraduate education that is responsive to social challenges. While these two references clearly do not represent the entirety of the students' experiences, they are elements of the course to which these presenters opted to draw attention and, one might thus assume, of value for these faculty members. They pointed to one student's comment that he "hope[s]to come back there [to Belize] some day." Students' ability to return to a country visited in a service-learning course often has more to do with social class and race privilege and little if anything to do with justice. Indeed, service learning in international settings "face[s] … issues of fit, ethnocentrism, and imperialism [and] … issues exacerbated by global inequities and colonial histories" (Sutton, 2011, p. 126). The easy assumption that one can travel at will, because one has the resources to do so, points to a political economy of privilege and wholly ignores the supposed reason for the course, which was to consider community health needs in particular settings in Belize. Further, it potentially sets up the course as a kind of service-through-travel-light.

The privilege of access to travel also raises the question of the priorities and interests of the faculty members. I wondered: what had drawn these educators to do research in Belize in the first place? While Hart and Walker identified several components of their "personal and professional interest" related to the course – awareness of injustice, previous travel to "'developing' countries," the lack of practice-based activism in their own and other courses in their department – there was no attention to the reasons for Belize or health issues specifically. Again, the taken-for-granted ability to pick nations and issues at will, largely outside of enduring relational contexts, is problematic. Although Hart and Walker described the process of community building, they also mentioned that "no established relationships" were in place in at least one community in which the class made a stop. This can lead to students primarily inhabiting the role of "educated spectators who observe more than participate from the protection of their privileged positions and assumptions" (Kahn, 2011, p. 116). How does this effect possibilities for reciprocity? What might we learn from a political economy of travel in relation to service-learning programs, particularly as travel itself is not accessible in equitable ways?

A recent visit to the homepage for the Department of Communication at the University of Louisville, where Hart and Walker teach, revealed: "The Service Learning program offerings are expanding! Professor Joy Hart and Professor Kandi Walker are taking students all over the globe. Students now can go to Africa, Central America, Asia, and soon we will have a trip to Europe! Get in touch with one of them to find out more about these exciting opportunities" (University of Louisville, 2012). Although existing research does not offer careful attention to the conceptual assumptions embedded in such service-learning courses, or to the outcomes for students from North America who travel abroad as part of their educational experience, recent research on semester-long study abroad programs raises the possibilities that such travel may "result in the reproduction of [students'] privilege" (Waters & Brooks, 2010, p. 226), that the "restructuring and re-patterning of international student mobility ... is neither neutral nor random in its effects," and that mobility becomes a privilege of the "socially powerful, [who are] seeking to add value to their educational experience" (Findlay, King, Stam, & Ruiz-Gelices, 2006, p. 315). Especially when based in courses that profess at least some allegiance to social justice priorities, to simply avoid addressing the political economy of travel is problematic.

I was also struck by a story recounted by one of the presenters during the panel. As Hart and Walker explained, the class visited a community in Belize that was struggling with poverty and substandard housing. Upon arriving in this community, one student commented on the "low quality" of the homes and the cheap materials that individuals used to build them. Shortly before leaving Belize, this same student remembered his observation about housing and stated that even when struggling with persistent poverty, with its attendant effects on survival and resources, those in the community "have it right" in regard to their resourcefulness and generosity which he witnessed and experienced. For the presenters, the fact that the student demonstrated a higher level of compassion for community members, through his statement that community members "ha[d] it right," was clearly a significant learning outcome for this student.

I was plain about my critique of this assessment on the part of the presenters. I stated, "Justice is about adequate housing and the ability of individuals and communities to make decisions about the conditions in which they live. The point is not how privileged students feel

[handwritten: to student and not enough structurally focused]

about the conditions in which others are living." In relation to poverty, institutional and faculty members' service-learning efforts aimed at democratic outcomes will be centrally directed towards eradicating poverty at systemic levels. Even as faculty members might see this as "progress" for this student – in effect, "seeing beyond" poverty to a family's resourcefulness – I wonder about the consequences of "seeing beyond" any injustice in service-learning settings. "If we're concerned with social justice, who is service learning for?" I asked.

Scholars have noted the difficulty and perhaps undesirability of narrowly defining the priorities and forms of civic engagement and service learning. Developing compassion for individuals racially different from oneself may be part of a process that moves an individual or those in a course towards more rigorous analysis of systemic injustice. The student did shift his ideas, which is clearly a pedagogical outcome in that course. However, this panel, and many other parallel expressions of civic engagement and service learning, raise significant and pressing questions. What is democratic about service learning? What are the philosophical, ethical, and relational starting points for faculty members who pursue service learning? How do educators who are pursuing service-learning efforts understand power and institutional oppression? With which public concerns and outcomes is service learning centrally aligned? What is the role of institutional critique and attention to power and how are both present in service-learning and civic engagement efforts? To what extent are service-learning efforts that are aimed at increasing empathy and tolerance among students built on conceptual approaches that sustain relationships of privilege, entitlement, and domination? In the next section, I will address these questions through an overview of the literature on the scholarship of engagement, civic engagement, and service learning.

The Scholarship of Engagement, Civic Engagement, and Service Learning: An Overview

The engaged academy, civic engagement, democratic outcomes, service learning, social justice pedagogy: scholars routinely use these and other terms to describe a range of efforts in higher education that explicitly consider social needs and the work of teaching, research, and service. In this chapter, I organize this literature into three primary areas, including (1) the scholarship of engagement, (2) civic engagement, and

Table 3.1. Brief Snapshot of Scholarship of Engagement, Civic Engagement, and Service Learning

The term ...	includes concepts such as ...	is practised related to ...	can be defined as ...
scholarship of engagement	the "engaged academy," the "engaged university"	teaching, research, and service	the ways in which universities, through teaching, research, and service, orient themselves towards social needs
civic engagement	citizenship education, civic education, democratic outcomes	primarily teaching; secondarily, service and research	the ways in which universities and faculty members' practise investments in public concerns
service learning	democratic outcomes, civic education	teaching	instructional efforts that connect service in community settings with academic study

(3) service learning. Table 3.1 provides a brief snapshot of these three areas of work.

The Scholarship of Engagement

As noted in the introduction to this chapter, scholars frequently use the terms the "scholarship of engagement," the "engaged university," and the "engaged academy" to explicitly invoke the existence of a relationship between higher education and public life. At the same time, a consistent set of priorities essential to the scholarship of engagement is elusive. As with scholarly and institutional commitments to the social contract addressed in chapter 2, the types of "engagement" pursued are wide-ranging, and beyond occasional and broad references to democratic values such as tolerance and inclusion, rarely offer much depth to ethical commitments. In this section, I will address the context out of which this literature has emerged, provide a definition of the terms, discuss tensions within the literature, and offer a critique.

In many ways, the notion of an "engaged academy" or one that "respond[s] to the needs and expectations of society and engage[s] with multiple communities of interest, has become quite commonplace ...

and is therefore not seriously contested at the level of value or principle" (Singh, 2003, p. 273). In the midst of charges that higher education has shown a "lack of responsiveness to public concerns" (Kezar &
Rhoads, 2001, 152; see also Bok, 1982; Ehrlich, 1995; Hackney, 1994;
Rocheleau, 2004), scholars understand a focus on engagement, with
attention to institutional, programmatic, scholarly, and curricular initiatives, as one way to speak to these concerns. More specifically, the
scholarship of engagement has largely been a response to issues including the "increasing specialization of academic knowledge into discrete
disciplines" (Barker, 2004, p. 125), the rise of "technocratic politics" in
higher education, the "domination by experts removed from a common
civic life" (Barker & Brown, 2009, p. 42), and disproportionate attentiveness to corporate and economic priorities at the expense of consideration of social outcomes (Barker, 2004; Singh, 2003).

In relation to the increasing specialization of knowledge, especially
that which is based on "an objective set of truths, practices, and procedures" (Barker & Brown, 2009, p. 42), scholars have charged that such
approaches to knowledge and its uses "idealiz[e] distance from rather
than engagement with" social problems (Barker, 2004, p. 125). Further,
a range of scholars have claimed that in a context of increasing attention to market-based priorities, the lack of a firm insistence on the public responsibilities of institutions of higher education will lead to the
decreased abilities of universities to maintain public relevance (Polster,
2004, 2007; Singh, 2003, Turk, 2000, 2008). The "scholarship of engagement," then, has served as a primary means to reassert and recentre the
public purposes of higher education, a way of "holding on to a larger
conception of societal values and ideals that affect the lives of large
numbers of people" (Singh, 2003, p. 302).

While calls for "engagement" in the context of higher education have
been fairly broad, the literature on the "scholarship of engagement" is
more specific. Scholars generally agree that this literature rests on "two
founding principles": "(1) mutually beneficial, reciprocal partnerships
and (2) [the] integration of teaching, research, and service" (Sandmann,
2008, p. 96; see also Barker, 2004; Bringle, Hatcher, & Clayton, 2006).
Scholars have asserted that engagement should go beyond outreach
and that university-community partnerships ought to produce knowledge (Sandmann, 2008). In this sense, advocates of the scholarship of
engagement have stressed both reciprocal relationships and the potential of these relationships to result in scholarly outcomes, including
knowledge production and application (ibid.). Two publications, both

produced in the 1990s, have been central to this understanding of the scholarship of engagement.

In *Scholarship Reconsidered*, Boyer (1990) stressed that in addition to "discovering knowledge," it was crucial for institutions and faculty members to be committed to "the scholarship of *integration*, the scholarship of *application*, and the scholarship of *teaching*" (p. 16; emphasis in original). A few years later, Boyer (1996) affirmed the importance of universities articulating and pursuing a "larger purpose, a larger sense of mission, a larger clarity of direction" (p. 21). Both of these publications urged universities to "reexamin[e] their roles in extensive and measurable societal change" (Brabant & Braid, 2009, p. 62). For Boyer and his colleagues, it was crucial that educators "connect the campus to the larger world" and "integrate ideas, connect thought to action, and inspire students" (Boyer, 1990, p. 77). Particularly in "The Scholarship of Engagement" (1996), Boyer's "emphasis on institutional change" (Saltmarsh, 2011b, p. 346) went beyond his earlier focus on individual faculty member's work. "The Scholarship of Engagement" challenged conventional understandings of the relationship of universities and communities.

At the same time, while Boyer's work certainly drew attention to the social purposes of higher education, it also "buil[t] on established academic epistemology, [and] assume[d] that knowledge [was] generated in the university or college and then applied to external contexts." In contrast, more recent articulations of the scholarship of engagement "emphasize ... that the learning and teaching be multidirectional and the expertise shared. It represents a basic reconceptualization of faculty involvement in community-based work" (Rice, 2005, pp. 27–28). Traditional knowledge production "decontextualizes 'problems' from the civic life of communities ... privatizes the world and ... profoundly erodes the subjective experience of mutual respect" (Barker & Brown, 2009, p. 42). Further, in contrast to knowledge in traditional scholarship, which "is perceived to be disciplinary, homogeneous, expert-led, supply-driven, hierarchical, peer-reviewed, and almost exclusively university-based," engaged knowledge is "applied, problem-centered, transdisciplinary, heterogeneous, hybrid, demand-driven, entrepreneurial, [and] network-embedded" (Sandmann, 2008, p. 97). In sum, in relation to public life, the "scholarship of engagement" professes commitments to reciprocal forms of knowledge integration and application through teaching, research, and service.

Five approaches to the scholarship of engagement include public scholarship, participatory research, community partnerships, public information networks, and civic skills or civic literacy (Barker, 2004). Public scholarship is focused on the ways in which deliberative practices can contribute to creating a community's sense of the public good. Participatory research is primarily attentive to the processes of participation. The community partnership approach places an "emphasis ... on social transformation" and is "concerned with power, resources, and building social movements" (p. 130). Public information networks are adept at working with communities to locate and utilize "resources and assets" (p. 131). Finally, a civic skills or literacy approach is committed to identifying and furthering "skills that are relevant to political participation and democratic decision making" (p. 132). While the above taxonomy suggests directions for practices of engagement, it also adopts a loose understanding of engagement.

Even when Barker and other scholars make explicit reference to democratic and public priorities, they for the most part do not thoroughly explore the particulars of these priorities, the ways in which they do or do not require an allegiance to specific values, or whether or not they necessitate the willingness and ability to consider competing interests. In fact, the most common thread in the variety of expressions of the scholarship of engagement may be the "growing acceptance of a problem-driven approach to the epistemology and methodology of contemporary scholarship" (Barker, 2004, p. 133). One can read a great deal about the process of engaged scholarship and far less about desired outcomes, particularly at concrete levels. Further, uses of the term public are various and often conflicting. Most scholars adopt broad understandings of the term public, and thus the term can include any number of concerns, including those that have little connection to democratic values or practices.

The scholarship of engagement may have succeeded in raising a certain set of questions about the production of knowledge, the responsibilities that universities have to public life, and the role of communities in defining and shaping responses to public concerns. However, in the context of articulating democratic commitments and the possibilities for justice, it has not been nearly as successful in (1) defining the specifics of "public" priorities or (2) addressing the ethically laden outcomes of engagement. Attention to engagement does open up the question of the connections and commitments that universities have with and to public life. To a large extent, faculty members have stepped into this opening to examine the processes of knowledge production and to emphasize that knowledge should be accessible and applicable. This focus on accessibility and applicability in no way ensures justice. Democratic commitments and justice require an interest in and alignment with a specific set of outcomes, a bold claim on what will be materially necessary for justice to occur. In a society in which large numbers of people are wholly unaware of, for example, the state's complicity in the death of men like Frank Paul, educators must identify the concrete desires of the practices of engagement. In settings in which faculty members choose both "the subject," and how that subject will be represented, engagement that leads to justice must go far beyond broad commitments to "public" priorities.

Educators increasingly pursue reciprocal partnerships with a range of groups and concerns, including social service organizations; small and large businesses in medical, technological, and other industries; and public institutions like the one complicit in Frank Paul's death. Concerning the service-learning examples discussed earlier in the chapter, the knowledge pursued may be collaboratively produced and applicable in specific settings. Who is that knowledge designed to serve? What does it aim to achieve? What does it seek to change? What does it choose to leave unexamined? In much of the literature on the scholarship of engagement, the process itself is what qualifies it as "engagement." In contrast, undergraduate education that opens up possibilities for democratic practices and the public good will need to articulate a relationship to and pursuit of specific priorities. It will concern itself with just ends and practices, and not only with the implementation of processes that espouse loose notions of justice and fairness, often with no attention to power or to the ongoing violence of injustice.

Knowledge always supports specific ends. When individuals and communities use knowledge, it has concrete outcomes that bear on how people live. With regard to the video that the presenters on the panel addressed, and its attention to Latino/a's families' "hopes and dreams," is this knowledge designed to educate whites in the community or to draw critical attention to federal and state immigration and labour policies? All knowledge use and application is ethical. Individuals in an organization or institution can rely on principles of reciprocity, partnership, and problem solving to ensure a wide range of outcomes, including those that might be unjust. All engagement is, in part, an articulation of the future in which we want to live, a set of cognitive and affective investments directed towards one way of living together and not another. Even as the scholarship of engagement may have compelled certain faculty members to acknowledge that knowledge production and teaching might pursue public commitments, it does not sufficiently explore the ethical components of those commitments, including whom they are serving, and in what ways.

In summary, the scholarship of engagement has been in part a response to overly technical and specialized knowledge that is far removed from public concerns, and it has stressed the importance of grounding knowledge production and application in community-academic partnerships with clear attention to community needs and priorities. While this emphasis on community partnerships opens up possibilities for democratic priorities, it in no way ensures them. Further, in the context of social issues that are profoundly entrenched and complex, the scholarship of engagement does little to sustain even an awareness of these issues, let alone consideration of their resolution. For example, Cindy felt quite justified in turning away from the realities of queer lives. Commitments within the scholarship of engagement literature would not necessarily ensure an educational framework that would habitualize the consideration of these lives with clear attention to power and injustice.

At another level, educators on the service-learning panel noted at the start of this chapter stressed outcomes that in many ways had little to do with changing social conditions and the institutional injustices that led to those conditions. The outcomes identified by the presenters had far more to do with students' comfort and individual gain and did little to shift their existing views of, for example, the systemic causes of poverty. Even as the scholarship of engagement has achieved discursive prominence and, in some instances, institutional support, such prominence and support in no way ensure any coherence or consistency in regard to what such scholarship looks like and requires. In the next section, I turn to a discussion of civic engagement, a term that more explicitly references the public components of engagement.

Civic Engagement and the Place of Democratic Commitments

The civic engagement literature has primarily emerged in the past two and a half decades, and has more directly and explicitly wrestled with the requirements of democratic and civic commitments than the scholarship of engagement. While the authors of one article assert that use of the term "civic" "should ... imply a set of public, democratic, and political (though not necessarily partisan) dimensions" (Saltmarsh & Zlotkowski, 2011a, p. 7), a concise definition of the civic components of engagement is not readily available in the literature. It may be most accurate to claim that scholarship that does discuss the assumptions and trajectories of the civic engagement movement offers far more attention to the difficulties of articulating and applying democratic commitments than to what these commitments actually are. In this section, I will discuss the history, expressions, and internal critique of civic engagement (i.e., critique offered by civic engagement advocates), and will then examine additional points of tension in the civic engagement literature.

Civic Engagement: History and Expressions

The civic engagement movement is closely linked with the "extant service-learning movement" (Brabant & Braid, 2009, 64), with adult education (Saddington, 2000), and with social justice pedagogical frameworks (Brabant & Braid, 2009; Brabant & Hochman, 2004; Koliba, O'Meara, & Seidel, 2000). Civic engagement draws on the land grant movement from the late 1800s, which stressed the responsibilities of universities and service to society. In the 1980s, there was growing concern that colleges and universities in the United States were "in danger of losing [their] public purpose" (Hartley, 2009, p. 12), which prompted a range of responses focused on the public dimensions of higher education (Boyer, 1990; Ehrlich, 1995; Newman, 1985). In the context of this concern, as well as in regard to economic pressures, an uncertainty about higher education's social role, young people's political disengagement, and students' growing interest in a degree for its money-earning potential, volunteerism and other forms of civic engagement in the 1980s and 1990s increased (Hartley, 2009). In the 1990s, "momentum around academic service-learning and civic engagement in general began to coalesce into a recognizable movement" (Saltmarsh & Zlotkowski, 2011a, p. 1).

This movement has resulted in a host of programs and activities. Reports (Boyer, 1990; National Commission on Civic Renewal, 1997; Newman, 1985), organizations and programs (Campus Compact, Learn and Serve American Higher Education), and institutions have all generally affirmed the importance of higher education considering its responsibilities to life beyond the academy. Civic engagement priorities have supported increased attention to service learning, civic learning, civic capacities, democratic and deliberative dialogue, and community service. Civic engagement has also led to university-community partnerships, the application of scholarly investigation to social concerns, the "integrat[ion of] community-based activities into courses" so that students address "complex real-world problems," and the "prepar[ation of] students to live in an increasingly diverse and interconnected world" (Hartley, 2009, p. 12). While educators' civic engagement work has significantly increased the depth, scope, and range of activities over the past two decades, recent scholarship questions civic engagement's success in changing academic norms (Saltmarsh & Zlotkowski, 2011a) and its alignment with democratic purposes (Saltmarsh & Hartley, 2011a, 2011b; Saltmarsh, 2011a; Saltmarsh, Hartley, & Clayton, 2009).

While the "civic" aspects of the term "civic engagement" point to public and democratic concerns and priorities (Saltmarsh & Zlotkowski, 2011a), "engagement" refers to the participatory nature of all academic work, and especially epistemology and the importance of "relational, contextual, participatory, and localized ways of knowing" (Saltmarsh, 2011b, pp. 346–347). Likewise, civic engagement scholarship and practices have been especially attuned to behaviours and dispositions that connect one to others and encourage a sense of responsibility, to the "establish[ment] of civic engagement projects as a legitimate activity" (Saltmarsh & Hartley, 2011a, p. 9), and to the role of community organizations in informing both knowledge production and pedagogical practices. The work and consequences of civic engagement have changed higher education. However, civic engagement efforts have not rested on a "concerted action around a set agenda" (Saltmarsh & Hartley, 2011a, p. 3). Recent literature makes serious and far-reaching charges about what exactly civic engagement has changed and whether or not it can fulfil the democratic commitments that many scholars see as a necessary component of the civic engagement movement.

Civic Engagement: An Internal Critique

Recent scholarship on civic engagement has made two important assertions: the "civic engagement agenda ... does not have clear goals or outcomes" (Saltmarsh, 2011a, p. 31) and "the dominant paradigm of civic engagement in higher education does not fulfill a democratic purpose" (Saltmarsh & Hartley, 2011a, p. 1). Over the past decade, scholars have acknowledged that even as civic engagement efforts and activities have increased, particularly in the 1990s, "engagement" is too often used as a kind of catch-all phrase that "can say everything and nothing at the same time" (Saltmarsh, Hartley, & Clayton, 2009, p. 5). Concerning the "civic" challenges of engagement, "the question before the movement now is whether an ill-defined and rather conventional – often bland – conception of engagement will be adequate to the task of inspiring people to undertake the difficult transformational change our democracy needs" (Hartley, 2011, p. 44; see also the National Task Force on Civic Learning and Democratic Engagement, 2012; Saltmarsh, Hartley, & Clayton, 2009). Scholars have further claimed that institutional change related to civic engagement has been insufficient (Saltmarsh, 2011b) and that civic engagement work has "been accommodated to the dominant culture and structures of higher education" (Saltmarsh & Zlotkowski, 2011b, p. 354).

Major institutional reports on civic engagement make several assertions relevant to questions of how higher education acts on public commitments. These include the claims that "there is considerable evidence that deep engagement is rare" (American Association of State Colleges and Universities, 2002, p. 13), that civic engagement has not "been embraced across disciplines, departments, and institutions" (Burkardt, Holland, Percy, & Zimpher, 2004), and that the "civic engagement movement has not reached its full potential" (Saltmarsh & Hartley, 2011a, p. 5; emphasis in original). Even as this literature acknowledges the necessity for civic engagement work to challenge institutions and societal norms, to explicitly embrace a democratic agenda, and to demonstrate the capacity to critique the status quo, it also unambiguously claims that most civic engagement efforts have fallen short of these demands. As recently as 2011, more than 20 years after the origins of the civic engagement movement, one of the movement's key proponents asks a foundational question: "What are the responsibilities of colleges and universities in our democracy?" (Hartley, 2011, p. 44).

Those who have worked at furthering civic engagement continue to grapple with this central issue. Their efforts have "challeng[ed] what counts" in higher education (Saltmarsh & Zlotkowski, 2011a, p. 2; emphasis in original) and have drawn attention to higher education's deep investments in conventional teaching and knowledge production. However, according to scholars central to the field, civic engagement has not succeeded in "changing what counts" (p. 2; emphasis in original). According to these scholars, three important obstacles to more significant shifts include (1) a focus on activity and place rather than purpose and process, (2) a preference among those in higher education for what are often purported to be apolitical or neutral forms of knowledge, and

(3) epistemological approaches that are primarily or exclusively technical and expert-driven. Civic engagement efforts have overwhelmingly
focused on carrying out "activities," such as volunteer work, intern-
ships, field placements, or a course or research project. Such activities
occur in a specific setting or place, nearly always based on broad understandings of "community" that are not necessarily linked to democratic
commitments. Further, these activities are commonly supported by centres, offices, or programs, which are frequently although not exclusively
distinct from academic disciplines. Such activities demand little to no
institutional change and offer scant attention to the "underlying assumptions" that infuse "institutional behaviors, processes, and products"
(Saltmarsh, Hartley, & Clayton, 2009, p. 6). In addition, this focus on
activity and place rarely, if ever, insists on explicitly democratic objectives or processes.

The focus on activity and place, alongside a lack of attention to process and purpose, is intimately aligned with a firm and largely unre-
marked insistence among many proponents of civic engagement to
"sidestep ... the political dimension of civic engagement" (Saltmarsh &
Hartley, 2011a, p. 6). The routine and consequential existence of power
and of "competing ... positions and opposing ideologies" are present
in all aspects of public life (Saltmarsh & Hartley, 2011b, p. 19), yet civic
engagement advocates have long and repeatedly opted to ignore questions of politics and power and to insist on "academic neutrality," as
does the 1999 Declaration on the Civic Responsibility of Higher Education. Without explicit ties to democratic outcomes, civic engagement
efforts are "remarkably apolitical" (Saltmarsh, Hartley, & Clayton, 2009,
p. 8). Finally, this widespread preference for a supposed neutrality has
close ties to technocratic, expert-driven forms of knowledge, "which
have robbed the academy of its ability to effectively challenge society
and to seek change" (p. 5). For civic engagement scholars, there is wide
support in higher education for conventional forms of knowledge production, and their insistence on detachment and the removal of context. This ensures that many scholars continue to perceive conventional
forms of knowledge as far superior to forms of knowledge that have a
connection to public questions, that rely on community experience and
expertise, and that consider the complexities of lived reality.

Given the prevalence of models for epistemological authority that
rely on conventional expectations of distance and detachment, introducing and sustaining alternative epistemological models is rarely if ever
straightforward. Epistemological norms have important consequences

related to civic engagement: faculty members and students easily and routinely assume that conventional forms of academic knowledge, including the ways in which social issues are identified and defined, are far more legitimate than community-based forms of knowledge; students become experts who provide service to communities and "fix" community problems; and faculty members and students actively deny the significance of power (Saltmarsh, Hartley, & Clayton, 2009). Indeed, when my student Cindy felt justified in suggesting that in a course on gender, it was not necessary to consider queer lives and experiences, she was, in effect, privileging the conventional forms of knowledge that had to date shaped much of her university education.

In response to this weakened and, many would argue, ineffectual model for civic engagement, scholars central to the civic engagement movement have suggested that "democratic engagement" or "democratic civic engagement" might serve as a more appropriate and meaningful framework for institutions and faculty members committed to the democratic and public purposes of higher education. Explicitly attentive to "reciprocity (processes) and ... democratic dimensions (purpose)" (Saltmarsh, Hartley, & Clayton, 2009, p. 11), democratic engagement "seeks the public good *with* the public and not merely *for* the public" (p. 9; emphasis in original). Drawing on scholarship on public work (Boyte, 2008) and on democratic professionalism (Dzur, 2008), democratic engagement emphasizes democratic values such as "inclusion" and processes that are collaborative, multidirectional, and problem-oriented.

Democratic engagement also draws attention to the necessity of second-order change in pursuing democratic outcomes, a type of change that "reflect[s] major dissatisfaction with present arrangements" and that challenges "underlying assumptions and institutional behaviors, processes, and products" (Saltmarsh, Hartley, & Clayton, 2009, p. 13). The processes noted above – collaborative, multidirectional, and problem-oriented – do not currently shape the majority of educators' work. Civic engagement efforts most often fit too easily within existing academic structures, which largely prevent what scholars such as Saltmarsh and Hartley call democratic engagement. Civic engagement, in this sense, is not up to the tasks and demands of democracy. In contrast, democratic engagement, which requires significant institutional change in academic settings, can speak to pressing social concerns in relevant and effective ways. In sum, while civic engagement efforts have directed attention to the "civic" aspects of engagement, scholars

have also pointed out that the results of this attention have emphasized activity and place at the expense of process and purpose. These
scholars claim that "democratic engagement" is more likely to lead to
democratic outcomes.

The Persistence of the Political and the Liabilities of Liberal Norms:
Additional Critique of the Civic Engagement Movement

Recent scholarship has suggested that this attention to democratic
engagement might be more able than civic engagement to support lasting, systemic, and significant shifts in higher education related to democratic outcomes (National Task Force on Civic Learning and Democratic
Engagement, 2012; Saltmarsh, Hartley, & Clayton, 2009). In considering
possibilities for pursuit of the public good and justice, two additional
claims are necessary. First, the refusal of civic engagement scholarship
to take on the embedded and interest-driven nature of all scholarly
work has supported an understanding of mainstream scholarship as
neutral and interest-free and made largely invisible its commitments
to the status quo and existing social arrangements, including those
that are unjust. It has likewise perpetuated the idea that only scholarship that is explicit and transparent about its agenda has one. Second,
civic engagement scholarship's uncritical acceptance of liberal norms
and values systematically and thoroughly obscures both the reality of
routine injustice and the possibilities for justice. Before addressing the
service-learning literature, I examine these two claims.

The Impossibility of "Opting Out" of Engagement:
The Necessity of the Political
As discussed earlier in this chapter, work addressing the "scholarship
of engagement" and civic engagement has asserted that higher education must "play a role in responding to social challenges" (Saltmarsh,
Hartley, & Clayton, 2009, p. 3). This assertion can easily lead to the
assumption that one can engage in forms of teaching, research, and service that do not "play a role" or are not a response. On the whole, the
civic engagement movement has not made the claim that all educational
work plays a role and is a response, albeit with varying priorities. The
civic engagement movement has sustained the idea that engagement is
optional and that the bulk of teaching and knowledge production is, in
fact, disinterested.

   All educational practice, whether teaching, research, or service, is engaged and has consequences that will bear on the social. Educational work grapples with and is committed to a large range of interests and outcomes. Whereas civic engagement scholars have insisted on civic and public outcomes, a lack of transparency among other scholars does not remove the existence of an agenda from the work these scholars perform. Educators who are not explicit about their research and teaching priorities are supporting a host of interests, including maintenance of the status quo, profit-seeking endeavours, an orientation towards increased individualization and privatization, and an acceptance of and support for existing social relationships and structures. Educational work that is outside of social relations and contexts, that is unimplicated, is not possible. Had scholars working in the field of civic engagement drawn attention to this premise, this might have enlarged the conversation and encouraged a broad discussion of the range of ends that we, as faculty members, pursue through our work.

Scholars have claimed, in various ways, that all teaching, research, and service are consequential and go beyond the walls of the academy. In this sense, inasmuch as students use knowledge to affect how people live, engagement is inevitable, and is itself a "default" component of all scholarship and teaching. All universities are inevitably committed to some set of ends, be these ends related to social challenges, the public good, and/or to economic competitiveness. The question is to *which* assumptions, desires, priorities, and needs faculty members' work commits itself and not *if* one commits to specific assumptions, desires, priorities, and needs. As I will discuss in more depth in chapter 4, asserting (explicitly or implicitly) that the functions of teaching, research, and service can be systematically contained and are, in effect, wholly resistant to any form of embeddedness and consequence beyond the academy is a profoundly unsustainable claim. This is far less a question of what one desires (e.g., to continue working with the assumption that educational institutions and practices are neutral) than an issue of what is ontologically and epistemologically possible.

Civic engagement scholarship has opted to not rigorously examine the fault line that arises when scholars assert that "disinterested" scholarship and teaching are possible. This group of scholars engage in a particularly debilitating move when they assert a set of priorities regarding democratic outcomes and then exercise caution in articulating the values inherent in such priorities. Ideally, all academic work will be explicit about its engagements, and faculty members will opt to be transparent about that to which we imagine our teaching might lead. At its best, education will prepare students to wrestle with the meanings, expressions, and realizations of democratic values. Educators who opt to ignore these questions do not operate as if they are separate from particular priorities and interests. Instead, they are committed to a different set of investments. Education, inevitably, bears on the material. It affirms and challenges norms and moves towards certain futures. All "education has politicity, the quality of being political ... it is never neutral" (Freire, 2001, p. 148). The choice of civic engagement scholars to not rigorously examine the reality that all institutions, departments, and faculties are implicated in some set of value-laden and politically and materially active priorities has had three concrete consequences.

 First, it has left the civic engagement movement open to critique from more conventional scholars, who can charge that civic engagement advocates are burdening universities with the inappropriate educational objective of considering how institutions are invested in particular ends. Dismissing the civic engagement agenda as antithetical to the fundamental work of education itself becomes possible and even logical. Second, civic engagement work has been highly cautious in relation to articulating the values central to countries with democratic aspirations and has openly refused to consider the political nature of civic engagement and education in general. Civic engagement scholars may have opted to be cautious in relation to explicit political priorities in order to increase the possibilities of integration into mainstream academic frameworks. The consequences of such a choice, whether consciously pursued or not, in effect, empty out the very core of democratic work, which is to pursue equitable ways of living together.

 As a result, the civic engagement movement has not been able to unambiguously address the role of power. Even as it refers to democratic values such as inclusion, respect, tolerance, and dialogue (see, e.g., Saltmarsh, Hartley, & Clayton, 2009), the civic engagement movement rarely names concrete priorities, such as the reduction and elimination of state-sanctioned violence against Indigenous and Black Canadian and African American communities, inequitable graduation rates by race, and educational environments that are absent of homophobia. Finally, a third consequence is that conventional forms of scholarship maintain centrality and enjoy high levels of legitimacy in the academy, and they appear as if they transcend interests. Increased attention to the implicatedness of all scholarship would more effectively reveal that with regard to those institutions and faculty members who claim neutrality or a firm remove from any kind of interests or agenda, "when we try to be neutral … we support the dominant ideology" (Freire,2001, p. 148). All of these consequences have limited the effectiveness of civic engagement.

The Problem with Liberal Norms

A second point of critique related to civic engagement work is its routine endorsement of a liberal framework in regard to democratic practices, broadly understood. I make reference to liberal orientations to social, political, and educational projects throughout this book, and in chapters 4 and 5 will present a more extended critique of liberal norms, particularly in educational settings. My objective in this section is to draw attention to the ways in which civic engagement scholarship seemingly effortlessly embraces and affirms what one scholar refers to as the "norms of democratic culture" (Saltmarsh, 2011b, p. 348). Such norms often include values civic engagement scholars reference in their work, such as "inclusiveness" and "an equality of respect" (Saltmarsh, Hartley, & Clayton, 2009, p. 6). These references are rarely accompanied by any discussion of these values in public life in North America, particularly in relation to the concrete practices of injustice at individual and systemic levels.[2] By largely ignoring or minimizing the existence of injustice, this endorsement of liberal frameworks insistently obscures inequitable power dynamics and ultimately harms the possibilities for justice. Two concrete issues are (1) the civic engagement literature's refusal to identify and name the existence of violence and oppression against subordinate groups, and to offer a parallel analysis of the mechanisms and consequences of injustice, and (2) insufficient consideration of what it means to value democratic practices in a context in which long-standing and supposedly "democratic" structures have been used to anti-democratic and unjust ends.

Naming Injustice. Social change requires that individuals and communities name injustice. Identification of injustice is an obvious requirement of pursuing justice. Such identification informs people who may be unaware of occurrences of injustice, specifies the problem to be addressed, and offers an indication of what might be different once justice is achieved. When civic engagement scholars profess a commitment to justice, and yet largely refuse to name the material practices and consequences of injustice, how can one be certain about what these scholars actually want to change? A great deal of the civic engagement literature says little to nothing about injustice – where and why it occurs, what it looks like, who it affects, and what will contribute to its undoing. Service-learning literature does often make explicit reference to community settings, and thus might reference specific issues, such as the examples I note at the start of this chapter. Yet, in the scholarship addressing civic engagement as an educational orientation from conceptual and philosophical perspectives, one might assume that injustice, and especially systemic inequity, is simply not present in North America. This turn away from the material and lived reality, a focus on aspirations with little to no attention to the real and urgent harm that injustice does, and a lack of consideration of systems, power, and competing interests are all markers of liberal work, particularly in educational contexts.

Although the use of words such as "inclusiveness," "transformation," and "enlightened and productive citizenry" (Saltmarsh, Hartley, & Clayton 2009, pp. 6, 3) in a recent critique of civic engagement may be interpreted to point to the broad purposes of civic engagement efforts, only one sentence in the 15-page document invokes the material. This sentence refers to "persistent poverty in our inner cities," "our failure to have a meaningful dialogue about the war in Iraq and Afghanistan," and our "fragile economy" (p. 3).These issues are noted as "significant societal challenges" (ibid.). None of these references clearly identifies those responsible for these issues or acknowledges in any clear way the significance or locations of power.

The language scholars use to identify and describe "societal challenges" is crucial. Such naming communicates, in various ways, if these are forms of institutional injustice or individual failures, if they are systemic and ongoing, and if they are isolated and infrequent. Is poverty primarily the fault of individuals, or is poverty connected to institutions? When we refer to the "fragile economy," do we raise the possibility that business and government leaders have had a role in creating this fragility and that these individuals and institutions thus have responsibility in addressing the consequences of such fragility? In terms of Iraq and Afghanistan, in addition to the goal of dialogue, which in no way necessitates an end to war and violence, do we raise the issue of imperialism? Do institutions have any responsibility in responding to "societal challenges"?

The absence of terms that reference concrete ends and institutional responsibility in the civic engagement literature, unfortunately, renders largely invisible not only the materiality of "significant societal challenges," but also the ways in which such challenges may be rooted in institutions. Further, as I commented at a conference on personal and social responsibility in higher education that I attended in 2011, we are not talking about issues that will occur 50 years in the future, or issues concerning which we can afford a kind of comfortable patience. "Significant societal challenges" are bearing on lives now. When a body of scholarship repeatedly refers to the concepts of democracy and to the desirability of justice, yet seems to simultaneously render invisible the lived experience of that injustice, what does this scholarship seek to change? To whom does it speak? Particularly if one assigns any sense of urgency to the day-to-day violence oppressed groups experience, what is there to reassure these communities that the civic engagement scholarship has an awareness of, let alone a concern with, such violence?

"Democratic" Norms. The easy reference to "democratic norms," "inclusion," and "respect" constitute a second component of liberal shortcomings in the civic engagement scholarship. The suggestion that "democratic norms" have been beneficent to all in equitable ways represents a dismissal of history and a radical denial of current practices. This acceptance of democratic practices is largely supported by liberal scholarship in political, social, and educational discourse. In fact, it has been well established that liberal and democratic norms have been a significant source of violence in North America (Smith, 2001; Smith, 2006). As one scholar notes, "it has never been against US law to commit genocide against Indigenous peoples – in fact, genocide *is* the law of the country" (Smith, 2006, p. 70; emphasis in original). In other words, democracy is "actually the alibi for democracy" and "covers up United States control over Indigenous lands" (ibid.).

When considering the most entrenched and harmful of "democracy's discontents" (Schneider, 2000, p. 107), what do commitments to "inclusion" and "collaborative processes" articulated by those who already have considerable amounts of power offer to marginalized groups, and how will such commitments lead to justice? When I think about students like Cindy and Allison, and preparing them for life in a world in which injustice is routine, deeply rooted, intricate, and messy, I am particularly aware that education that fosters a willingness and ability to address competing interests and move towards justice will require far more than the desire to include, which can be interpreted to mean "inclusion" based on the dominant group's norms and terms.[3]

On the one hand, Cindy's call for "streamlined" education was, in some ways, a straightforward rejection of inclusion. In stating, "I thought this course was going to be streamlined," Cindy might have been declaring, "I expect this course to address gender, narrowly understood, and to stay away from a discussion of queer lives that in any way challenges the status quo." In response to Allison's claim of her disconnect with nation, educators might understand an epistemology of inclusion as an appropriate and sufficient response. In other words, course content might include or recognize racism in North America. Clearly, faculty members can opt to "include" queers and racial minorities as subjects. Indeed, faculty members have relied on political and social frameworks of inclusion to pedagogically and epistemologically "include" bodies that knowledge and course content continue to leave out of educational and public discourse. Yet, the logic of inclusion often rigorously denies power. It also requires those in subordinate groups to fundamentally reject their own humanity and possibilities for sovereignty. Inclusion works if and when those in the subordinate group wholly and without critique accept the norms of the dominant group, which have created and continue to maintain inequity in the first place. In practice, whether implemented politically, socially, pedagogically, or epistemologically, or as is most often the case, from a combination of these modalities, the realities and demands of inclusion can be devastating for subordinate groups and are squarely in opposition to forms of justice that require "determining the conditions of one's action" (Young, 1990, p. 37).

The concept of inclusion has long been central to liberal political thought. In the context of liberal democracies, "there is a common assumption ... that they are and should be incorporative ... Inclusion implies the state will tackle and resolve problems of, for instance, inequality and access" (Macdonald, 2008, p. 341). Yet, whatever the liberal state's discursive allegiances to inclusion, there are "ideological limits to liberalism's incorporation of difference" (p. 342). When considering the capacities of civic engagement to address entrenched forms of injustice, moving towards justice will require possibilities for oppressed groups to, "on their own terms," interact with and challenge those in power (ibid.). Inclusionary frameworks necessarily preclude such engagement. Indeed, while seldom acknowledged in public discourse, which frequently lauds countries such as Canada for its "forward looking" policies of multicultural inclusion (Mackey, 2002), inclusion "legitimates the status quo" (Preece, 2001, p. 1). Inclusion reflects the "attempt to perfect, to master or make normal (that which is other)," and to ultimately "turn everyone into ... one kind of being, at least at some level" (Dunne, 2009, p. 52).

Although I cannot know, I wonder if Allison's choice to articulate her understanding of living in Canada as a racial minority woman in a response paper rather than to the class as a whole was, in effect, a strategic move that would reduce the chance that other students in that class would respond with a discourse of inclusion. She was, in effect, refusing to participate on her peers' terms, which can also be read as insisting on forms of subjecthood which, as least for that moment, were less burdened with liberal contradictions than might have been the case had she made the statement to the class as a whole. Even as I, as the faculty person, might have responded within the logic of inclusion, Allison did not give her classmates such an opportunity. Inasmuch as pedagogical practices always invoke ontological associations, how do educators, in invoking a discourse of inclusion, demand a "form of 'personhood'" of our students, especially those students who are in subordinate groups, which requires that they "relinquish their own" (Macdonald, 2008, p. 348)? In sum, easy support for inclusion within liberal discourse and within the civic engagement literature may feel familiar, reassuring, and worth defending to many educators. Yet such support ultimately works to "transform the colonized population into subjects who align with [dominant] norms" (Coulthard, 2007, p. 443). Within such norms, "values that challenge the homogenizing force of Western liberalism and free-market capitalism" (Alfred, 1999, p. 60) are rarely if ever present.

In refusing to name injustice, and in uncritically accepting "democratic norms" and discourses of inclusion, the civic engagement scholarship effectively denies, or at least dilutes, the daily reality of oppression of marginalized groups and simultaneously obscures the workings of privilege and power. To name the existence of injustice and the desirability of justice at conceptual levels and, at the same time, to refuse to consider the materiality of oppression, does harm. Such forms of naming remove the reality of oppression from public discourse. "Democratic norms" continue to privilege some and harm others. Frank Paul is dead. Cindy would have liked to ignore queer lives. Allison felt separate from nation. A white man treated boys of colour in a library computer room as less than human. Injustice is everywhere, and it acts on bodies. Whom is civic engagement scholarship serving? What realities and norms does it seek to make public, to bring into both higher education scholarship and other discursive arenas? Whose lives is it designed to change? Even as civic engagement scholars have stressed the importance of democratic purpose, references to this purpose are largely in the abstract and favour rhetorical over material commitments. Inasmuch as civic engagement efforts are concerned with deeply rooted forms of injustice, the articulation of purposes will need to be much more specific and concrete.

Service Learning

Service learning represents an institutional, curricular, and pedagogical set of efforts to integrate a variety of forms of community service into academic study. While faculty members, staff, and administrators might often use the terms service learning and civic engagement interchangeably, these terms are most accurately viewed, from historical, conceptual, and programmatic perspectives, as parallel yet not necessarily overlapping. As explained earlier in this chapter, endorsements on the part of faculty members or institutions of civic engagement work are most often an acknowledgment of public and democratic priorities. While the classroom is one setting in which to enact these public commitments, research and service can also further civic engagement efforts.

Service learning, in contrast, is nearly exclusively carried out in curricular contexts. Further, early service-learning activities were often aligned with the public and democratic components of civic engagement, and some scholarly discussions of service learning assume the integration of civic outcomes as a priority. At the same time, faculty members can pursue service learning with little or no attention to civic priorities. While faculty members and institutions have made explicit and substantive commitments to service learning, they have not found consensus as to whether or not service learning has significantly altered higher education. Below, I offer an overview and discussion of service learning in higher education.

The term service learning was "coined in the late 1960s" (Saltmarsh, 1996, p. 14). Service learning efforts draw on educational theorists such as Paolo Freire and John Dewey, and on a variety of educational philosophies and programs including community service, volunteerism, experiential learning, social justice movements in education, and student-centred and experiential pedagogies (Rocheleau, 2004; Varlotta, 1997). Scholars have also made strong connections between service learning and pragmatism, even as these connections are "rarely ... directly formulated and attributed" (Saltmarsh, 1996, p. 14). Service learning, routinely understood as one form of experiential education, has been defined as occurring when "students participate in activities that address human and community needs together with structured opportunities intentionally designed to promote student learning and development" (Jacoby, 1996, p. 5). The combination of experiential and academic learning is crucial, as is the connection to a specific community setting or organization. In effect, service learning "uses 'service' as a text" (Varlotta, 1997, p. 453).

Philosophical and Historical Underpinnings

Service learning requires a curricular component focused on "community needs" or "community service." Thus, one's approach to "community" is crucial in regard to service learning. According to one article, "the history of what we have come to call community service actually entails three different and continuing cultural responses to the individual and social dilemmas that emerged from the crisis of community at the turn of the last century" (Morton & Saltmarsh, 1997, p. 137). In brief, these three understandings of community include (1) an emphasis on the non-profit and social service sectors, (2) the importance of educated citizens acting as democratic agents paired with "support for a large, powerful state" (p. 138), and (3) an explicit rejection of "most of the assumptions and values underlying both capitalism and democracy" (p. 137). As proponents of each response, Jane Addams, John Dewey, and Dorothy Day all grappled extensively with the challenges of charity, a mode of responding to social issues that "assumes the continued and necessary existence of a dependent and 'lower' class to be the recipient of the kindness of their superiors" (Dewey, 1978, p. 348).

Over time, there was a crucial shift in the language on which Addams, Dewey, and Day relied, namely, from terms such as charity and philanthropy to service: "A dominant language of charity and philanthropy was replaced in the popular vernacular and public discourse sometime later in the 20th century with a language of 'service'" (Morton & Saltmarsh, 1997, p. 146). The tensions surrounding this shift in language explicitly and implicitly align with many of the shortcomings of civic engagement and service-learning work that I identify in this chapter. Morton and Saltmarsh conclude that this shift in language does not represent a "fundamental reframing" (p. 146) in regard to the conceptual underpinnings of service learning. In other words, the current reliance on a service model is significantly tied to long-standing notions of charity. While Morton and Saltmarsh conclude their analysis with the assertion that community service "does contain an antidote to the crisis of community" (p. 148), they do not fully address how this antidote will be put into practice. I have included attention to the historical and philosophical foundations of the term "service" because these issues are at the heart of what service learning will offer to both students and to public life. Unfortunately, the type of analysis found in Morton and Saltmarsh's article, which examines the central assumptions and objectives of service learning, is rare. In the 17 years since their article has been published, there has been little to no scholarship produced that offers a thorough conceptual investigation of the deeply rooted underlying assumptions that drive service learning.

While a rigorous conceptual analysis is lacking, there has been some attention to the concrete expressions of service learning from a charity model and how such a model limits considerations of justice. Within the service-learning literature, scholars have asserted that while charity refers to the "provision of help," social justice "refers to the state of institutional or structural arrangements" (Marullo & Edwards, 2000, p. 899). Others have addressed the ways in which service learning based on notions of charity might encourage victim blaming and a retreat from the consideration of contextual and structural factors (Hollis, 2004). As one scholar asserts, service learning for social justice makes significant demands on the instructor. When considering the charity vs. the social justice approach to service learning, "it is important to evaluate which type of service learning has the greater impact on the community and the greater possibility of social transformation in the long run" (Lewis, 2004, p. 107). Consideration of questions of impact, the priorities and objectives of service learning, and the philosophical and ontological foundations from which service-learning work emerges is crucial when engaging questions of social justice. At a broader level, scholars have addressed the limits of charity and approaches to justice that go beyond charity (see, e.g., Shaikh, 2007; Young, 2006). As one public intellectual from the United States succinctly states, "Well, charity ain't justice. Charity is beautiful, but you ain't got to be charitable to me if I already got justice" (Dyson, 2005). In sum, the extent to which notions of charity underpin one's approach to service learning and to justice is critical.

Existing literature has identified specific approaches to service learning, even as the discussion of these approaches, for the most part, does not include in-depth attention to issues of power. These are the philanthropic, civic, communitarian, and social justice approaches. Philanthropic approaches draw on the idea that "service is simply a natural

philanthropic approach to SL

(1) social responsibility of those who can offer assistance grounded in the context of charity" (Abel & Sementelli, 2004, p. 61). In this model, while social challenges exist, they can best be addressed by those who are sufficiently privileged to be able to offer resources and assistance to those who are "less fortunate." Philanthropic approaches require little to no critical analysis or reflection concerning the conditions that created the social challenges in the first place. As this model "creates and supports dependency" (p. 61) and discourages partnerships and reciprocal relationships, some believe that it "undermine[s] many of service-learning's objectives" (p. 65). Another important component of the philanthropic approach is neutrality with regard to social issues (Abel & Sementelli, 2004; Hoppe, 2004). Academic discussions about "the good life," for example, should be abstract and should not attempt to come to any conclusion in relation to specific social or political positions. Even as many proponents of service learning might agree that a philanthropic approach is "paternalistic and marginalizes those it seeks to help" (Hoppe, 2004, p. 140), one can identify traces of this approach in many service-learning efforts.

(2) *civic approach to SL* In contrast to the philanthropic approach's emphasis on altruism, the civic approach focuses on mutual responsibility and begins with the premise that "democracy demands equal participation and voice by all citizens" (Battistoni & Hudson, 1997, p. 5). Civic approaches to service learning consider democratic activities (voting, civic participation, etc.), and go beyond these forms of involvement to emphasize the role of higher education in addressing "pressing social problems" through relationships with community stakeholders (Watson, 2004, p. 77). For those who support a civic approach to service learning, ideally, students will learn through participation in community work, and knowledge will be centrally directed at "improving human welfare" (Hoppe, 2004, p. 141). At the same time, civic approaches often fail to encourage "broad social critique" and consideration of systems and power (Westheimer & Kahne, 2004, p. 261). Building on liberal understandings of public life and social issues, the civic approach seems to suggest that encouraging civic considerations – reciprocity, community building, democratic ideals – will be sufficient to ensure democratic outcomes.

(3) *communitarian* A communitarian approach to service learning emphasizes the social nature of all public life. Directly opposing the civic approach's affinity for liberalism's "fixation on the sovereign autonomy of rights-bearing individuals" (McClay, 1998, p. 101), communitarianism shifts the gaze from the individual as autonomous to the individual as a "member of a larger social fabric" (Colby, Ehrlich, Beaumont, Rosner, & Stephens 2000, p. xxvi). Those who advocate this approach believe that through, with, and in community is where the work of democracy occurs. However, critics have argued that this approach is "much too closely bound to the very liberalism it would correct" and that it downplays the importance of defining what type of community we desire, overstates the existence of shared values, and is naive in its estimation of how community-based dialogue and action will address social challenges (Murphy, 2004, p. 126). Further, communitarian approaches to service learning "tend to romanticize the idea of community and to sentimentalize the idea of the situated self" (Boyte & Farr, 1997, p. 6). On the whole, communitarian approaches also fail to sufficiently address particular and competing interests.

Alongside these three approaches to service learning, the social justice understanding has offered the most explicit attention to oppression, power, and social change. Social justice approaches consider institutional and systemic issues. Likewise, students must learn to consider competing interests, the significance and uses of power, and the ethical priorities a democratic agenda requires. Even as many faculty members link their own service-learning efforts with social justice priorities, the limits of such efforts are often easily visible, particularly when one looks closely. Raising questions about how service learning considers institutional injustice, power, and systemic change can quickly reveal the lack of anything beyond a verbal commitment in service learning to social justice. A study of 600 service-learning programs found that a mere one per cent included a "focus on specifically political concerns and solutions such as creating or working with groups to represent the interests of a community" (Colby, Beaumont, Ehrlich, & Corngold, 2007, p. 5). Indeed, the panel presentations I discuss at the start of this chapter, all of which in some way referenced social justice, point to several conceptual questions about the ways in which service learning orients itself towards social justice outcomes. The philosophical and historical underpinnings of service learning, as reflected in these four approaches, have a direct bearing on the implementation of service-learning efforts.

Purpose, Objectives, and Pedagogical Components

For Brabant and Braid (2009), service learning has a "dual purpose: (1) to stimulate students' interest in, and ability to digest, course content as they relate to practical experiences beyond the classroom and

(2) to aid in the process of inculcating values we deem essential to the well-being of any *civic* construct – humility, efficacy, and empathy" (pp. 67–68; emphasis in original). Service-learning outcomes often include an integration of competencies in the disciplines and in civic areas, enhancement of civic responsibility, development of personal and social responsibility, community activism, enhanced academic learning, and intercultural competency (Brabant & Braid, 2009; Hironimus-Wendt & Lovell-Troy, 1999; Westheimer & Kahne, 2004). While much of the attention to service-learning outcomes notes the importance of civic-related learning, prominent scholars in the field have also questioned the ways in which service-learning efforts, over time and across institutions, have maintained a commitment to civic engagement priorities. Beginning in the 1990s, in regard to the combination of service and academic study, instructors focused most consistently on "reflective, community-based pedagogy" and, secondarily, if at all, on civic learning outcomes (Saltmarsh, 2011a, p. 30). Indeed, the focus on "the technical aspects of a discipline" resulted in even the "most exemplary models of service-learning" offering no attention to civic dimensions (p. 30). While educators have been able to adapt civic content to service-learning courses, ensuring civic learning outcomes is less common. In regard to this analysis, then, service learning may or may not foreground or even consider civic, public, or democratic outcomes. Indeed, it is possible to shape service learning around conventional disciplinary norms, as long as the course includes a community component.

Faculty members incorporating service learning into their courses have long considered both pedagogical components and desired outcomes. Pedagogically, service learning, to some extent, shifts the space of learning from being primarily or exclusively the classroom to occurring in both the community and on campus. Other aspects of teaching change as well. Faculty members must increase their knowledge of community networks and stakeholders; offer considerable attention to the process of learning as it occurs while linked to a community setting, which often involves shifting time frames and revisiting assignments and expectations; and balance between discipline- and civic-based knowledge, inasmuch as service-learning faculty members are interested in the public and democratic aspects of service learning (Peters, 2004). In sum, service learning rests on pedagogies that are centred on "connecting structured student activities in community work with academic study, decentering the teacher as the singular source of knowledge, incorporating a reflective teaching methodology, and shifting the model of education, to use Paulo Freire's distinction, from 'banking' to 'dialogue'" (Saltmarsh, Zlotkowski, & Hollander, 2011c, p. 288).

The pull between disciplinary knowledge and content vs. civic knowledge, content, and capacities is one of two tensions that are acknowledged by proponents of service learning. Further, service learning is always positioned within university structures. In the context of faculty members' and departmental understandings of service learning as problematic or a threat to disciplinary learning, service-learning advocates must consider whether to align with traditional academic structures or to find support elsewhere in the university. Ideally, institutions and faculty members will "position service learning as a core academic effort … an activity belonging to the primary systems and structures of higher education – departments, curricula, and activities that constitute the faculty domain" (Saltmarsh & Zlotkowski, 2011a, p. 3). When faculty members and institutions situate service learning as a necessary part of disciplinary knowledge, rather than as an optional or even undesirable addition to it, service-learning efforts will usually be more sustainable.

At the same time, such an approach has been rare. Even as service learning has prioritized the importance of becoming recognized as a "legitimate form of scholarship … for some the very idea of organizing in a way that recognized the legitimacy of disciplinary units and cultures was inherently problematic … the disciplines themselves were a large part of the problem" (Saltmarsh & Zlotkowski, 2011a, p. 3). While this tension is at first glance primarily a structural question – i.e., where to "house" service-learning programs – it simultaneously raises questions about outcomes and how and to what extent service learning becomes an integral part of students' education. When a department prioritizes service learning within its curriculum, this will significantly bear on the education of students in that department. In contrast, for students who take service-learning courses outside of their department (courses housed either in other departments or in non-departmentally based programs on campus), service learning may be, proportionately, a very small component of one's education.

In relation to all three presentations discussed at the beginning of this chapter, I wondered how the faculty members were defining social justice. As all of the papers primarily addressed individuals, attitudes, and behaviours, rather than institutions, power, and systemic patterns and practices, did the presenters assume that social justice might be accomplished in the absence of attention to the latter group of concepts? In the

case of the course that designed a film that portrayed Latino/as as having "hopes and dreams" and the "important part [Latino/as] play in
the local and state economy," I can see how this might, for non-Latino/
as, slightly shift their understanding of individual Latino/as. As the
educators stated, they hoped to interrupt stereotypes, offer a critique of
anti-immigrant rhetoric, and portray Latino/as more positively. These
goals are clearly components of moving towards justice and point to
the possibility of awareness of the complexities of injustice and how it
works, as well as the workings of power, specifically in the context of
students and their relationship to migrant workers.

This course, which closely aligns with the social justice approach to
service learning, raises questions we might ask of all service-learning
courses. To what extent does the class focus on discursive and rhetorical vs. material realities? A film positioned as an educational tool that is
directed towards reducing stereotypes is addressing injustice at a representational level. Where is the material, or change focused on living
conditions for Latino/a workers? Is power analysed primarily in relationship to students, in broader contexts, or not at all? To what extent
do service-learning courses pursue increased dialogue, tolerance, and
inclusion, rather than the elimination of "institutional conditions which
inhibit or prevent people from participating in determining their actions
or the conditions of their actions" (Young, 1990, p. 38)? Dialogue, especially in the absence of a clear set of priorities for change at material
levels, may be primarily successful at easing the consciences of the
dominant group and offering to faculty members a sense of "making
a difference." Particularly when commitments to empathy, tolerance,
and inclusion are emphasized, this can set up a framework in which the
dominant group sets the terms. To offer inclusion into unjust systems
seems a questionable and destructive objective, particularly when one
is in the subordinate group.

Two aspects of service learning that limit its ability to contribute to
democratic practices and to justice are (1) a lack of institutional analysis
and an insufficient language for power and (2) service learning that is
constructed as "application" vs. "implication" (Britzman, 1995, p. 163).
Apart from service-learning scholarship that explicitly addresses social
justice, the service-learning literature offers little attention to institutional injustice and change. Further, faculty members can make verbal
and conceptual commitments to social justice, and might simultaneously pursue pedagogical practices and learning outcomes that are
largely aligned with a philanthropic approach to service-learning and

charity-based approaches to justice and equity. For faculty members who do attempt through service-learning courses to integrate careful attention to systemic injustice, a multitude of social and institutional constraints make such goals particularly challenging to achieve. Service-learning courses often reduce democratic practices to individual actions, draw attention away from power relationships, and give visibility and priority to concepts such as dialogue, inclusion, and tolerance. They also simultaneously render invisible systemic practices of injustice and the inevitability and complexity of competing interests and power. Courses that do either or both are, in fact, reducing the capacity for the students in these courses to understand and analyse the requirements of democratic practices.

 Inasmuch as students learn that democratic values and possibilities for justice are achieved solely or primarily through attention to individual behaviours and require no consideration of power, they will very likely be opposed to ideas that insist on the primacy of the relational and the role of institutions. When students repeatedly learn that responding to social needs and considering justice and the public good are matters of attitudes and individual behaviour, they can be quite confident in rejecting course content that challenges this approach. Thus, service-learning courses, especially those that focus on the individual and lack attention to power, can, in effect, support a vigorous resistance to instructors who offer content that questions the role of institutions. Particularly in educational and social frameworks that routinely affirm "a sense of being individual, disconnected from older social ties and able to pursue one's own particular dreams and aspirations ... [and] individuals are affirmed for their human capital ... [and the] freedom to choose and consume" (Seddon, 2011, p. 176), normalizing a critique of institutions is challenging and can easily be overlooked in the interests of what seems possible in a term.

To pose a second set of questions related to service learning, I will borrow from Britzman's idea of education as "application" vs. "implication" (1995, p. 163). In the context of considering undergraduate education and civic outcomes, we are all positioned as ethical agents, as people who are situated within a complex set of relationships and who are always choosing how to live within those relationships. In this sense, we are always and everywhere implicated. "Application" privileges a separation between "the interpreter and the interpreted" (Britzman, 1995, p. 163). I would claim that, on the whole, service-learning courses are based on a model of "application." Though the courses might lead to a sense of implication, they are conceptually and programmatically set up as "applications." As a form of engaging the social, service-learning programs privilege application. This has a couple of concrete and problematic results that are highly relevant. To a large extent, service-learning courses are constructed as curricular programs that should meet the interests of the faculty person, who within the context of the course has the most power. Within the framework for the course (duration, desired outcomes, level of course, etc.), student and community organizations are expected to fit within faculty members' expectations, even when faculty members can and do make serious attempts to offer something of value to the community organization.

At the same time, the structural model for all service-learning courses, regardless of the faculty member offering the class, raises several questions and risks. It potentially furthers the idea of democratic work as charity, repositions educators and students as the primary beneficiaries of civic or social justice service-learning work, locates relationships with community organizations as secondary to pedagogical and curricular objectives, and rearticulates and normalizes problematic power relationships. As Walker and Hart's (2011) account of their service-learning course that involved community work in Belize demonstrates, at times such courses place multiple demands on a community with which the educators and students have no long-term or even recently formed relationships. Despite calls for partnerships, reciprocity, and mutuality, the reality of most service-learning efforts is that the educators and students have significantly higher levels of power, access, and control than the community organization. These limits are inherent to nearly all service-learning efforts. As a model for education, service learning runs a high risk of furthering such dynamics, often with the participating faculty members offering no critical assessment of the foundations and consequences of these dynamics.

In contrast, entering a course with the goal of grappling with the idea of implication sets up a radically different set of objectives and a different process for learning. Admittedly, a model of education as "implication" is, in many ways, more time-consuming and elusive and places different demands on faculty members than a model of education as "application." Within a context of democratic engagement, relying on a model of implication begins with assessing, reflecting on, and critiquing the relationships in which students are already situated, rather than constructing a course in which they are placed into a specific setting. Students are always already variously implicated: at work, in campus organizations, as members of a community, as constituents of political representatives, in housing/rental infrastructures, and as students. How might they consider power, injustice, and possibilities for justice from one of these locations, from "their own spaces" (Boyte & Farr, 1997, p. 7)? Organizing a course around students coming to a critical understanding of their own existing locations, which will be complex and related to power, may lead to concrete work with a community or other organization. As I will discuss further in chapter 7, starting from one's own implicatedness, rather than from a position of application, has significant consequences related to considering democratic practices, the public good, and justice.

Conclusion

This chapter has examined philosophical and pedagogical components of the scholarship of engagement, civic education, and service learning in order to better understand the ways in which all three might potentially limit consideration of undergraduate education, democratic practices, the public good, and justice. As asserted in chapter 2, literature has claimed that institutions of higher education have an obligation to consider social needs. Within a focus on civic engagement, colleges and universities in North America have explicitly acknowledged that institutions of higher learning "are among the nation's most valuable laboratories for civic learning and democratic engagement" (National Task Force on Civic Learning and Democratic Engagement, 2012, p. 2). A recent report boldly "call[s] on the higher education community – and all of its stakeholders – to embrace civic learning and democratic engagement as an undisputed educational priority" (p. 6). The report goes on to assert that "there is a civic dimension to every field of study" (p. 16), and that education will ideally prepare students "*with* knowledge and *for* action" (p. 10; emphasis in original). Such reports, part of a wide body of scholarly work, firmly establish civic engagement as a concern central to higher education at a broad level.

Such robust support for careful attention to the public good and "democratic purposes" (p. 83) in the context of undergraduate education points to larger questions. How do existing philosophical and epistemological frameworks set up norms and possibilities for understanding self and other, for naming injustice, and for moving towards justice? How can educators ensure that ideas about civic engagement and democratic practices fully acknowledge the embodied, urgent, and often violent consequences of routine injustice? As I argued in chapter 1, we reveal the most about ourselves as a society in terms of how we repeatedly turn towards "too much wrong." Similarly, how do the scholarship of engagement, civic engagement, and service learning unambiguously urge us to turn toward "too much wrong," or to consider and act against state-sanctioned violence directed at Black and Indigenous men, differential graduation rates by race, and the removal of queer lives from public spaces? In what ways are the scholarship of engagement, civic engagement, and service learning embedded within liberal norms, and how do such norms themselves impose constraints on how civic engagement and service learning might name injustice and imagine justice? For educators disturbed by a white man's communication in a library computer room, by the deaths of men like Amadou Diallo and Frank Paul, and by our students' refusal to consider injustice against queer communities on our campuses, what do the scholarship of engagement, civic engagement, and service learning offer?

In this chapter, I have claimed that these three bodies of work carry a set of assumptions and conceptual legacies that, on the whole, negate the very analysis and practice that attention to democratic practices, the public good, and justice require. More than a matter of "not going far enough," I would argue that these three bodies of work, paired with liberal norms, are far too invested in maintaining allegiances to the individual as primary, to the illusion of neutrality, and to existing power arrangements to effectively take up questions of injustice and pursue the possibility of justice. Further, even as the scholarship of engagement, civic engagement, and service learning represent the most institutionally affirmed responses to the question of democratic practices and undergraduate education, numerous faculty members and departments pursue their work with little to no consideration of this scholarship and its relevance for undergraduate education. In the next chapter, I continue to examine the reach of liberal norms, and the ways in which these norms bear on educators' work more broadly. In many ways, the first component of moving towards a different set of practices is ensuring a full understanding of the ways in which existing assumptions move and breathe just under our skin.

4 "What Do You Think? 41 Bullets?": The Relationship of the Subject and the Social

It is the fall of 2003. I am in my second year as a faculty member at a public university in northeastern Indiana. I am teaching a course on intercultural communication for the second time. About 25 students are enrolled in the course, we meet three times a week, and it is a Friday, the end of the second week of the term. The students come from a variety of departments. Five African Americans are in the course. The rest of the students are white. The topic for this week has been history and intercultural communication. Students have read a chapter from the textbook on history, watched a film on religious and racialized violence in the United States, and listened to a presentation that I gave that examined how educational institutions have historically attended to difference and thus potentially shaped what students know about intercultural communication. I have also asked the students to consider how history and communication work in their own lives, and they have written brief reflection papers on this topic. Today, I am wrapping up the unit with a brief presentation on how history is relevant to intercultural communication. Before I start, I let the students know that throughout my presentation, I would like to hear examples from them that pertain to the points I make in the presentation. For these examples, they might consider their reflection papers, my earlier presentation, the reading, the film, and other sources of knowledge.

I make the first point: "History functions as a socializing force." From history, and from the ways in which individuals, media, and institutions represent that history to us, we learn about what is appropriate and inappropriate, and about what is considered acceptable and desirable. Once I am finished with this point, the first of three that I will make, Gloria, one of the five African Americans in the class, responds to my request for examples: "The Diallo killing is important in my community. We know we can't trust the police. That's a lesson for us." Following Gloria's reference to the African American community's distrust of the police and to the killing of Amadou Diallo, I turn to the class as a whole, and ask: "How many of you have heard of the Diallo killing in New York?" The students shake their heads. "Maybe Gloria would like to tell us about the Diallo killing," I suggest, which allows her to add to her account if she chooses to do so, "or I can talk about what happened to Amadou Diallo. Other students can tell us what they know of the situation."

Gloria gives a brief description of what happened: "This Black man, Amadou Diallo, was standing in the doorway of his apartment building, and four white policemen put 41 bullets in him. And they all got off. Forty-one bullets, and nothing happened to those policemen." I explain that yes, the policemen saw Diallo reaching towards his back pocket, and while Diallo was reaching for his wallet to get his identification, the policemen saw something different. They said later that they thought Diallo had a gun. The police never did find a gun in Diallo's possession.

Paul, a young white man who sits in the back corner of the classroom, adds his knowledge of the situation. He quickly fills the room with his presence. It is the first time that Paul has shared strong feelings on any topic with the class as a whole: "41 of those bullets were necessary. Every one of them. Those policemen were doing their job." Paul's tone is unwavering. He is angry and certain.

Robert, a young African American man sitting towards the front of the room, turns his whole body to face Paul. "What?" Robert is aghast: "41 bullets? Are you kidding? He had a wallet, and they needed 41 bullets?" Robert's voice is angry, and incredulous. Paul talks back: "They were acting in self-defence. You expect them to see him pull a gun and do nothing?" The conversation between the two men continues. "It wasn't a gun. And 41 bullets? There were four of them. He had a wallet in his hand. Not one of those 41 bullets was necessary." "They did exactly the right thing. They had to defend themselves. That was their job." "If they wanted to kill him, one bullet would have been enough."

There is a pause. Paul and Robert seem to be finished. In my experience, such classroom interactions are often where the most significant possibilities for learning take root. They are also cognitively and affectively demanding. Educators are always navigating a complicated map of power and priorities. Standing in the uneven geography of my students' knowledge and ideas, I am doing the best I can to sort out my pedagogical priorities with the possibilities and responsibilities of my role as the course instructor. As I consider what might come next, I also observe a rush of ideas tracking through my head and heart: Gloria's choice to risk this insertion in a classroom where the white faculty person might not have her back; my awareness that she is also very likely an astute observer of racial dynamics and knows what she is doing; for Robert, the utter weariness of sitting in a room with others who believe that the particular combination of a Black male body, four white policemen, and a moment of uncertainty requires 41 bullets, representing nothing less than a form of ontological devastation; for Paul, the depth of that which he feels he needs to defend; my own longing for pedagogical spaces that can bear such devastation, and for moments, however fleeting, in which those in the room commit to the ongoing relationality of knowing with others in ways that begin to crack open the glacier-like presence of injustice.

Again, I sense a profound brokenness among those of us in that space. There is too much wrong. I wait. Once we see differently, will we act differently? If we act differently, how often, in what settings, and for how long will we do so? As Paul and others who see clearly the necessity of 41 bullets consider whether they will opt to question their deeply held beliefs, what are the costs to Gloria and Robert? How are we all thinking and feeling our way through a different way of knowing, affectively and cognitively sustaining or not investments in the work of being together, three times a week, for an hour? The demands, in that moment, feel overwhelming. Paul is utterly convinced of the need for 41 bullets. He seems, in fact, angry that someone has dared to question this use of power. I am aware that in only the second week of class, we have moved close to issues that may be entirely new for most students in the room. The existence of strongly felt emotions and conflicting interests, all playing out in a formal classroom setting, may also be unfamiliar for many students. I stand in that pause, feel caught by the difficulty of what I see.

An unarmed Black man, four white policemen, and 41 bullets. I see state-sanctioned violence. Gloria has identified with her community's distrust of the police. Questions persist. Inasmuch as democratic living requires at least a minimal consideration of justice, what is the subject? Whose lives are considered, and how? Students note the ways in which instructors foreground seemingly neutral disciplinary content and, simultaneously, retreat from the complications of inequity (Simpson, 2007). Related to such classroom contexts, I hear students assert that they have learned to expect education that only lightly brushes up against questions of injustice, that maintains a firm distance from deep-seated social issues, and that for the most part remains within the confines of dominant educational and social norms. In what ways do, for example, a white man's treatment of four boys of colour in a library computer room, Amadou Diallo's death, and differential graduation rates by race enter the content and conversations that shape what students learn as they complete their degrees?

Scholarship on higher education, civic engagement, and service learning has offered extensive attention to the social contract, the general aims of a university education, and public and democratic commitments in teaching, research, and service. In the last chapter, I began to address how liberal norms act to constrain these three areas of work in regard to possibilities for considering democratic practices, the public good, and justice. In this chapter, after considering a classroom situation in which students and I were again negotiating the contours and limits of the subject, I make several claims about social life and provide a rationale for these claims. I next place liberal and critical work in conversation with each other, particularly with regard to questions of undergraduate education, democratic practices, the public good, and justice. An identification of the central starting points for each of these bodies of work points to the ways in which scholars working in these areas consider power, competing interests, and institutional forms of injustice.

Democracy's Agenda: 41 Bullets and Negotiating the Subject

Stories of practice often carry a wealth of information about the desires of our students and ourselves. While analyses that remain at the conceptual level run the risk of oversimplifying, dismissing, or distorting lived reality, engaging the material or beginning with how power acts on bodies in concrete situations often lends a concreteness to the subject in ways that resist such oversimplification, dismissal, or distortion. In the course in which we had a discussion of the choice of four white policemen to kill Amadou Diallo, the students and I were negotiating the connections between a reading on the relevance of history to intercultural communication and the in/justice of the policemen's actions and Diallo's death.

In 1999, in New York City, four white policemen fired 41 bullets into the body of Amadou Diallo, a Black man standing in the vestibule of his

apartment building. When a student in the Intercultural Communication course brought the subject of the Diallo killing into our conversation, there was quick and sharp conflict among the students. The first
student's reference to the Diallo killing and the presence of disagreement presented me with multiple avenues to pursue. I could engage,
ignore, or openly reject the subject of Diallo's killing. I could opt to take
a break, and not return to the subject of the Diallo killing, or I could
make a quick reference to "unfortunate deaths" and move on to the next
point of discussion. I could also place the possibility of systemic racism
squarely on the table and ask for discussion.

Beyond these specific and immediate concerns, this classroom interaction points to several broader questions. What is the role of the
instructor in regard to education that considers social challenges? What
kinds of risks do students from non-dominant groups take when they
bring what some, particularly those in dominant groups, perceive as
"difficult" subject matter to the table? When such subject matter is on
the table, what kinds of norms and priorities do faculty members keep
close and rely on to navigate such situations? When the subject matter
on the table explicitly evokes the well-being of individuals and communities, is it possible for a faculty person to be neutral? Whether or
not educators rigorously consider such questions in relation to the story
in this chapter or to other classroom situations, such issues persist. The
ways in which we invite, refuse, and consider such topics and conversations constitute part of our educational practice whether or not we
acknowledge this.

I appreciated Gloria's comments about the Diallo killing and its significance for the Black community. I had asked for examples, and the
one she provided was highly relevant to the material we were covering during that class. I was familiar with the Diallo killing. For me,
the actions of four white policemen who chose to shoot 41 bullets into
Amadou Diallo, as well as the general lack of accountability for Diallo's
death among the structures within which those four policemen worked,
point to racism within the New York police services. Police officers are
always part of a larger system. In the case of Diallo's death, institutional
structures undoubtedly contributed to a professionalization process in
which shooting 41 bullets at an unarmed Black man seemed sensible.
These structures have also ensured that 15 years following the shooting, routine violence by institutions purportedly set up to serve communities is ongoing. As I work on this chapter, George Zimmerman,
previously a neighbourhood watch volunteer in Sanford, Florida, killed

Trayvon Martin, an unarmed 17-year-old African American.[1] At the same time, I am aware that not everyone sees the issues of responsibility for Diallo's death in the same way that I do.

However we see this situation and questions of responsibility, Gloria is right: this is an example of history as a socializing force. As Gloria finishes talking, I am aware that she has taken a risk. In this classroom and at this institution, as well as in the broader community in which she and her peers live, most will perceive her way of seeing as a challenge and will likely mark it as angry, misplaced, and/or "militant." Gloria "use[d] transformative knowledge to challenge" (Richardson & Villenas, 2000, p. 268) the actions of an institution that most of us in that classroom rarely questioned. In articulating "transformative knowledge," Gloria has disrupted the "common sense knowledge" that asserts that the police services represent an institution that the public can trust. In this sense, she has called into question the taken-for-granted assumptions and loyalties of many students. She has attempted to redirect, if only for a moment, the incessant normalcy and flow of dominant knowledge. Agendas are most visible when they challenge what we assume to be true, and can bring into stark relief that which we often do not even see. I had asked for examples, and Gloria provided one. In so doing, Gloria had called into question the agenda of dominant knowledge – the belief that institutions are fair and that the police offer the same level and type of protection to individuals and communities regardless of race (Staples, 2011).

I understand Diallo's death to be part of the subject in this course on intercultural communication. A priority in all of my courses is to ensure that students can link concepts with concrete social issues. In this course, I hope that students will develop a more complex understanding of how intercultural communication plays out in people's lives. Naming injustice, allowing this topic to be present in the room, is a crucial step towards envisioning the ways in which communication might play out differently, so that Diallo might have lived, and so that police officers use the power of their roles differently. To be in such an educational space is in this sense a relief. We have begun to name the mess, which is no longer "behind my back, outside of my vision, beyond my memory," particularly for those in positions of privilege (Simpson, 2003, p. 49).

When it seems that, for the moment, the students have stepped back from making comments, I offer my own thoughts: "Gloria has brought up an issue that is clearly about intercultural communication, and about history and the lessons it teaches us. Also, I am glad that Robert and

Paul could say where they are at, that they can disagree. This is part of talking about race, of talking about culture and history." I know I want to expand the conversation about responsibility, accountability, and the ways in which institutions protect and kill. I am not quite sure what to do or say next. I look at the students, who are momentarily silent. "What do you think?" Gloria asks, leaning towards me in her seat, "Forty-one bullets?"

Faced with Gloria's question, Robert and Paul's disagreement, and a room full of students who have never heard of Amadou Diallo, what are my own educational investments? What will I do with the power I have, with my agency as the instructor for this course? Whether I plainly acknowledge the conflict Robert and Paul have had; comment on what it means for a community to distrust an institution whose mandate is to "enhance the quality of life in New York City ... [and] to enforce the laws, preserve the peace, reduce fear, and provide a safe environment" (City of New York Police Department, n.d.); move on to my second point in the presentation; end class early; or remain with my students in the very real ethical questions that are always part of the social, I need to respond. Whatever I do next will move us in one direction and not another. Such moments are wrenching. They press, scrape, and make demands. In such moments, we do our work as educators.

This example from the classroom has strong links with the three central questions I raised in chapter 1. First, what are higher education's obligations to the social? Does higher education have a responsibility to consider Diallo's death, so that students might grapple with difficult social issues during their university education? Second, what is the subject? Content that challenged many students, as well as the demands of dialogue, were both in the room when Gloria asked about 41 bullets, when Robert and Paul disagreed about the police services' uses of those bullets, and when students and I listened. Within broad conceptual frameworks, such as history and intercultural communication, what do we expect our students to learn? Finally, how do constructions of the subject and the social inform each other and teach our students about their implicatedness in an unjust world? This classroom example raises another crucial question: What is the role of the faculty person? Finally, how does a concern for justice, a hope that my students will expand their capacity for considering the public good, inform my response? In what ways is any response an indication of one's investments? "What do you think?" Gloria asks me, "41 bullets?"

The Parameters of the Social

For Gloria, the Diallo killing and its significance for her community were clearly subjects with relevance to that class. Prior to that class meeting, other students had absolutely no knowledge of Diallo, the four white policemen who killed him, and the response of the New York Police Department. Immediately after that class, returning to my office, I ran into a colleague who taught in my department. As I briefly mentioned the exchange to him, it became clear that like many of my students, he also had no knowledge of the Diallo killing. Teaching is always a way of mapping our engagement with the world in which we live. Many educators opt to teach courses on intercultural communication or other subjects with little attention to the material, and with an extensive focus on the norms of dominant groups, and/or with the assumption that power is irrelevant or exists only at the individual level. These faculty members, on the whole, offer a map of, for example, intercultural communication that is largely accepting of existing social arrangements, that communicates to students that such social arrangements are desirable and appropriate, and that critique or resistance are unnecessary. To what extent do we as educators have an awareness of broad and specific institutional injustices that have a connection to content in the courses we teach? Although we may not often carefully consider the ways in which our thoughts about the world in which we live form a kind of weave with the ways in which we teach and how we conceptualize content and subject matter in our courses, that weave is there.

Likewise, even before Gloria leaned towards me with her question about 41 bullets, I knew that I wanted this class to enliven students' awareness of the ways in which intercultural communication contributes to unjust interactions and also opens up possibilities for more just relationships. I wanted students to understand, as Gloria had so aptly pointed out, that we are not equitably situated. I hoped that students might then further develop their understanding of the relevance of communication to forms of inequity. If educators aim for our work to be relevant to the world outside of the classroom, the particulars of that world are vitally important. Four characteristics of public life are especially salient in regard to the questions to which this book responds: (1) all social life is insistently relational, (2) inequity exists, (3) power matters, and (4) a language and imagination for the public good are necessary for living together well.

The Relationality of Public Life

In connection with the first claim, that public life is insistently relational, I am asserting that how we live together is relationally, and not individually, constituted. Even as we might consider ourselves a free-standing, independent "I," this is materially impossible. All of our choices implicate us within an ever-present set of relationships. The choices that individuals make are necessarily situated within a broad set of social and institutional constraints and expectations. We cannot set ourselves outside of, or "free" ourselves from, the social. My struggle, for example, to respond to the white man in the library was necessarily tied to a set of inescapable social arrangements: the presence of other adults in the room, the absence of any library personnel who might have considered it their responsibility to step into the situation in a direct way, and/or the possibility of those in the room, including myself, holding stereotypes towards the boys of colour (Fleras, 2011; Jones, 1997).

How we interact with other individuals involves the interplay of agency and structure, and is a negotiation of the possibilities we engage within the constraints and expectations that social norms and structures impose. As I decided first whether and then how to respond to the man's hissing in the library computer room, my decisions and actions were intertwined with a host of realities. Agency and institutional constraints are mutually constitutive. In brief, we cannot escape our sociality. However this sociality is felt – as labour, burden, possibility, or even absent, a non-presence – it exists, always. We are enmeshed. Even as public discourse and popular culture increasingly insist on a language of an "I," on the discursive and rhetorical reality that we act and live primarily or even exclusively as individuals, such perceptions and frameworks fundamentally betray the assertion that to be human is to be situated in a set of relationships.

Inasmuch as to be human is to be enmeshed, situated within relationships that are simultaneously historical, immediate, and anticipatory, and inasmuch as we have agency, that agency is always ethical. All choices have consequences and bear on the self and on others. From my response to the white man in the library, to how I addressed questions of 41 bullets, to educational stakeholders who accept differential graduation rates by race, to Canadian officials who leave Indigenous men in the cold to die, we cannot opt out of the inevitability of ethical consequences. Ethics, centrally about the ways in which individual and institutional practices harm some and benefit others, is necessarily bound up with being enmeshed. In a framework in which democratic values have currency, asking the questions, "Who benefits, and how?" and "Who gets hurt, and how?" can start to reveal the intricacies of how our choices bear on the self and others.

In sum, then, we are always positioned as ethical agents. We act, and these acts have consequences. Within the ever-present set of constraints imposed by institutions, we have relationships to power through which we variously accept, confirm, resist, disturb, upset, sustain, and invest in the communities within which we live. Further, as educators, when in any way we endorse theories, epistemologies, or ontologies that foreground the individual, that dilute the inevitability of a relational, context-bound existence, we are necessarily distancing our work from the material and weakening its capacity for considering the practices of injustice and the possibilities for justice.

Existence of Injustice

A second component of public life is that inequity and injustice exist. A white man's treatment of four boys of colour in a library computer room, the repeated removal of the banner of the queer student group at my university, the death of Frank Paul, disproportionate graduation rates by race, pay differentials related to gender, high numbers of Black and Indigenous youth in the criminal justice systems in Canada and the United States: in concise terms, there is too much wrong. When individuals carry out discriminatory behaviours in cooperation with reinforcement linked to institutional forms of power, "gross social, political, and economic inequities result" (Dugan, 2004). Such inequities have a relationship to the existence of dominant and subordinate groups. Dominant groups "set the parameters within which the subordinates operate ... and determine how" the power the dominant group holds "may be acceptably used" (Tatum, 2000, p. 12). The existence of dominant and subordinate groups, paired with dominant groups' uses of power, have ensured that subordinate groups are significantly worse off in terms of quality of living, income, mobility, life chances, etc., and that subordinate groups are often represented and treated as less than human, particularly in relation to the dominant group. Numerous reports and studies have demonstrated the existence, deep roots, and widespread consequences of racial, gender, and economic inequities, both in North America and globally (Bauer, Travers, Hammond, Boyce, & Anderson, 2007; Hausmann, Tyson, & Zahidi, 2011; Klugman, 2011; Mohamedou, 2000).

Inequitable relationships of power play out across dominant and subordinate groups and are central to injustice. If social justice can be defined as "the institutional conditions for promoting self-development and self-determination of a society's members" (Young, 2000, p. 33), then injustice is the lack of these conditions. I assume that injustice exists and that it is defined by two social conditions, that of oppression and domination:

> Oppression consists in systematic institutional processes which prevent some people from learning and using satisfying and expansive skills in socially recognized settings, or institutionalized social processes which inhibit people's ability to play and communicate with others or to express their feelings and perspective on social life in contexts where others can listen ...
>
> Domination consists in institutional conditions which inhibit or prevent people from participating in determining their actions or the conditions of their actions. Persons live within structures of domination if other persons or groups can determine without reciprocation the conditions of their action, either directly or by virtue of the structural consequences of their actions. (Young, 1990, p. 38)

I rely on understandings of justice that are grounded in relationships of power rather than those originating in systems of rights, distribution, or procedures. Considerations of inequity must examine the conditions for agency and not be reduced to notions of individual rights and the mechanisms and consequences of distributive processes.

A central component of injustice is that while individuals can and do carry out discriminatory acts, practices of injustice are also embedded in institutions, which have significant rhetorical and material forms of power. Concerning the complicity of the state in killing men such as Amadou Diallo and Frank Paul, individual police officers and other state employees acted within and to a large extent were supported by the norms and expectations of their respective institutions. "Oppression is in this sense structural, rather than the result of a few people's choices or policies. Its causes are embedded in unquestioned norms, habits, and symbols, in the assumptions underlying institutional rules and the collective consequences of following those rules" (Young, 1990, p. 41; see also Young, 2011). Particularly in mainstream contexts, the profound lack of attention to any form of institutional response or responsibility for Diallo's death, and the nearly total focus on four white policemen, wholly cut off from any broader structural reality (a "bad apple" approach), demonstrate the power and reach of individual approaches to justice. The question of how institutions were responsible for expecting and demanding the actions of the four white policemen that led to Diallo's death is rarely asked. In effect, reducing in/justice to individual acts removes the possibility that institutions are actors with considerable power. (For rare analyses of institutional accountability for Diallo's death, see Center for Constitutional Rights a and b; Pastor, 2002.) In sum, when identifying central components of public life, it is necessary to assert that injustice exists and relies on both individuals and institutions for its persistence. Injustice is normal, routine, and ubiquitous. Resisting injustice – moving from too much wrong to less wrong to possibilities for justice – will require that individuals and communities critically analyse relationships of power and grapple with changed practice at institutional levels.

Significance of Power

A third component of social life relevant to this book's consideration of undergraduate education, the public good, and justice, is that power matters. Directly linked to both constitutions of the social and to practices of injustice, power can be defined as the processes by which individuals and institutions make decisions about, and create, maintain, and resist the conditions in which we live. Individuals and institutions exercise power in relationships that are fluid and dynamic. Scholars frequently conceptualize power within a distributive paradigm and treat it as a "kind of stuff possessed by individual agents in greater or lesser amounts" (Young, 1990, p. 31). Such understandings deny the relational reality of power, misname power as primarily or exclusively dyadic, and obscure the structural nature of power (Young, 1990). In contrast to these understandings, power can be viewed as "something that circulates, or rather something which only functions in the form of a chain" (Foucault, 1980, p. 98). In this sense, power is not fixed in one discrete location or possessed entirely by one individual. Rather, individuals "circulate between [power's] threads," and are "always in the position of simultaneously undergoing and exercising their power" (ibid.). In this sense, power is always multifaceted and embedded in relationships that involve multiple institutions and individuals, as well as layers of acquiescence, complicity, and resistance.

Again, a concrete example illustrates the complexities of power. As a productive and constitutive force, power was present in the library computer room in several ways. First, the mainstream media were shaping the conditions in that room. Even as the media do not control how those of us in that room viewed boys of colour, and even as each of us might have responded to that media in different ways, the media undoubtedly shaped a context in which the white man felt hissing was an acceptable form of communication and in which only one of the adults in that room felt his behaviour necessitated a response. Several of us as individuals opted to shape the conditions in which we were living: the white man who hissed, the boy who opted to challenge the white man, and myself, as I questioned the man's mode of communication. The dozen or so other individuals in the room remained silent, a way of accepting conditions in which the boys were treated as less than human.

Further, paralleling the Black community's distrust of the police referenced by Gloria, the boys in the library were most likely fully aware of the risks of challenging white men. Related to any resulting conflict that might draw in law enforcement or library personnel, those boys could not necessarily expect just interactions with individuals and institutions that had power. In this sense, even as they were not physically present in the room, these institutions exercised power, in ways that ensured both domination and oppression (Young, 1990). The possibilities of institutional involvement, and what that involvement might mean for their own lives, likely contributed to the ways in which the boys decided to respond. In order for undergraduate education to make it possible for students to turn toward "democracy's discontents" (Schneider, 2000, p. 107), for students to consider and negotiate the failures and possibilities of democratic practices in shaping the communities in which we live, attention to the workings and consequences of power is crucial. Refusing an analysis of power, failing to consider its centrality in constituting social relations, is a way of refusing materiality. By refusing to attend to power, we choose to move away from the practices of sociality in which we are all enmeshed.

Importance of Democratic Values, Public Good, and Justice

A fourth and final assumption that I make about the parameters of the social is that individuals and institutions in North America, including institutions of higher education, must have a language and imagination for democratic practices, the public good, and justice. Individuals and institutions in Canada and the United States profess an allegiance to democratic modes of living. Even as such allegiances may not be systematically realized, and even as the benefits of democracy are clearly more available to some groups than others, democratic societies do profess certain priorities. Educational contexts are settings in which we can wrestle with such priorities. When we consider students like Cindy and Allison, calling for "streamlined" education and noting a disconnect from nation, as we draw attention to Gloria's marking of her community's distrust of the police, or as we wrestle with the ways in which the state continues to exploit Indigenous communities and consider how the university positions itself in relation to this exploitation, what norms, ethical commitments, and hopes for the future do we as educators pursue?

At a minimum, the obligations and promise of the public good and of justice ought to bear to some degree on our work as educators. Throughout this book, I am positioning democracy not in the narrow political sense of a form of government, or individualized forms of behavior (such as voting). Rather, I am interested in democratic practices as modes of sociality, in the possibilities that democracy as a form of "associated living" (Dewey, 1998, p. 390) offers for considering justice. As I have noted earlier in this book, democracy is contested terrain. Scholars have relied on the term democracy and on supposed support for democratic practices to ideologically construct a veneer of openness, inclusion, and fairness that obscures multiple forms of violence exercised by state-sanctioned institutions. Even "as these scholars are interested in the theoretical idealism of democracy, they appear amnesiatic toward the continued lived realities of democratically induced oppression" (Richardson & Villenas, 2000, p. 260). As one scholar asks, "Can the 'good life' be built on the deaths of thousands" (Grande, 2004, p. 32)?

When possibilities for democracy are grounded in attention to "issues of power, dominance, subordination, and stratification" (Grande, 2004, p. 34), to how democratic practices might move communities towards justice, and to the ways in which democratic modes of living might be detached from a liberal and Western emphasis on rationality, universality, and the individual, such possibilities might open up spaces for more just forms of living. The term democratic practices refers to modes of sociality that account for the relationship of agency and structure and the role of power; that identify domination, oppression, and dispossession; that envision and work towards the reduction of inequity and injustice; that grapple with the inescapable presence of ethical relationality; and that insist on a language for the practices of democratic values and priorities, including the public good and justice.

Democracy carries with it certain values. Even as there have been and continue to be immense gaps between the "appearances and realities" of "democratic" policies and practices (Richardson & Villenas, 2000, p. 266), democracy has long professed commitments to both the public good and to justice. Societies with high levels of inequity will be significantly constrained in their realization of democratic practices. Even as its meanings, expressions, and possibilities are fluid and contested, democracy has an agenda. It leans towards one set of values and away from another set. Ideally, communities will grapple with these values, will rigorously examine and question what they will look like in practice and how they might be realized.

Most would agree that the public good and justice constitute two crucial values within democratic societies. Intimately connected, the public good and justice point to modes of living that stress the importance of the reduction of suffering, practices of sovereignty and "determin[ing] the conditions of one's actions," and structural conditions that support equity and a high quality of life for everyone (in terms of health, education, meaningful work, leisure, legal systems, etc.) (Grande, 2004; Young, 1990, p. 37). The public good, too often defined in exclusively or primarily economic terms, refers in this book to an ethical and relational concern for community well-being and for justice, and it is directly contrasted to a privatized, competitive, and economic prioritization of efficiency and individual gain. The public good has a connection with understandings of power that are "rooted in concepts of respect, balance, reciprocity, and peaceful coexistence" (Grande, 2004, p. 61n33). Considering the public good also requires an active regard for one's agency, choices, and allegiances and their consequences at local, regional, and global levels.

As stated earlier in this chapter, justice is defined as "the institutional conditions for promoting self-development and self-determination of a society's members" (Young, 2000, p. 33). In sum, then, democratic modes of living assume ethical agency and responsibility in numerous settings and related to multiple interactions. A white man's disregard for four boys of colour in a library computer room, the repeated removal of the banner of the queer student group on my campus, the choice of four white policemen to fire 41 bullets into Amadou Diallo: we routinely constitute the social, constructing how we will and do live, together. Further, invoking the concept of democracy, noting both its deeply embedded violence, and its potential for more equitable forms of living, makes claims on what it means to live well together. Put simply, democracy requires us to consider justice and the public good. Finally, such consideration requires both a rigorous engagement with the reality of injustice, as well as a language and imagination for more just and equitable modes of living. Those living in democratic societies must be able to, over and over again, name injustice and imagine justice.

This section has made four assertions about public life. As this book is centrally interested in the question of higher education's obligations to the social, and especially to what undergraduate education might offer to democratic life, what is foundational and enduring about the world in which we live? As faculty members, our understandings of the social inevitably bear on how we conceptualize the subject. Four claims I make about the social include (1) public life is insistently relational, and we are enmeshed and cannot escape ethical agency; (2) inequity exists; (3) power matters; and (4) democratic modes of living require a language and imagination for the public good and for justice. How do these four parameters bear on the ways in which educators define "the subject" in any given course or discipline? If we start with a bold acknowledgment that we live in relation, that injustice exists, that power matters, and that we value the public good and justice, what do these claims have to do with our work as faculty members? In what ways do such claims necessitate careful attention, with our students, to agency, positionality, and power? How might such claims construct the subject as the material expression of living together well, of the realization of the public good, and of justice?

Undergraduate Education and the Obligations of the Social: An Overview of Liberal and Critical Scholarship

For Paul, Robert, Gloria, and myself, the issues of Diallo's death, the actions of four policemen who fired 41 bullets, and the complicity of the institutions within which those men worked were clearly on our minds. I was again standing on that epistemological fault line, and I felt acutely the question of what is the subject. Whether or not the lived expressions of the concepts we address in our courses enter the classroom, lean towards us with their urgency and weight, they are among us, in our midst. That is, whether or not in a class on intercultural communication the students and I take up Diallo's death, this issue and others are undeniably part of the social and have links to communication. Diallo is dead. State-sanctioned violence directed at communities of colour continues at alarming levels, and this and numerous other interplays of violence, power, and responsibility have a connection to intercultural communication, whether or not my students and I grapple with these subjects. "What do you think?" Gloria asked me, "41 bullets?"

In this section, I consider liberal and critical educational scholarship that implicitly and explicitly grapples with such questions.[2] Liberal assumptions are largely taken for granted in educational settings and, on the whole, fail to offer rigorous examinations of injustice and justice. Critical scholarship continues to offer direct attention to questions of power and of the public good, yet largely exists on the periphery of educational work. Further, among liberal scholars who opt to consider critical work, deep engagement with the central tenets of critical thought is rare. The tensions, gaps, and silences that exist across liberal and critical bodies of work, which play out in departments, at conferences, and in other locations of scholarly discourse and practice, are significant and consequential. In terms of constructing institutions of higher education that might substantively consider the relationship of democratic practices, the public good, and justice to the "subject" of undergraduate education, liberal and critical scholars must be in direct and ongoing conversation with each other about the issues this book raises.

Critical scholars openly discuss questions of systemic injustice and the possibilities for justice. Liberal colleagues dismiss such work as "advocacy." Even as critical scholars hope that our work will be convincing to faculty members who largely rely on liberal norms, when we do participate in robust conversations about these issues, we most often do so with other critical scholars. At the same time, liberal educational assumptions are central to nearly all teaching, research, and service. Liberal scholarship continues to have considerable discursive and material power for the work of nearly all educators, including the work performed by faculty members who adopt critical perspectives.

Particularly in day-to-day university work, liberal faculty members rarely have to "defend" or even acknowledge their primary assumptions. Critical scholars have increased in numbers and visibility over the past two to three decades, yet we still work in relatively small numbers in most departments and within other institutional structures. As liberal norms hold sway, mainstream educators often expect critical scholars to explain and defend our starting points and objectives, particularly when we bring our concerns from the periphery into the educational centre. In the end, all of us together – those working with both liberal and critical frameworks – shape what our students know. The differences in these two frameworks, while often discussed in primarily abstract terms, are not only conceptual. They matter to what and how students learn.

As a critical scholar, I am committed to education that grapples with the material conditions in which people live, with power, and with change in the interests of justice. I work among large numbers of scholars who implicitly and explicitly embrace liberal norms and priorities and in so doing turn down the volume of the material, offering cursory nods to 41 bullets but little more. Liberal and critical scholars work side by side in many departments and within most if not all disciplines. How do we as educators, liberal and critical, navigate questions about the subject, about epistemological norms, and about the relevance of 41 bullets and other social issues? In order to consider the "we" of my own educational work, the ways in which I am embedded with my colleagues and the institutions and contexts within which I work, I am concerned in this chapter and the next with the limits and possibilities of liberal educational norms. These are norms that are both widely embraced and yet have not adequately responded to the demands of the material, of the public good, and of justice.

Representatives of the Canadian police services leaving Indigenous men in the cold to die, Cindy calling for streamlined education, and Allison identifying her lack of connection to nation: I do not believe that all "social needs" are similarly urgent and relevant. A quick glance at research priorities across departments at a university can reveal a wide range of pursuits: holding criminal justice institutions accountable for the deaths of Indigenous and Black men, design possibilities for MP3 players, young peoples' uses of social networking, how health organizations can communicate with specific groups, or the role of public transport in reducing pollution. I do not advocate a simplistic, formulaic, or deterministic approach to considering research and curricular priorities. However, a wholly relativistic approach is also problematic. In democratic societies, faculty members will ideally grapple with the burdens and costs of inequity, with how we can move from too much wrong to less wrong to justice. While the approaches and responses to such questions will ideally be intellectually, philosophically, and politically varied, democratic modes of living do encourage us to keep questions of the public good and justice in the foreground. The equation is not a simple one: these issues count, and these do not. Rather, we must consider how, in democratic societies, we place different and sometimes competing social issues in relation to each other.

As with any group of scholars, those who adopt a liberal approach to higher education demonstrate a variety of understandings of education and its purposes. Their perspectives and beliefs are not homogeneous or even. Liberal scholars do not uniformly reduce complexity or deny the existence of inequity. They do not consistently or always embrace liberal assumptions, and they may at times be critical of such assumptions. At the same time, it continues to be rare, particularly in mainstream educational settings – disciplinary conferences, department and other university meetings, etc. – for there to be any collective commitment to critical norms and assumptions or for critical educational ideas to be collectively taken for granted. Further, the fundamental tenets of liberal scholarship and social thought, including the ways in which those tenets are enacted by liberal scholars across North America, obscure and constrain possibilities for justice and democratic life. Inasmuch as education concerns, as Dewey asserted, habits and dispositions, what habits does undergraduate education affirm? What dispositions does it deny?

I hope that the discussion in this section offers a way to better understand the primary intellectual and epistemological tenets and consequences of liberal and critical scholarship. For any faculty person, liberal or critical, who is interested in undergraduate education that speaks to the concerns of public life, we will need to have conversations with our colleagues, across liberal and critical leanings, that can grapple with theoretical differences in regard to the work of undergraduate education. I am also attuned to a certain level of caution among nearly all faculty members when it comes to directly and transparently embracing the social purposes of undergraduate education, particularly in public settings. I continue to hear from faculty members at my institution, and at conferences and in other academic settings, of deep-seated reservations in exploring questions of power and social life. Again and again, liberal and critical educators note the fear they have of being charged by students, faculty colleagues, and administrators with "being political" or "taking sides." For pre-tenure faculty members and instructors in limited-contract positions, this fear can be connected to possibilities for advancement and promotion, particularly when a senior faculty member and/or administrator at that faculty member's institution has made it clear that any perceived allegiance to particular social or political values will be problematic. This fear may well be linked to central assumptions within liberal educational thought. In this, and other ways, liberal assumptions bear on educational practices.

Liberal Perspectives

Liberal perspectives on higher education are long-standing and broadly accepted. Indeed, it might be argued that these perspectives inform a great deal of activity in higher education, including curricular norms and objectives; the production, evaluation, and representation of knowledge; and disciplinary structures. Those who write about higher education from a liberal perspective clearly assert that education should include the "development of the whole person" (Axelrod, Anisef, & Lin, 2001, p. 50; see also Nussbaum, 1997, p. 9) and "responsible independence of mind" (Rothblatt, 1993, p. 63; see also Bok, 2006; Nussbaum, 1997). Further, undergraduate education should ensure that graduates are able to think well, to live with diversity in a global society, to consider the perspectives of others, and to competently analyse competing claims (Axelrod, 2002; Bok, 2006; Nussbaum, 1997; Rothblatt, 1993).

Liberal educational thought also places a clear emphasis on the individual and rationality (Axelrod, 2002; Kimball, 1995; Nussbaum, 1997; Rothblatt, 1993). The following definition of liberal education is useful:

> Liberal education in the university refers to activities that are designed to cultivate intellectual creativity, autonomy, and resilience; critical thinking; a combination of intellectual breadth and specialized knowledge; the comprehension and tolerance of diverse ideas and experiences; informed participation in community life; and effective communication skills. (Axelrod, 2002, pp. 34–35)

Many liberal scholars explicitly or implicitly refer to the social. They recognize, as Axelrod does, the importance of consideration of "community life" and "diverse ideas," state the relevance of "responding to the concerns of society" (Fallis, 2007, p. 115), and acknowledge the important role of "citizenship" (Nussbaum, 1997, p. 9). On the whole, liberal scholars believe that an inculcation of these capacities in students is one central objective of undergraduate education. Further, these capacities are discussed as ends in themselves. These scholars do not offer in-depth analysis of the ways in which these values are practised and are inherently ethical. For most liberal scholars, questions of ethics, and particularly prioritizing one set of ethical ends over any other, should not form the substance of university education.

Three assumptions central to liberal scholarship addressing higher education include the idea that universities and other social institutions have been generally beneficent and adequate to society's needs, that knowledge is a value in its own right, and that the individual is the preferred starting point for all knowledge production, for curricular and pedagogical practices, and for consideration of questions of meaning, justice, and the challenges of living together well. These assumptions are crucial: they inform multiple aspects of undergraduate education, often in very subtle ways, and they set up a framework for thinking about education and its scope and effects. I would also assert that many educators ascribe to these assumptions and act on them in most, if not all, of their teaching and research. Liberal understandings of society and of education have informed much of public life and educational practices in North America for the past three to four centuries. In many ways, liberal approaches to both public life and education are quite naturalized, appearing as a given.

Institutions as Beneficent

Liberal scholars often assume that institutions of higher learning, and other public-serving institutions, have for the most part had a positive influence on society. A belief exists, largely unstated in the literature, that in general institutions have served individuals and groups in beneficial ways. Liberal scholarship assumes that occurrences in which institutions have harmed individuals and groups are rare and largely a problem of the past. Further, for the most part, institutions and social systems work well and are fair. Even though these systems may occasionally malfunction, or temporarily fail, they are, by and large, evidence of enlightened and advanced approaches to living together well in the twenty-first century. For those adopting a liberal approach, the deaths of men like Frank Paul and Amadou Diallo are understood as exceptions, and represent a failure of individuals within the system, rather than pointing to collective failures within and across systems as a whole. Likewise, when one considers a range of social issues – disproportionate high school graduation rates by race, high numbers of Indigenous and Black youth in the criminal justice system, homophobia in schools, or growing income gaps – these issues are primarily an indication of individuals within specific institutions acting badly, or of minor and temporary shortcomings that can be remedied through repair of a specific problem rather than through rigorous attention to, at a minimum, how institutions variously serve different groups.

Disinterested Knowledge

This belief in institutions as largely beneficent is directly connected to a second assumption. For liberals, knowledge itself, wholly detached from context, its uses, and its consequences, is a sufficient and desirable objective for undergraduate education. The belief that social institutions have been both adequate and fair has implications for knowledge. If institutions have been and are fair, one does not need to consider the ways in which these systems are unfair, or to ask how knowledge itself leads to a specific worldview. In such a framework, to state that knowledge exists separately from context makes sense. Knowledge becomes a desirable outcome in its own right. A student's grasp of specific concepts, detached from context or interests, is a positive outcome. This outcome is positive regardless to what extent these concepts speak to lived reality; account for or ignore, deny, or distort the experiences and knowledge of non-dominant groups; and move students and educators towards an understanding of the public good and justice or not.

In this framework, knowledge as a set of concepts or ideas exists independently of the material conditions of how people live. Concerning the earlier examples from the courses on gender and communication, knowledge for knowledge's sake would have ensured that both Cindy and Allison could explain the idea that gendered communication behaviour is socially constructed at a conceptual level. Cindy might have come to realize that her understanding of herself as a woman and what that means was learned. She might also have assumed that her understanding of gender, of herself as a woman, had nothing to do with being straight. Thus, the removal of the banner of the queer student group, the ways in which Cindy and her peers were unaware of challenges for queer students on campus, or any one of the issues that queer people face were simply irrelevant to constructions of gender and to Cindy's consideration of gender and communication. Questions of the material – how real life complicates knowledge, and challenges it; the effects of knowledge, what it leads to or denies in terms of seeing self and other – fall outside of "knowledge."

As I thought more about Cindy's hope for a "streamlined" course on gender and communication, I also wondered how Cindy's education so far had taught her that this was a reasonable expectation. How had the approximately 30 courses that she had taken before she enrolled in the gender and communication course systematically taught Cindy that queer people and communities were not part of the subject? Such systematic narrowing and elimination in educational spaces is common. Within a discourse of tolerance and inclusion, it is sufficient to superficially acknowledge non-dominant groups, and to fully retreat when the realities of those groups in any way challenge those in the dominant group. (For additional discussion of the problems with such superficial acknowledgement, often presented as an approach of "inclusion," see chapters 1 and 3.) Faculty members rarely rigorously question existing practices or the assumptions supporting these practices. Finally, Cindy's insertion also illustrates that all knowledge is interested, even as many liberal scholars deny this claim. Knowledge about gender that denies the relevance of queer lives and communities is interested in maintaining social relations that centre and normalize straight lives. All knowledge has interests. Yet, Cindy had learned to believe that it was appropriate for herself and her peers to ignore, for example, the presence of queer individuals and communities.

The Individual as Primary

Finally, throughout liberal understandings of social life and of education, the individual is in the foreground. Liberal understandings of justice focus on individual rights and freedoms, on goods being adequately distributed to individuals, and on individuals being able to achieve their own particular version of "the good life," most often with little or no regard for how this version impacts the whole (Hollenbach, 2002; Sandel, 2008). Likewise, liberal understandings of education repeatedly stress education of "the whole person," capacities that each student should develop, and individual intellectual development. Even as these capacities should offer some benefit to others, the focus is on individual development. This orientation to the individual is crucial, and was perhaps active in Cindy's "streamlined" comment. For Cindy, any education she could accept and endorse needed to serve her individual needs well. Public or relational aspects of course content in that class, such as the routine and repeated removal of the banner of the queer student group on campus, an issue students raised in class, were not part of the subject for Cindy. Further, she felt she could legitimately defend her individualized understanding of that subject. Even as these liberal assumptions about knowledge and institutions are rarely spelled out, particularly in the classroom, they are nonetheless profoundly significant.

Taken to their logical end, these practices ensure that liberal educational scholarship will actively sustain existing norms and relationships of power. Those working within a liberal educational framework might moderately question current practices or acknowledge the existence of difficult social issues. However, liberal scholars often make a quick and thorough retreat when addressing the fullness of the damage done by racism and other forms of injustice, or when pressed to articulate ethical commitments that will make justice possible. Further, these scholars also exercise caution when it comes to fully considering the institutional causes and devastating and urgent consequences of any injustice related to bodies and communities. On the whole, for liberal scholars, institutions are beneficent, knowledge is useful as a set of ideals separate from its uses, and the individual is primary.

In reference to the four parameters of the social I articulated at the start of this chapter – (1) all social life is insistently relational, (2) inequity exists, (3) power matters, and (4) democratic societies value the public good and justice – liberal educational scholarship is ill-equipped to seriously consider these parameters. There is a profound lack of fit between (1) the four components of the social that I assert and (2) the three primary assumptions within liberal scholarship that I articulate above. In a very basic example, any scholar who believes that institutions are beneficent, that knowledge is disinterested, and that the individual is primary would have been fully justified in turning away from Gloria's knowledge about Diallo's death. I might have noted that Diallo's death was unfortunate, and moved right back into my presentation. In sum, in theory and in practice, I do not believe that liberal scholarship substantively contributes to what is needed for undergraduate education that considers the public good and justice. More than this, liberal educational scholarship can obscure considerations of power, agency, and the role of institutions.

Critical Theory

Like liberal scholars working in higher education, critical scholars are also concerned with the conceptual foundations and desired outcomes of undergraduate education, as well as with disciplinary content and pedagogical approaches. Most iterations of critical educational theory either explicitly or implicitly assume that domination and injustice "shape the lived world" (Kincheloe, 2008, p. 46) and that higher education has a role in reducing human suffering. Critical scholars insist

on the ongoing existence of oppression and on the existence of imperialism, racism, sexism, heterosexism, and classism; they see reality as
fundamentally complex, non-linear, and embodied; and they claim that
theories of knowledge must address "ethics, human values, desires and
interest, as well as how politics structure the understanding of human
relations" (Dei, 2000, p. 50).

Critical scholars address the limits of social and educational priorities that focus on "the system of production and accumulation in
which knowledge is reduced to its economic functions and contributes to the realization of individual economic utilities" (Morrow 2006,
xxxi). Further, they are interested in theories and epistemologies that
are transgressive (Grande, 2004), that invoke a "visionary pragmatism"
and "pursue justice" (Collins, 1998), that analyse "what limits seeing"
(Razack, 1998, p. 14), that support study for the purpose of "future
relationship that is mutually beneficial" (Maracle, 2005), and that offer
a "deepening of the political" (Mohanty, 2003, p. 191). In these ways,
whereas liberal scholars implicitly and explicitly foreground the individual, critical scholars are centrally concerned with the social and with
the ways in which a variety of "publics" negotiate the possibilities for
democratic life and for justice.

Perhaps the most significant contribution critical theory and pedagogy have made to higher educational practices is increased visibility
of the relationship of knowledge and power (Collins, 1998, 2000; Giroux, 2007b; Giroux & Searls Giroux, 2004; Kincheloe, 2008; Mbembe,
2001; Said, 1979; Smith, 2001). For critical social theorists, "material relations of power and the production of social meaning do not cancel each
other out but constitute the precondition for all meaningful practices"
(Giroux & Searls Giroux, 2004, p. 90). Close analyses of knowledge and
power will significantly contribute to stronger intellectual frameworks
for understanding the social, for articulating the complexities of power
and agency, and for considering the ways in which the "uses of power
normalize oppressive conditions and practices" (Simpson, 2010a,
p. 372). Likewise, critical theorists hope for the classroom to be a place
where students can embrace a culture of critical questioning, including
the ways that taken-for-granted knowledge has made it difficult to consider the reality of injustice and possibilities for justice.

Three assumptions central to critical theory in education include the
belief (1) that institutions are not just and ongoing institutional practices ensure high levels of social inequity; (2) that knowledge has interests and is necessarily linked to context; and (3) that in order to move

towards justice, it is necessary to foreground the social rather than the individual.

Institutional and Social Inequity

Whereas a basic belief in the adequacy of public-serving institutions shapes much of the work of liberal scholars, many critical thinkers start with the belief that these institutions, including higher education, have been inadequate and have acted to constrain people's lives in significant ways. Critical scholars believe that the institutions on which we rely have not adequately or equitably met society's needs. Institutions do both good and harm, and most often act to maintain and/or further the interests of those in power. These interests often limit the choices and autonomy of those within subordinate communities and groups.

Knowledge as Interested

This critique of institutions leads to a second assumption of critical scholars: the idea that knowledge acts to hurt and to help, to maintain and to challenge relations of power. Knowledge is not disinterested or neutral. The assumption that knowledge exists for knowledge's sake denies the ways in which what we know sets up parameters for how we see, necessarily influences how we act, and bears on how people live. In other words, knowledge does not simply exist. Knowledge is not contained within a conceptual assertion about, for example, how gender and communication work. Rather, critical scholars assert that the formation, representation, and effects of knowledge are always bound up with power and interests. Knowledge acts on lives. In a course on gender and communication, I could have opted to offer knowledge that downplayed or ignored queer realities. When students raised the issue of the repeated removal of the queer banner, I might have minimally acknowledged this reference, and then moved back to the reading. In contrast, I could also opt to make this a part of the subject in that course. I could choose to connect the repeated removal of the banner, as well as how the university, through the lack of a public institutional response, contributed to ideas about sexuality and about gender. Similarly, when Gloria raised the issue of the Diallo killing, and I took up this topic, I was indicating to students that I was interested in knowledge that could consider Diallo's death at the hands of four white policemen, rather than knowledge that could not hold this reality.

The Social as Primary

A third assumption for critical scholars is that questions of the social, of how various groups construct and imagine the "we" of public life, should be foregrounded. The uses of knowledge, critical questioning, the workings of power, how relationships shape meaning: these issues, all central to critical thought, are social questions. They insistently draw attention to how we live, together. Higher education might both encourage knowledge that orients itself towards the social, towards living together well, and it might provide an opportunity for students to work at the challenges and promise of forms of sociality that offer rigorous attention to the public good and to justice. The classroom itself is a space in which students can learn to engage, through intellectual analysis and the labours of dialogue, the possibilities for democratic hope (Simpson, 2010b). Indeed, in communicating that she expected that the course on gender would be streamlined, Cindy was indicating her interest in eliminating queers as subjects. Cindy and other students will rely on what they have learned to construct patterns of belonging, to imagine who is a part of their "we" at work, in their communities, and in a range of public settings. Knowledge is always active in constructing the "we" of public life.

On the whole, over the past two to three decades, critical scholars have undoubtedly brought commitments and content into higher education that were previously absent from universities. The visibility of material, lived practices in a range of scholarship, and the existence of institutional spaces for scholars to do critical work have increased. Likewise, this increase in visibility and space has, in many instances, ensured that critical work in university settings has made a difference not only for students, but also for the public good and for justice. Critical thought now has a presence in many departments in the traditional disciplines. It has also lent its support, in various ways, to the establishment of new areas of study, including performance theory; queer studies; African American, Latino, Asian American, Black Canadian, Asian Canadian, and Indigenous studies; and disability studies. While many university departments may have only one or even no critical scholars, some departments may have a few or even several critical scholars working together. At the same time, in most institutions, of the 40 or so courses students take to complete a degree, most students may take no courses, or perhaps one or two, that are taught from a critical perspective. Furthermore, much of public discourse for the most part mimics and strengthens the liberal educational assumptions named above: institutions are beneficent, knowledge is disinterested, and the individual is primary.

Student learning is never even or predictable. However, the educational frameworks that are offered, and particularly those that are offered repeatedly, shape what these students can imagine, inform what they believe is normal and possible, and become part of their sense-making frameworks and how they see the world around them. Again, returning to the four parameters of the social I outlined earlier, where do students learn to ethically navigate agency and structures? When do they hear about and have the opportunity to grapple with the public good, democratic values and practices, inequity, and power? What is the relationship of disciplinary content to lived reality, and how is that relationship brought to the fore in courses students take? This chapter centrally asserts that in relation to the primary components of public life – the inevitability of being enmeshed, the presence of injustice, the role of power, and the need for attention to the public good – liberal educational assumptions reduce possibilities for engaging the materiality of public life and for moving towards justice. In the next chapter, I will examine liberal assumptions in regard to specific educational practices.

5 Liberal Norms and Questions of Practice: Education, Ethics, and Interests

About three years after the class meeting in which students disagreed about the death of Diallo and four white policemen's use of 41 bullets, I was attending a conference at my institution which drew faculty members and administrators from across the region. At the time of the conference, as when I taught the course itself, I was an untenured faculty member at a university in northeastern Indiana. As the conference wrapped up, I found myself talking to the Vice Chancellor for Academic Affairs at one of the participating institutions, a woman with whom I had spoken once or twice before and did not know well. I had just presented at the annual meeting of the Association of American Colleges and Universities (AAC&U), and had addressed in my presentation the discussion my students and I had had about Diallo's death. In conversation with the administrator at the regional conference, I briefly mentioned a connection I saw between the theme of the conference we were attending and the AAC&U meeting at which I had presented a couple of months earlier.

The administrator asked for more information about my presentation at AAC&U.

"Well," I said, "related to the interaction I addressed at the conference, the students and I were discussing intercultural communication and history. I was presenting information on how history functions as a socializing force, and I asked the students for examples. A woman brought up the Diallo killing in New York as an example of history as a socializing force for the Black community. The students got into a conversation about the Diallo killing, and there was very quickly disagreement."

"How did you respond?" she asked.

"I knew that I basically agreed with the initial comment, that racism was a part of the Diallo killing, although I did not say this to the students," I said to her. "I wanted to keep all students in the conversation. I sensed that if I explicitly stated that the killing involved racism, I might lose students. So I opened up the possibility of racism, asked about how the police might serve some communities well, and for other communities, represent an institution that does not serve them well. I hoped that we might think about questions of ethics in democratic societies."

By this point, I was a bit taken aback by her interest. We were standing between tables, and when we began talking, she seemed to be on her way out of the conference room. At the same time, I cared about the issues I had addressed in my AAC&U presentation. I was brief in my response to her questions, yet also clearly interested in the exchange. After I had summarized my take on what was occurring in the classroom, her next comment ended the conversation immediately: "That's what you think? You sound like a moral dictator." Her tone was steady. Her face wore a slight smile. She seemed almost amused by my foolishness regarding the matter I had raised. I said nothing, and she left the room.

The above conversation offers a stark indication of the administrator's priorities and commitments. Although I knew there was resistance to transparent and critical educational investments, the swiftness and, for me, seriousness of the label "moral dictator" still caught me short. I thought back to the AAC&U presentation I had made. My Dean, a mathematics scholar whom I did not know well, was at the AAC&U conference and attended my presentation. In subsequent conversations I had with him, during and following the conference, it was clear that he had understood the issues that I had addressed in my presentation. Further, he had indicated his own willingness to consider these questions. He seemed to respect the fact that I was struggling with the concerns the interaction raised.

Although the Vice Chancellor for Academic Affairs and I had several interactions following our conversation that day at the conference at my institution, we never again addressed the classroom discussion, or her response to my explanation of what I thought about the exchange. Administrators routinely indicate, in a variety of settings, what types of educational conversations they will support. At the end of that conference, I believe that the comment from the Vice Chancellor was abundantly clear: stay away from such topics. In contrast, my Dean understood that even as not all faculty members would understand the policemen's actions as racist, Gloria's point, as well as my desire to grapple with questions of the public good, were educationally relevant and appropriate in that course.

As I noted in chapter 4, liberal educational norms can be simultaneously subtle yet powerful. They can assert, without ever making direct or transparent claims, that education must be disinterested and that faculty members should therefore retreat from questions of practice, politics, and power. I wonder what prompts any educator to label a colleague a "moral dictator" when that colleague affirms the possibility of police racism in the United States and also communicates the importance of grappling with a pedagogical response that considers democratic priorities. To some extent, her comment was not primarily a reflection of my intellectual commitments, but centrally a claim about the ways in which my commitments offended her own. In this way, her calling me a moral dictator was, at least in part, an assertion of what she took for granted and held close about the work of education. Clearly, I had crossed an intellectual, pedagogical, and moral line for her. Such lines are of our own making. They do not magically or mysteriously appear. Rather, they are sustained in the day-to-day practices of research and teaching. Further, I wonder what made me a dictator in her mind: the type of views I held, the fact that I communicated these views and made them public, or both.

The administrator unabashedly made her views quite public, and with no apparent hesitation. She also firmly refused any further intellectual exchange, rather than making it possible for us to learn from the views that each of us held. In some cases, we might believe that with certain colleagues, we have nothing to say to each other, given the perceived differences in intellectual perspectives. Charging a faculty person with being a moral dictator goes well beyond the usual acceptable interaction between faculty members, yet this administrator made the charge with no apparent caution or remorse. What sort of educational parameters support such a charge and render it normal and appropriate? What are the components of intellectual and pedagogical assumptions that ensure that such a charge is infinitely more legitimate than a faculty member's efforts to, with her students, grapple with 41 bullets, intercultural communication, history, racism, and the public good?

Articulating the charge of moral dictator was for that administrator a fairly blatant way to let me know that she disapproved of my teaching. At a minimum, it seemed that the ways in which I was attending to issues of communication, history, and racial difference were not something that she valued. I would argue that for many educators, the core assumptions that infuse the underlying legitimacy of charges like the one of "moral dictator" are so broadly and deeply accepted as to be virtually unassailable. That is, even as faculty members and administrators inhabit a profession that purportedly values intellectually engagement with a variety of perspectives, it can be problematic to question the veracity and implications of assumptions like those made by that administrator.

Thus, when I drew attention to a presentation that I had made at a conference that flatly refused some of these norms – that knowledge is disinterested, that education should not enter the realm of political or social values, that as faculty members we should not allow ourselves to become entangled in the intricacies of real life such as racism and police violence – the administrator with whom I was in conversation felt entirely justified in calling me a moral dictator. Identifying and stepping back from routine assumptions and practices, such as making judgments when another's work challenges our own, can be difficult, given that these assumptions and practices are often "prereflective and habitual. [Such practices] come to be experienced as necessary rather than contingent, constitutive rather than regulative, universal rather than partial" (Tully, 2002, p. 547). This is particularly true, it would seem, for practices shared by the majority of those in any group. For those who attach themselves to less mainstream commitments, the articulation of such priorities will usually need to be intentional and constantly reviewed, as they will not be granted an easy reception.

I would assert that liberal educational thought has become, as Tully states above, "prereflective and habitual" in ways that implicitly and explicitly condone the rejection of even moderate challenges to its core assumptions. In this chapter, I will address two largely naturalized sets of practices in higher education that are profoundly active in how faculty members conceptualize the subject. In particular, I will first discuss the silence of liberal thought on the question of the ends education is serving and the intertwined emphasis on education of the "whole person" detached from any particular ethical practice. Second, I will examine the routine acceptance and reinscription of ontological and epistemological dichotomies, forms of acceptance that reject basic research on what it means to be human. My objective here is to contribute to a broader process of undoing the reach of liberal educational norms. I will conclude the section with further discussion of the conversation my students and I had about Diallo, and with consideration of educational starting points with regard to undergraduate education and democratic forms of sociality.

The Inevitability of Ethics and the Dangers of Dichotomies

Two areas in which the "shared patterns of thought" (ibid.) are particularly persuasive in the context of liberal educational norms involve (1) claims of educating the "whole person," with no ongoing attention to ethics and consequences and (2) routinely endorsed dichotomies related to ontology and epistemology that are intellectually and scientifically unsound. I will enter these two areas through the work of Martha Nussbaum and Derek Bok, two individuals who have been especially noted for their scholarship on undergraduate education and what it might offer to students, particularly in relation to questions of civic life, social needs, and critical reflection. Nussbaum and Bok have offered consideration to these questions over several years and in multiple publications, and their work has been prominent in higher education discourse. Faculty members offer routine support for education of the "whole person" and for ontological and epistemological dichotomies, support which over time ensures that these ideas receive ongoing legitimation. In this way, educational assumptions become simultaneously invisible and necessary, and those engaging in such practices cognitively and affectively bypass what informs their constructed particularity. One can, of course, opt to see differently.

Educating the "Whole Person" and the Inevitability of Ethics

Perhaps the most often cited strength of a university degree is that education prepares students for "life generally," and "cultivat[es] ... the whole human being" (Nussbaum, 1997, p. 9; see also Axelrod, 2002; Kimball, 1995; Rothblatt, 1993). Indeed, two themes that are clearly present in Nussbaum's and Bok's work include (1) education of the "whole person" and (2) the objectives of university education, such as capacities for citizenship, diversity, and communication. Together, this emphasis on the whole person and on specific objectives has become legitimate and desirable for many educators. At the same time, Nussbaum's and Bok's scholarship offers very few resources for considering entrenched social issues and challenges. Nussbaum's work has been widely recognized for its attention to education, human rights, the capabilities approach, philosophy and public life, and law and morality. She has won numerous awards for her teaching and research. Indeed, when I hear faculty members and administrators in conversation about higher education and the social contract, Nussbaum's name often enters the conversation.

Two of Nussbaum's books, *Not for Profit* (2010) and *Cultivating Humanity* (1997), the latter of which won the Ness Book Award from the Association of American Colleges and Universities in 1998, are both strong defences of liberal education. They also offer extensive discussion of the goals to which higher education, the humanities, and curricular and pedagogical practices ought to aspire. In *Not for Profit*, Nussbaum makes clear references to democracy and encourages a "more inclusive type of citizenship" (p. 7), notes the importance of being able to "imagine the experience of another" (p. 10), and stresses the relevance of "sensitive thinking about distribution or social inequality" (p. 22). According to Nussbaum, in a "humane, people-sensitive democracy," citizens need multiple capacities, including the ability to "think well" about social and political issues, to view "fellow citizens as people with equal rights," to demonstrate concern for others, to understand the consequences of policies for different groups, to "imagine well" the ways in which complex issues affect human experience, to critically evaluate political leaders, and to consider the "nation as a whole" and as "part of a complicated world order" (pp. 25–26). Moreover, she argues, citizens need a "narrative imagination" to "relate well to the complex world around them" (p. 95).

At many levels, Nussbaum's articulation of educational priorities does begin to make space for curriculum and pedagogy that can grapple with inequity and injustice. Indeed, when considered in light of the work of more conservative scholars (see, e.g., Bloom, 1987; Fish, 2008), Nussbaum might in some ways seem quite progressive. In *Cultivating Humanity* (1997), her references to "our nation's legacy of vicious racism" (p. 151), "racial obtuseness" (p. 110), the limits of "factual logic and knowledge alone," and the problems with the belief that "we are all alike under the skin" (p. 111) all point to intellectual positions that, on the surface, indicate a possible openness to educational discourse that might be more concerned with the material consequences of injustice than most liberal scholarship.

Nussbaum's work is so often cited by liberal scholars perhaps in part because of its ability to seemingly acknowledge democracy's failures, yet at the same time, to stay firmly entrenched in a liberal educational framework. Nussbaum makes multiple references to tolerance, inclusion, compassion, critical reflection, empathy, pluralism, and the world citizen. She makes few claims that explicitly name how power is negotiated and/or who holds it, nor does she thoroughly discuss power's relationship to competing interests and social inequities. One must take as a given that her defence of and urging towards empathy and inclusion, for example, will be sufficient for practising justice. Nussbaum seems to assume that critical thinking and reflection will inevitably lead to democratic outcomes. Further, she is much more attentive to abstract liberal priorities and norms than to moving towards just practices in material and embodied terms. For example, her attention to "inclusion" is far more an indication of her alignment with liberal practices that allow oppressed groups into an existing framework that those in power have undemocratically constructed and continue to control, than of her commitment to making existing systems more equitable.

Nussbaum's consideration of compassion neglects to carefully attend to power. Nussbaum states that compassion requires "a sense of one's own vulnerability to misfortune. To respond with compassion, I must be willing to entertain the thought that this suffering person might be me ... Compassion, so understood, promotes an accurate awareness of our common vulnerability" (1997, p. 91). Even a cursory examination of relationships among groups in North America demonstrates that we are not, as Nussbaum claims, commonly vulnerable. It is, of course, possible to argue that we are all at risk of misfortune generally. A more telling and complex assertion is that our level of risk (in terms of direct threats to life and well-being) is primarily determined by our relationship to specific forms of individual and institutional power. As I write this chapter, I am also reading reports of the killing of Trayvon Martin, an unarmed 17-year-old African American killed by a neighbourhood watch volunteer in Florida. Black, Indigenous, and Latino youth and adults are far more often the victims of police violence than those in white communities. Life expectancy rates, levels of wealth and education, health status, and other quality of life indicators are not equitable across racial lines. Nussbaum's discussion of compassion makes no reference to power or social status, yet such factors ensure that Martin and other Black and Latino youth and men are at risk of death and violence in ways that I, for example, am not.

Nussbaum's attention to compassion rests on the liberal norms discussed earlier in this chapter, including a focus on the individual and an implicit belief that institutions have generally been beneficent. For

Nussbaum, compassion will be supported by individuals recognizing that "their own possibilities are similar to those of the suffering person," and the idea that we are "imperfect human beings" (1997, p. 91). While compassion, according to Nussbaum, does require the knowledge that one "has suffered some significant pain or misfortune in a way for which that person is not, or not fully, to blame" (pp. 90–91), Nussbaum's discussion makes no reference to institutions or to the ways in which "misfortune" arises through the ways in which individuals and institutions use power.

In this same discussion, Nussbaum defines empathy, another capacity frequently referenced by liberal scholars, as "the ability to imagine what it is like to be in that person's place" (1997, p. 91). Empathy is a quality often mentioned as desirable by students in the intercultural communication courses that I teach. On the whole, practices of empathy exist at a discursive level, and they often have a link to feelings of pity or charity for an "unfortunate" or "disadvantaged" other. Identifying, for example, police violence and working at its reduction and cessation does not require empathy. Because in the process of expressing empathy, those in privileged groups retain the power of constructing and defining another's reality, empathy can allow for and support a distancing from the lived reality of subordinate groups.

When I can listen to my student Gloria, and consider Gloria's own representation of the Black community's distrust of the police on Gloria's terms, rather than inhabit a reality for Gloria that I might "imagine," empathy is irrelevant. In some ways, empathy becomes useful in cases when listening to another's experience becomes uncomfortable for whatever reason (Young, 1990). It is indeed convenient to "imagine" what it is like to be another person when listening to an individual or community becomes challenging or presses at the limits of knowledge for those in privileged groups. Empathy may, in this way, be a particularly opportune device for liberals who are finding it difficult to take in the hard truths of injustice. Students and scholars alike vigorously defend the importance of empathy when I question its purposes, and are reluctant to consider its limits.

Indeed, once I can "imagine" how such a reality feels for Gloria, I no longer need to listen to her at all. Empathy has the most shelf-life when it retains ties to notions of a benevolent and charitable subject. When students such as Gloria raise issues such as institutional complicity in racism, thereby contradicting a liberal world view, class discussions often move to a denial of racism. Further, Nussbaum's consideration of the "whole person," inasmuch as it refuses to attend to a material, embodied reality and to ethical priorities, is quite limited. As one scholar asserts, examining possible parallels between Nussbaum's work and the political agenda of Jörg Haider, an ultra-conservative Austrian politician, Nussbaum "advocates a social program based on Western liberal values ... but app[lies] it hegemonically" (Ling, 2000, n.p.). Nussbaum's "insistence on liberalism as the philosophy of all that is right and good" supports the "lack of a relational understanding between Self and Other" (Ling, 2000, n.p.; see also Ray, 2003).

In sum, while it may be difficult if not impossible for many educators to disagree with Nussbaum's exhortation of education of the "whole person" and of such values including tolerance, inclusion, and compassion, her discussion of higher education is generally aligned with liberal norms. I am not so much "arguing against" these values or educational priorities, or declaring that they are intrinsically problematic in a strictly conceptual sense. I am asserting that such values will not, ultimately, lead us to justice. Further, the ways in which those in power have employed these values have often been in the interests of (1) downplaying or avoiding entirely the role of institutions in injustice and (2) maintaining dominant paradigms for both understanding the social and responding to social challenges. The employment of these values by those in higher education has firmly (yet often subtly) removed the identification of injustice, and possibilities for justice, from a range of educational spaces.

Back in the classroom, when Gloria asks me what I think about 41 bullets, she seems most interested in her community's safety, rather than in any "tolerance" or "empathy" I might offer in regard to Diallo's death. Indeed, in this sense, a focus on tolerance and empathy can be a means for those in power to completely bypass the need and possibilities for institutions to ensure justice and equity for all communities. "Tolerating" Gloria's frustration with a policing system that wrongly and disproportionately kills those in the Black community, or offering "empathy" to, for example, Diallo's family, most often represents the limits of liberalism, rather than the attainment of democratic practices, equity, or justice.

Derek Bok has also authored two books that substantively consider the social contract that higher education has with public life and the significance and objectives of university education. Known for his role in university administration, including two terms as the president of Harvard University, Bok has authored six books on higher education and has been recognized for his advocacy of student participation in public service programs. In two of these six books, *Our Underachieving Colleges* (2006) and *Beyond the Ivory Tower* (1982), Bok considers the ways in which universities balance teaching and research with service to society, and discusses the primary purposes of university education. In this section, I am primarily concerned with the aims of undergraduate education that Bok addresses in *Our Underachieving Colleges*, and with the earlier text's distinction between what one reviewer describes as a "centrist" and "activist" view (Kezar, 2005, p. 474).

In *Beyond the Ivory Tower*, "Bok attempts to provide a framework and rationale for how, why, and when universities should be involved in meeting social needs and how they can best serve the public good" (Kezar, 2008, p. 474). In this book, Bok notes that universities "have a clear obligation" to "tak[e] account of society's needs" (1982, p. 301) and to consider the role of faculty members in regard to these needs and to questions of governance, leadership, and implementation. In chapter 3 he asks, "Who is to define these needs and determine the priorities to assign among them?" (p. 78). At the end of this chapter, Bok offers his response, stating that "universities have an obligation to serve society by making the contributions they are uniquely able to provide" (p. 88). In offering these contributions and considering the university's response to social concerns, academic leaders must protect a range of values and interests, including academic freedom, rigorous intellectual standards, and the ability to pursue scholarship without "outside interference" (p. 88). Bok's discussion may manage to appear exhaustive and thorough, particularly to those who are advocates of his views. In the end, however, beyond apparently assuming that academic leaders will be able to navigate "the difficult task" (p. 88) that confronts them, Bok's work offers little specific guidance to those considering equity and social issues, particularly when social needs and priorities conflict.

Again, on the whole, Bok's discussion offers little analysis of or even reference to power, ethical priorities, or the material conditions of how people live. Also in chapter 3, Bok criticizes faculty members who take an "activist view" (1982, p. 78) and scholars who "allege that the modern university has become a handmaiden of the establishment" (p. 79). He questions the view that "presidents, faculty members, and students ... ought to take more initiative to frame a conception of the good society and to pursue this vision aggressively by refusing to support certain programs while striving to develop others" (p. 79). In his more recent book, *Our Underachieving Colleges*, Bok (2006) suggests that "promoting certain values and behaviors" can "amount to indoctrination" (p. 64). This is a convenient suggestion to make: any intentional and robust consideration of the public good and democratic values amounts to indoctrination, which clearly violates liberal scholarship's belief in disinterested knowledge.

In such frameworks, consideration of ethical practices in support of the public good and in the context of injustice might make one a "moral dictator." Once faculty members or administrators make the charge of indoctrination, they also legitimize and embrace a full and exhaustive retreat from questions of the public good and of justice. It then becomes desirable to talk in largely conceptual terms about "compassion," "inclusion," "empathy," and "tolerance." As I claim in chapter 2, the lack of a rigorous consideration of the public good is common in liberal scholarship. In this sense, Bok's work is quite adept at seemingly advocating for liberal values such as compassion and tolerance, yet simultaneously saying little to nothing about power and possibilities for justice. Further, his work clearly critiques educators who offer transparent attention to values and interests.

Our Underachieving Colleges examines the purposes of undergraduate education. Bok clearly affirms that attempting to confine the purposes of universities to "intellectual development" is "too narrow a view of the undergraduate experience … colleges should pursue a variety of purposes, including a carefully circumscribed effort to foster generally acceptable values and behaviors" (2006, p. 66). In the remainder of the book, Bok devotes a chapter to each of eight aims, which have "broad enough applicability to be appropriate for virtually all undergraduates" (ibid.). These aims include the ability to communicate, to think critically, to engage in moral reasoning, to consider the obligations of citizenship, to live with diversity, to demonstrate readiness for a global society, to acquire broader interests, and to prepare for a career. In his discussion of each of these purposes, Bok provides general parameters for what each includes. He also references studies of faculty members' consideration of such issues, as well as research on students and learning practices. In-depth examples are rare, as are connections between concepts and embodied practices.

Again, at one level, one might easily endorse these purposes. In many ways, they represent the possibility of careful attention to social issues much more explicitly than previous scholarship in higher education authored by those situated within mainstream educational discourse. At the same time, Bok's aims do not necessitate any specific set of ethical priorities. Even as Bok refers to "generally acceptable values and behaviors" (p. 66), one might wonder: acceptable to whom? In practice, "generally acceptable values and behaviors" will most often benefit and sustain those in the dominant group. Bok asserts that faculty members must consider how students will "use knowledge to analyze problems in the field" (p. 139). His summary of the aim of living with diversity states: "The challenge is to determine how to help students learn to live together with understanding and mutual respect while not appearing insensitive to the aggrieved, unfairly accusatory to the majority, or rigidly doctrinaire to larger society" (p. 75).

I do not know exactly how Bok's purposes and his explanation of them might have aided in the classroom with Gloria, Paul, Robert, and their peers. In defining the bounds of "generally acceptable values and behaviors," in regard to the police force's use of 41 bullets, from whom should I draw authority? If students should, indeed, be able to "analyze problems in the field," as Bok states, this was clearly a problem relevant to the study of intercultural communication. Would venturing into this particular issue automatically indicate, for Bok and others, that I was inappropriately taking sides, or "indoctrinating" students? Finally, should my objective, in the midst of the conflict and disagreement in the classroom, have been to encourage students like Paul to "appear" sensitive, or, as Bok states, "not appear ... insensitive to the aggrieved" (2006, p. 75)? Pursuing this objective in such a way seems potentially anti-intellectual, as I would presumably expect Paul and myself to simplify the particulars of the Diallo situation in the interests of "appearing" sensitive. Suggesting that we educate students to "not appear ... insensitive" is a particularly destructive and offensive educational objective when it comes to addressing racism and other forms of oppression. "Not appear[ing] ... insensitive" seems to be wholly directed at maintaining existing power relations and releasing those in higher education settings from the need to carefully consider inequity and oppression.

In his broader discussion of appropriate purposes for undergraduate education, Bok addresses indoctrination in the classroom:

Institutional efforts to build character or change behavior should include only goals with which no reasonable person is likely to disagree. For example, virtually no one would quarrel with attempts to encourage students to be more honest, more scrupulous about keeping promises, more understanding of those of different races, backgrounds, and religions ... It is only when professors use their classrooms to influence which promises students keep, how they vote, or what kind of community programs they support that their teaching is open to criticism. (2006, p. 64)

This statement makes a clear break between, for example, "understanding those of different races, backgrounds, and religions" and the links between conceptual understanding and one's actions. That is, Bok seems to imply that education can draw a firm line between thinking about and doing. Further, Bok implies that it is impossible for instructors to, with their students, consider specific promises and refrain from "us[ing] their classrooms to influence which promises students keep." This is a fairly unsophisticated view of the practices of teaching. This statement also points to several tensions concerning liberal educational assumptions in relation to the material conditions of how we live.

First, Bok does not discuss the parameters of "reasonable." Paul, Gloria, and Robert probably each felt that the sets of beliefs they held, while sharply conflicting, were deeply reasonable. Each student's knowledge base and experience had, at least in his or her own mind, reasonably led to the conclusions that he or she held. Likewise, as can be seen in the range of analyses of the Diallo killing and New York City's response, these students were not alone in holding conflicting conclusions about the situation. Individuals usually view their own beliefs about any given social issue as "reasonable." This includes scholars, who often readily provide evidence and rationales supporting the reasonableness of their positions. Bok also encourages students to be "more honest" and "more scrupulous about keeping promises" (2006, p. 64). At the same time, faculty members should not consider with students which promises they might keep or break. Perhaps Bok is suggesting that learning can be acontextual, that we keep discussions at a general level and step back from including, as part of our instructional and professorial role, an examination of the complexities such as intercultural communication, history, and a community's distrust of the police.

In relation to "reasonableness" and to his support for honesty and scrupulousness, Bok does not thoroughly discuss where the complexities and consequences of inequity fit. It is almost as if expressions of reason and honesty exist above the fray, concepts to be readily and easily applied without difficulty or debate. In this framework, I might present a course on intercultural communication with little to no attention to material realities and social issues. Such an approach seems to be

keeping its own promises, however naturalized. Commitments to "reasonableness" most often support an allegiance to existing forms of sociality and interaction. To what conclusion does such an approach lead?
It seems that by not considering the question of which promises with
my students, I am, in effect, endorsing existing promises, which at least
at present, support police brutality directed especially at Indigenous,
Black, and Latino communities in North America.

Finally, Bok and other educators will likely hold substantively conflicting views of institutions and the ways in which they justly or
unjustly serve different communities. These differences in assessing
reality do not constitute the central issue at stake. Ideally, a rigorous
consideration of intellectual differences, and the evidence that supports such differences, is a hallmark of good scholarship, and must be
a crucial component in any discussion of social needs and inequities.
The assertion that education can avoid keeping promises is a highly
problematic starting point. As educators, we might, at a minimum, be
transparent about our central claims and assumptions and provide evidence for how we arrived at such starting points. We are all, through
our approach to our disciplines and course content, keeping promises
that have a connection to the material reality of how people live.

In the class addressing intercultural communication and history, on
the day during which our attention to Diallo began and in subsequent
class meetings, I never felt the need or desire to tell my students which
promises to keep. Contrary to the assessment of many liberal scholars,
the ways in which faculty members teach are far more complex and
nuanced than Bok's analysis of indoctrination implies. It is possible to
in the classroom openly acknowledge that individuals and institutions
are always "keeping promises," and to have a robust intellectual discussion about how we all, in the various ways in which we are implicated, act to maintain and pursue specific promises. Exploring the
existence of specific "promises," and how these might be constructed
differently, does not require me to demand that students endorse any
particular political or ethical position. I also have seen, over and over
again, that students are aware of complexity and appreciate the educational spaces in which they can grapple with such complexity. In
my experience, students are far more interested in discussing their
views and engaging with their peers than with learning how to offer
the appearance of sensitivity or similar qualities. As scholarship has
documented, and as I hear directly, students learn from hearing ideas
that are different from their own and from being in conversation with

students from cultural backgrounds different from their own (Gurin, 1999). Further, even as such classroom discussions can be difficult, I take Paul, Robert, and Gloria, and their potential contributions to the communities in which they live far too seriously to settle for encouraging a lack of the "appear[ance of] insensitivity to the aggrieved" (Bok, 2006, p. 75).

The minute we turn towards the material, link course content to, as Bok articulates, "problems arising in everyday life and experience" (2006, p. 68), we are invoking promises and their inherent complexity and entanglements: the historical weight of commitments that have led to where we are now; the press of living with those commitments and promises; an assessment of, acceptance of, or resistance to their burdens and possibilities; and the inevitability of shaping the promises with which we will live tomorrow. Faculty members and students have ontological and ethical responsibilities for promises that will shape our future. Education can be the work of asking, with students, what these promises look like in various settings, and how such promises might change when democratic practices, the public good, and justice matter.

The ways in which students and faculty members articulate possible responses to social issues in any given course can, in practice, be far more complex, hopeful, and intellectually rigorous than any form of indoctrination. In democratic societies in North America, it ought to be possible to boldly and repeatedly affirm the public good, justice, and ethical uses of agency. Such priorities are not indoctrination, but a leaning towards values to which we have, as nations, at least discursively committed ourselves. The realization of those values, the ways in which they become real in communities, will by necessity be worked out, over and over again, in particular contexts in ways that are neither fixed nor predictable. As a faculty member, the best and the most I can do is to encourage a language and imagination for such values in ways that can intellectually and practically stand up in the midst of social issues.

For many faculty members, support of liberal educational norms, such as Nussbaum's endorsement of the importance of education of the whole person, and the purposes of university education such as those outlined by Bok, are deeply convincing and sensible. Such scholarship ensures that it is reasonable and defensible to downplay or minimize the role of ethics, politics, and power. For educators comfortable with liberal norms, higher education, in communicating knowledge that is

both disinterested and that retreats from particular ethical commitments, performs an important societal function. In sustaining liberal
norms, educational institutions endorse and naturalize existing forms
of sociality, as well as dominant ontologies and epistemologies. Further,
in the interests of maintaining one's belief in beneficent institutions
and disinterested knowledge, it is crucial that individuals are willing
to resist understandings of society and knowledge that question these
institutions or suggest that knowledge is interested.

In a liberal framework, faculty members who do consider concrete
political and ethical questions – what about the use of 41 bullets? – are
potentially indoctrinating students, moving into educational practices
that contradict our roles as educators. Inasmuch as such understandings of educational practice are contingent, how might a critical exploration reveal the "limits imposed on us" (Foucault, 1997, p. 133) or shed
light on the "conditions of possibility" (Tully, 2002, p. 534)? In other
words, how might faculty members step outside of arguments such as
Nussbaum's and Bok's and risk an open engagement with the questions of which promises? How might we accept the inevitability of, and
commit to engaging with the complicated demands of, interests, benefit, and harm that all knowledge invokes?

When Gloria asks, "What do you think? 41 bullets?," I can turn
towards and affirm, offer information and context: yes, Diallo is dead;
four white policemen who fired 41 bullets at an unarmed man have
been excused of responsibility for his death; formal institutions have
not addressed larger issues of accountability; and in democratic societies, all communities should have equal protection under the law. I can
affirm Robert's, Paul's, Gloria's, and their peers' agency. We can ask in
the classroom: what does all of this mean and why, and for whom? What
kind of world do you envision for yourselves? As faculty members,
when we teach, we will articulate our longings. We cannot escape communicating our construction of the social. What types of assumptions
about the self and about knowledge have obscured the ways in which
educators, through our teaching, necessarily keep our own promises?
How do we, through curricular and pedagogical choices, indicate our
own allegiances to particular and material understandings of the world
in which we live? How have educational frameworks made the split
between concepts and practice seem so logical, necessary, and natural
to many faculty members and students? In the next section, I will examine the significance of dichotomies in higher education and how they
bear on educational practices.

The Dangers of Dichotomies

One important component of liberal educational norms is a widespread and often unconsidered acceptance of ontological and epistemological dichotomies or dualisms. Indeed, this acceptance can be seen in common defences of liberal education. Education should be about the intellect and not about emotions. Faculty members can offer disciplinary knowledge and content but cannot influence behaviour or students' practices once they leave the classroom. Legitimate forms of knowledge have been shaped through objective reasoning. Subjectivity, often a way of referencing values or emotions, has no place in higher education or the classroom.

Dichotomies or dualisms can be defined as ontological and epistemological assumptions of opposing and often mutually exclusive characteristics, or "the division of any given area of reality into two contrasting and possibly conflicting areas" (Jenkins, 2005, p. 5). Central to theories of being and of knowing, dualisms have long been a topic of discussion in philosophical and epistemological discourse. Within higher education and the production of knowledge, positivist and empiricist epistemologies have heavily relied on minimally a separation of mind and body, as well as on dualisms including objectivity/subjectivity, rationality/emotion, and detachment/investment. Even as such dualities have been thoroughly critiqued (Flax, 1990; Smith, 2001), they are still profoundly active among both students and faculty members.

Theories endorsing the necessary separation of mind and body in the context of knowledge production and education have significant ramifications for setting up not only what is possible in educational contexts, but also in responding to the question of the subject. As scholars have claimed, dualisms play a profound role in (1) regulating knowing, learning, thinking, feeling, and doing in educational settings and (2) assigning value to different bodies and thus deciding who can know (Collins, 1998; Mbembe, 2001; Smith, 2001). While the mind-body dualism is perhaps the most referenced and analysed dichotomy, it has integral links to a secondary set of dualisms including objectivity/subjectivity, reason/emotion, detachment/investment, thinking/doing, and theory/practice. On the whole, scholars have valued the first attribute at the expense of the second, and have supported the idea that such attributes are, indeed, separable in relation to being and knowing.

Educators, including faculty members and administrators, use these dualisms as forms of gatekeeping and regulation, and as systems of legitimation and refusal when considering, for example, Bok's distinction between the value of keeping promises generally (named as "detachment" or "reason" by liberal scholars) and the inappropriateness of faculty members and students together considering which promises to keep ("investment" or "emotion" for liberal scholars). Because reason is valued over and assumed to be separable from emotion, once I consider with my students not only that history functions as a socializing force (reasoned detachment), but that the police might inequitably serve communities based on race (emotional investments), I can now be charged with indoctrination. Such charges are far more frequent than careful consideration of how, for example, the fact of history functioning as a socializing force acts on bodies and, for example, kills men like Amadou Diallo and Frank Paul and boys like Trayvon Martin. These dichotomies can be as prevalent and as invisible as air in educational settings. For faculty members interested in considering democratic practices, the public good, and justice, it will be necessary to consider the possibilities for interrupting and refusing them.

Dualisms are particularly powerful in the ways in which they regulate consideration of the subject and what is worth knowing, as well as the ways in which they impose values on particular bodies. The separation of mind and body, reason and emotion, and theory and practice (or theory and experience) "help determine what counts as real" in epistemological discourse and pedagogical contexts (Smith, 2001, p. 44). The separation of subject and object and of knower from known, and the requirement of distance for objective research "impl[y] a neutrality and objectivity on behalf of the researcher" (p. 56). As scholars have asserted, this valuing of objectivity effectively severs the relationship between the researcher and researched and the knower and the known, and simultaneously removes consideration of power. Put another way, the claim of objectivity is an "ingenious strategy" for "avoiding responsibility": "the prevailing position does not present itself as simply that – prevailing in a specific social constellation – but rather claims to be transcendent and justified beyond a discourse" (Danelzik, 2008, p. 215). In this sense, dualistic positions "immuniz[e] themselves" (ibid.) from any form of criticism, examination, and review.

While these dualisms have been substantively critiqued (Collins, 2000; Harding & Hintikka, 2003; Jaggar & Bordo, 1992; Smith, 2001; Stanley & Wise, 1993), such dualisms are still significantly prevalent in a great deal of discourse and practice in higher education. Particularly in relation to the idea that knowledge is disinterested, or void

of ethical priorities, values, or any form of implication with social life,
dualisms have significant consequences for scholarship on higher education and for curricular and pedagogical norms and expectations. In
this sense, dualisms regulate the possible and construct what is real.
Bok can devote an entire book to the purposes of education and never
plainly address how such purposes bear on the material and have a
connection to the body and to lived experience. Cindy felt justified in
calling for the removal of bodies and lives that challenged her own constructions of gender, constructions that also privileged separation (of
gender from sexuality) and distance (from queer lives on campus and
in other contexts). Such regulation, supported and rationalized by the
dualisms noted above, profoundly constrains how one might respond
to the question of what is the subject.

For some, "the political implications of the dominant knowledge
system are inconsistent with equality and justice" (Shiva, 1993, p. 60).
Further, the roots and effects of epistemological frameworks and dualistic understandings of being and knowing are not confined to the
assumptions faculty members make about our work, but rather have
a necessary connection to the social and political. Indeed, knowledge
systems inform socio-political norms and practice: "through the oppo-
sitions of reason/body and culture/nature, a relationship of exterior-
ity to 'nature' is established. This is a condition for the appropriation/
exploitation that grounds the Western paradigm of unlimited growth"
(Lander, 2009, p. 41). In sum, dualisms provide a specific regulatory
system for considering the social that presents itself as universal. They
legitimize, in implicit and explicit ways, (1) the dismissal of ethical priorities that are grounded in the material rather than the abstract, (2) the
repudiation of the social and political content and interests of all academic work, and (3) the refusal of knowledge and faculty members'
practices that grapple with, for example, the significance of 41 bullets
for the well-being of various communities.

This system of regulation has also ensured that any community, reality, interaction, or experience that transgresses Western understandings
of being human, of understandings of time and space, and of reasoned
knowing, is deemed to be lesser than the Eurocentric and Western norm
(Lander, 2009, p. 40; see also Fabian, 1983; Mbembe, 2001; Mignolo 2009).
Once Western epistemologies assign non-Western bodies to the "realm
of the physical and irrational," these bodies "are denied full humanity
itself" (Hokowhitu, 2009, p. 102; see also Goldberg, 1993). Such valua-
tion systems simultaneously reinscribe Western forms of knowing as

"transcendent," in effect, beyond the body, and persistently undercut and deny forms of knowing and being that suggest that Western forms of knowledge might be limited and particular.

It may be impossible to fully articulate the ways in which Western epistemological dichotomies have served to define the subject in narrow, hierarchical, and rationalistic ways, and have subsequently radically constrained ways of being and knowing in higher education and other settings. One point of critique of Western epistemologies is to assert that they are particular rather than universal and that they might be understood as such. In the context of such a critique, in which Western epistemological claims to universality are thoroughly examined, it might be possible for educators to begin to consider the legitimacy of other epistemological frameworks. It is noteworthy that dualistic epistemological norms prevail, even as abundant evidence, produced by scholars working within Western knowledge frameworks, demonstrates that the supposed split between mind and body, or reason and emotion, flatly contradicts what it is to be human. This persistence likely reflects both the deep-rootedness of dichotomies, as well as their value to normative educational discourse. As one scholar states, "It is ironic that the duality between reason and emotion that has been perpetuated through the ages is a distinction that is not honored by the architecture of the brain" (Davidson, 2000, p. 91). In other words, many faculty members heavily depend on dichotomies in relation to being, knowing, and doing that are fully contested by ongoing research.

Particularly in the past decade, research in fields including affective neuroscience has repeatedly demonstrated that "emotions play a vital role in determining decisions" (Meshulam, Winter, Ben-Shakhar, & Aharon, 2012, p. 11), that evidence in regard to "various aspects of emotion-cognition interactions points to dynamic interplays between separate but interconnected neural systems involved in emotional and cognitive/ executive functions" (Dolcos, Iordan, & Dolcos, 2011, p. 686), and that "emotion and cognition conjointly and equally contribute to the control of thought and behavior" (Gray, Braver, & Raichle, 2002, p. 4115). Given this research, any education of the "whole human being," such as that advocated by Nussbaum, must consider the cognitive-affective interplay that such research has confirmed. These challenges to a cognitive/ emotional dualism point to additional possible critiques. What if theories of being and knowing approached the body as a "thinking body; the ... body as a material producer of thought; the body as a holistic notion where physiology and the interplay between history, present, and future

interact to produce social meaning" (Hokowhitu, 2009, p. 114)? What if
faculty members started from the claim "that any absolute separation
between theory and practice is a mistake" (Hill & Morf, 2000, p. 218)?
What if we risked, whenever possible, refusing the dualisms that have
so inscribed liberal educational thought and practice?

In the interests of careful consideration of democratic practices, the
public good, and justice, redefining the subject will require a thorough
analysis of the ways in which the dualisms of mind/body, reason/emo-
tion, objectivity/subjectivity, and theory/practice underwrite much if
not all educational work. Further, educators must be willing to address
how this underwriting has led to a retreat from considerations of ethics
and interests. Institutions of higher education have significant investments in maintaining these dualisms. They have been in place for centuries, and are part of the fabric of institutional policies and practices.
They may have contributed to Cindy's swift and concise demand, once
the fact of queer bodies was in the room, for streamlined education
and for an education that could resist the intrusion of a "'messy text'"
(Cruz, 2001, p. 659). As one scholar, addressing the construction of the
disinterested knower, urges:

> It is not enough to change the content of the conversation … it is of the
> essence to change the *terms* of the conversation. Changing the terms of
> the conversation implies going beyond disciplinary or interdisciplinary
> controversies and the conflict of interpretations. As far as controversies
> and interpretations remain within the same rules of the game (terms of
> the conversation), the control of knowledge is not called into question.
> (Mignolo, 2009, p. 162; emphasis in original)

Rethinking the terms of the conversation requires that scholars rigorously and insistently question such dualisms. As Mignolo concludes,
when questioning the myth of disinterested knowing, "the basic
assumption is that the knower is always implicated, geo- and body-
politically, in the known" (p. 162).

For faculty members working in mainstream educational institutions, it will inevitably be difficult to change the terms of the conversation. Success at such changes will be fleeting and tenuous. It is always
necessary to work at such changes. Differently defining the subject
in our courses, and attempting to "change the terms of the conversation," might make it possible to pursue subjects that are engaged with
the materiality of too much wrong and with the practices of in/justice.

To pursue such subjects, one must thoroughly consider the ways in which we imagine our own educational desires, our constructions of self and other, and our investments in particular ways of seeing, all of which have ontological, epistemological, curricular, and pedagogical significance.

Conclusion: Starting Points for Constructing the Subject

If, as Mignolo asserts, "the knower is always implicated" (2009, p. 162), what might serve as starting points for all faculty members' work? How do we constitute the subject in our courses? Through this constitution, how do we construct the relationship between self and other? Cindy asked for streamlined education, Allison noted a disconnect from nation, Gloria asked me what I thought about 41 bullets, and an administrator labelled me a "moral dictator." What might ground an ontological, epistemological, ethical, and pedagogical relationship with such assertions? When we consider the purposes of education, the ways in which our courses might inform the lives of our students, what is the shape of our own implicatedness, as knowers and teachers? I have asserted in this chapter that liberal scholarship falls short in its responses to such questions, particularly in relation to its belief in beneficent institutions and disinterested knowledge. If we claim, as I did in chapter 4, that all life is social and ethical, that inequity exists, that power matters, and that in democratic societies, we ought to have a language and imagination for the public good and for justice, where might we begin?

For educators interested in considering such a language and imagination, and in examining, with our students, the reality of "too much wrong," we might opt to start from a rigorous and persistent commitment to the material, the social, and the ethical components of public life. When shaping course content, making decisions about what we understand as the subject, and critically analysing what we believe are the purposes of university education, the material, the social, and the ethical might serve as the central parameters by which we orient our work as faculty members. The material refers to lived reality and embodied practice, the ways in which living bears on being, the burdens of "too much wrong," the costs of inequity, and the particulars of living together well or not. The material encompasses the deaths of men like Paul and Diallo, educational systems that fail racial minority populations, the attempted removal of queer lives from public spaces, and a white man treating boys of colour in a library computer room as less than human.

The social refers to relationships of power, the negotiation of individual and institutional agency, habits of relationality, and the incessant hum of implication. The social encompasses a consideration of institutions, such as the criminal justice and education systems, that inequitably serve different communities; attention to how dominant norms and the practices of those in power narrow the space for what it means to be human; and the longing for a world in which everyone present in a library computer room might urge a white man to communicate differently. Finally, the ethical refers to a commitment to grapple with the public good and with questions of justice; to an ongoing consideration, through dialogue and practice, of the kind of future towards which we want to move; and to an active engagement with the shape of the communities in which we want to live. It encompasses patterns of caring, investment, and regard; questions of what went wrong – in that library computer room, when four policemen shot 41 bullets and killed Amadou Diallo, when individuals repeatedly removed the banner of the queer student group on campus; and a shared and hard-earned desire to ask, when the public good, democratic practices, and justice matter, what needs to happen next.

Epistemological, curricular, and pedagogical frameworks that turn towards the material, social, and ethical are not formulaic, predetermined, or fixed. They do not allow attention to one narrow set of subjects and refuse consideration of another set. Such frameworks are broad, subject to rigorous critique and analysis, and able to grapple with complexity and competing interests. In sum, such frameworks can meet the demands of real life. They encourage pedagogical and course-related attention to a range of subjects, always set in relation to questions of interests and consequences, the ways in which such subjects, and our understanding of them, will bear on how people live. (I will offer extended discussion of the relevance of these starting points to pedagogical practices in chapter 7.) An examination of the material, social, and ethical in no way establishes or determines ways of seeing, thinking, feeling, or acting. However, it does require habits of regard for living together well, for practices of the public good, and for the realization of equity and justice.

In addition to considering the material, the social, and the ethical, we might also begin with a willingness to grapple with the ways in which knowing is always a cognitive and affective process. To believe and act otherwise is to deny our humanity. Strongly held allegiances to the idea that the police services are not racist, to Nussbaum's encouragement to educate the "whole person" with little attention to concrete ethical commitments, or to Bok's mandate that we must stay away from discussing with our students which promises to keep are never exclusively intellectual or cognitive. They are intertwined with deeply held emotions, bound up with our sense of ourselves and patterns of caring constructed over years. Nussbaum's "reasonable pluralism" might be so appealing precisely because it affectively affirms our belief in a benevolent state, even as a detailed intellectual rationale does not follow, and as evidence suggests otherwise. Paul's insistence on the necessity of 41 bullets, as well as faculty members' support for liberal norms, are rarely if ever based on logic alone. Inasmuch as an allegiance to what is familiar obscures the existence of injustice, those interested in democratic practices, the public good, and justice must acknowledge the significance of affect and cognition, and must endorse forms of knowing and learning that thoughtfully attend to both.

When Gloria leaned towards me with her question of "What do you think? 41 bullets?," how did such a regard for the material, social, and ethical inform my work as a faculty person? First, in relation to the material, the press of real life was in many ways my first response to the question of what is the subject. Diallo was dead, and institutional accountability for this death seemed apparently irrelevant in much if not all of public discourse and institutional practice. As Gloria pointed out, this refusal of accountability has profound consequences for communities of colour. Further, I was aware that how we perceived and defined "real life," and how intercultural communication mattered to it, would be different among those of us in the classroom. Second, in attending to the social I was especially interested in power and institutions – how did both shape not only what happened to Diallo, but also how those of us in the classroom saw this issue and what we knew about it? Finally, in reflecting on the ethical, I was, in the classroom, full of the desire to enact the possibilities of the public good and justice with my students. As I had tried to explain to the administrator who called me a "moral dictator," I wanted questions of the public good, accountability, and the safety of Black communities to be in the room, a part of the subject.

At this point, as I have already stated, many scholars might charge me with indoctrination. Indeed, my desire to, as Bok might say, explore with my students which promises might be worth keeping, could for some mean that I was inappropriately influencing students. Learning happens when students make course content their own. Students will do this in various ways. When Gloria asked me about 41 bullets, what I felt most keenly was a desire that all of us could continue this conversation together, with an active regard for questions of the public good. As the instructor for that course, I had hoped to make available a way to consider ideas and practice that leaned towards the public good and justice. I had no desire to tell Paul, Gloria, or Robert what to think. I did, however, want all of the students in that class to have the opportunity to consider, first, the value of institutions that serve all communities equitably; second, the possibility that this was not occurring; and finally, the relationship of these questions to intercultural communication. In terms of the promises I chose to keep in that situation, I hope I found a way to betray the illusion of the promise that we are all equitably served by societal institutions, as scholarly research does not support this claim, and to keep the promise of my belief in the necessity of naming injustice and imagining justice.

My sense is that Paul, the student who vigorously defended the policemen's actions, for the most part, maintained his belief that the four policemen "did exactly the right thing." However, over the next several weeks, as we circled back and around questions of intercultural communication, racial privilege and discrimination, and institutional practices, I also believe that Paul gained a larger sense of both problems within and responsibilities of democratic societies. I think that this increased awareness occurred in relation to broad communicative practices, institutional injustice, and as Gloria brought to the fore, the Black community's distrust of the police. Following a charge of police brutality in Ohio directed at an African American man, which occurred during the term, I often walked into the classroom to find Robert, Paul, and other African American and white men enrolled in the course deep in conversation about the issue in Ohio. They punctuated their discussions with both laughter and heated exchange. They kept talking.

What is the subject? How are institutions unjust? In what ways is knowledge interested and is life insistently social? What is the fit of reason and emotion, detachment and closeness, object and subject, knower and known, mind and body? How are we always and everywhere implicated and interested, laden with ethical agency? University education offers profound, rare, and potentially far-reaching opportunities for us to consider a range of subjects with our students. "41 bullets?,"

Gloria asked, leaning towards me. "What do you think?" At its best, education might risk pursuing what it means to live together well, to resist a white man's racism in a library computer room, to name the state's complicity in the deaths of men like Diallo and Paul, to welcome Gloria's knowledge that the Black community does not trust the police, to suggest a language for the public good, and to name injustice and imagine justice.

6 Epistemological Architectures: Possibilities for Understanding the Social

In the Communication, Gender, and Culture course that I teach, I ask students on the first day of class what their expectations are for the course: "What do you want to know, or know better, in 12 weeks, at the end of the term, that you do not know now? Related to this course, what do you hope might be different for yourself in 12 weeks?" Many students state that they would like to better understand what "usual" behaviours are for men and for women. A woman might communicate that she wants "to be able to succeed in the workplace, where gender differences are important. If I know more about how women typically behave, and how men usually behave, it might be easier for me to succeed." A second student states that he "wants to be more aware of what is going on when I communicate with my girlfriend." For another student, "My parents expect very different things of me as a woman than of my brothers. Is that okay?" The students who made the first two statements may hold an underlying assumption that broad generalizations about men and women and their communicative behaviour are possible and desirable.

Also on the first day of class, I let the students know about my expectations. I tell them: "Constructions of gender and sexuality are important to how we live. Through communication, at numerous levels – in personal relationships, in the workplace, through the media, through public policies – we make meaning about gender and sexuality, set up norms for boys and girls, for men and women." I address their interest in "usual" communication patterns for men and for women: "This is not going to be a class that offers a fixed set of guidelines for what to expect from women and from men. I am not sure that such guidelines are possible, let alone useful." I let the students know that I hope that what they learn in this class "will strengthen your sense of agency related to gender and communication, lead you to more sophisticated and nuanced understandings of how gender, sexuality, and communication work." I am clear about why I am interested in such understandings: "I hope we can think about, over the next 12 weeks, how narrow and restrictive constructions of gender and sexuality can harm people and communities, and how we might opt to understand communication as a means to resist such narrowness and restriction." When I ask students about their interest in gender and communication, few of them make any explicit reference to queer lives and experiences. The course objectives directly reference sexuality. One reads, "To further your ability to make links between gender, sexuality, communication, and power in your day-to-day lives." Another objective is "to sharpen your sense of yourself as a communicative agent related to gender, sexuality, and the public good."

As students let me know about their expectations for the course, and I explain mine, we are already articulating spaces of epistemological (im)possibility, indicating the ways in which our mental and affective perceptual frameworks might invite new knowledge. In other words, on this first day, we are both opening up and placing constraints on what we consider to be relevant and worth learning. As I write this chapter, I wonder at my own use of the term "sexuality" in the course objectives. To my knowledge, the term sexuality is language commonly accepted in many social science disciplines to refer to all subject matter that somehow pushes beyond straight lives. Even as both queer and straight individuals and communities live beyond the "sexual" components of their identities, "sexuality" is the preferred term in a great deal of the social science and humanities disciplines to refer to queer lives and experiences.

The term "sexuality" seems to imply, at least at a literal level, that once you are not straight, as an identity and community, you are reduced to "sex." When I scanned the newspaper today, the front-page headline was a quote from President Obama: "'Same-sex couples should be able to get married'" (*Globe and Mail*, 10 May 2012, p. 1). The experiences and lives of queer individuals and communities go far beyond sexuality or sex, and have to do with law, public policy, family, employment, housing, and numerous other aspects of existence. The term "sexuality" is a particularly impoverished term to refer to all subject matter outside of straight norms. Such language normalizes an oversimplification of the lives of queer individuals, and strips down the complexity of living queer. Already, on the first day, through the syllabus and this discussion about our expectations, we are setting up frameworks for how we will know.

In another example of students and their teacher working out the possibilities of the subject, the administration at Pontiac Academy of Excellence, a middle school in Michigan, fired Brooke Harris in the spring of 2012 after she encouraged her students to hold a fundraiser for Trayvon Martin's parents. In Harris's class, students brought up the death of Trayvon Martin. While working on a writing assignment, students began discussing Martin's death. Noting their interest in the subject, Harris linked the assignment with students' interest in Martin's death. According to Harris, the students were "deeply affected [and] wanted to do more." Students decided they would like to do a fundraiser and "donate that money to someone else who they saw needed it [Martin's parents]" (Democracy Now, 2012). In response, the superintendent charged Harris with insubordination and unprofessionalism. In this situation, Harris affirmed her students' commitments, and connected a writing assignment with students' concern for Martin's death. In doing so, Harris marked educational spaces as those in which students can grapple with social issues, with priorities that were sitting against their skin, and with issues by which those students were "deeply affected." Harris and her students identified Martin's death as worth their attention. Her superintendent judged this attention inappropriate. Students in my course on gender and communication addressed their lives as men and as women and voluntarily offered no attention to queer lives. When do knowledge claims begin, and on what assumptions are they based?

Constructions of the subject across disciplines, departments, and courses are deeply bound up with epistemologies, or theories of knowledge. An epistemology "is a framework or theory for specifying the constitution and generation of knowledge about the social world; that is, it concerns how to understand the nature of 'reality'" (Stanley & Wise, 1993, p. 188). Epistemologies give us clues about what is worth knowing and who can know, and also support evaluative claims about differently situated knowledges and knowers. Epistemologies tell us, for example, that gender and sexuality operate largely independently of each other, or that gender and race are inseparable. When one scholar asserts that the police services are unjust and another firmly disagrees with this claim, our epistemological assumptions, even as they may not be visible, help us to interpret and judge such competing knowledge claims. "Inform[ing] descriptions, mental models, and accepted interpretations of the world" (Houghton, 2009, p. 99), epistemologies offer us ways to make sense of a range of social interactions, realities, and assertions.

Even as the most active regard for epistemological theory may occur in philosophical and educational discourse (Bernecker & Pritchard, 2011; Bernal, 2006; Hendricks & Pritchard, 2008; Huemer & Audi, 2002; Scott, 2010), as educators we inevitably rely on and express our own epistemological frameworks when, in the context of designing and teaching a course, we consider the "nature of 'reality'" (Stanley & Wise, 1993, p. 188) and make sense of the social. We routinely communicate epistemologies to students, through our construction of the subject, legitimation of different knowledges, and reliance on various forms of knowledge, such as textbooks or disciplinary concepts. Epistemology not only encompasses what knowers might assert as "true," such as the idea that gender is socially constructed. Epistemologies also tell us what forms of knowledge we can legitimately rule out, such as the possibility that queer lives have a central place in a class on gender. When a student tells a faculty person that in relation to a history of violence sanctioned and carried out by institutions, the Black community does not trust the police, our decisions about what to do with such knowledge are based in epistemological frameworks. Through such frameworks, we normalize ways of approaching and understanding the social world. Epistemologies construct possibilities for understanding the "we" of public life and the relationship of self to other.

I am interested in this chapter in what might be called epistemological architectures, or the ways in which epistemologies construct or close off spaces for what one can know. Epistemological architectures, which parallel what one scholar has referred to as "structures of believability" (R. Walcott, personal conversation), inform our responses to knowledge that is, at least for the knower, "not yet." Knowledge that is "not yet" – information, ideas, and assertions that challenge, stretch, or land outside of what one finds familiar. Knowledge that is "not yet" is a way of making meaning that is at once beyond what one knows and within reach of what one might come to know. Our "structures of believability," or our capacities for knowledge that is "not yet," are the doorways that we walk through to engage or refuse what we find challenging, new, or upsetting. Epistemological architectures act as a kind of cognitive and affective scaffolding that readily accepts some knowledge and rigorously rejects other knowledge. Epistemological architectures assert frameworks of possibility for what is not yet known. They offer clues to students like Cindy when they are confronted with queer lives in a course on gender, or to a faculty person unfamiliar with police violence against Black communities when students articulate the existence and consequences of such violence. When Cindy asked for streamlined education, and Allison noted a disconnect from nation, it was their epistemological architectures, or "structures of believability," that made such claims possible. In brief, Cindy's epistemological architecture could not accommodate the possibility of queer lives being part of the subject, while Allison's readily understood the idea of race and gender as interconnected.

How do representations of knowledge set up epistemological architectures and thus construct possibilities for understanding the social? Even as Cindy may not have previously considered the place of queer lives in a course on gender – for her, knowledge that was "not yet" – why did she opt to reject the possibility of this knowledge, rather than consider it? There is a relationship between epistemological content, or what is already part of what we know about the social world; and epistemological spaces of (im)possibility, or how we respond to knowledge that is new, unexpected, or challenging. Further, this relationship is ongoing, fluid, and intricate. In spaces of epistemological (im)possibilities, epistemological architectures provide a kind of map, offering routes for understanding, for example, the ways in which queer lives may or may not be part of the subject.

Particularly in pedagogical settings, in which learning is a central activity, epistemological architectures, or those spaces of epistemological (im)possibility, are crucial. They indicate to Cindy and Allison what they might know differently. When Cindy called for streamlined education, she was relying on a very particular epistemological architecture, constructed, in part, through her university education so far, that not only suggested but in some ways demanded the denial of queer lives. In contrast, what approach to knowing might have allowed and encouraged Cindy to more readily engage queer lives? What sorts of epistemological architectures have links to democratic practices and consideration of the public good? How do faculty members normalize these architectures?

This chapter's central contribution is a careful analysis of the links among streamlined epistemological architectures, routine classroom practices, and possibilities for understanding the social. I begin by discussing the ways in which the gender and communication course brought together a range of epistemological and pedagogical expectations and norms. I next discuss the possibility that Cindy's demand for "streamlined" education was a logical outcome of priorities and allegiances that one might trace through four primary "sites" of knowing: (1) student and faculty members' expectations, (2) traditional epistemologies, (3) epistemological approaches to gender and to difference, and (4) textbooks. I then make connections between the primacy of concepts, neoliberal ideologies, and neoliberal epistemologies, which work together to construct the social in ways that significantly narrow the space for what it means to be human. I conclude the chapter with starting points for epistemologies committed to "knowledge-making for well-being" (Mignolo, 2009, p. 177).

Pedagogical Sites of Knowing: Traditional Epistemology, Gender, and Textbooks

In this section, I examine a variety of epistemological entry points into the course on gender and communication. At one level, the students and I came with a set of expectations that certainly shaped how each of us took in and responded to course content and classroom discussions. In addition to students' expectations, traditional theories of knowledge, epistemological approaches to difference, and textbooks all significantly shape what students might already know and consider worth knowing.[1] All of these entry points, or sites of knowing, were operative when Cindy called for streamlined education and Allison noted a disconnect from nation. Indeed, the accumulation of epistemological leanings and preferences in all of these sites, over years and in numerous courses, shapes both what and how students know. What kinds of knowing do such sites habitualize? What types of subjects do they make desirable or unlikely?

Pedagogical Expectations of Students and Faculty Members

When I ask students in fourth year gender and communication courses about what they have learned in other university courses about queer communities, they point out that very few classes they have taken have offered substantive attention to life beyond straight norms. The students report that, for the most part, their previous courses have ignored content that suggested, in any way, that all of life may not be contained within the parameters of being straight. My students' interest in learning about "usual" behaviours for women and for men also communicates an expectation. How do educational practices inculcate a familiarity and comfort with, as well as a desire for, broad generalizations about people's lives? In what ways had the courses my students had had before the gender and communication class taught them to expect "usual" behaviours and little if any attention to queer lives? Educators have, at least for some students, sedimented which knowledge constitutes the subject, as well as legitimate forms and representations of such knowledge. What have my colleagues and I taught students about knowledge that does not fit into a landscape of "usual"? To what extent have we offered knowledge that is "unusual," that does not fit familiar categories? How does knowledge about what is "usual" disguise its partiality, and exert the ability to dismiss whatever challenges or refuses its parameters and assumptions? What kinds of epistemological architectures have we habitualized?

Students come with a range of expectations that in varying ways place into and remove from view certain possibilities for knowing. Cindy may have begun the gender course without ever having to thoughtfully and at some length consider the subject of queer lives, or the limits of straight norms. The absence of such content in undergraduate education has multiple consequences. In one respect, it removes a large segment of the population from educational discourse, and communicates that such individuals and communities are not worth knowing, particularly on their own terms. In a different respect, such absence constructs an epistemological landscape in which straightness becomes, for Cindy and others, a universal norm. Such norms become powerful even as they are intellectually and materially inaccurate. Thus students in the gender and communication course could have a lengthy discussion about the socially constructed nature of gender, with no reference to, for example, raced or queer lives, and assume that they were speaking for the whole.

The (il)legitimacy of certain areas of epistemological content is closely intertwined with acceptable forms of knowledge (Collins, 1998; Grande, 2004; Smith, 2001). As noted above, many students had likely been in courses in which faculty members routinely presented material about straight lives as a universal norm. Cindy may have been most at ease with knowledge that came in the form of broad, generalizable categories. Students' references to "usual" behaviours for men and for women also points to such preferences and norms. While knowledge is certainly about content (such as, for example, assertions about a community or social issue), it is also about form, or the conceptual containers which we construct for holding knowledge. In the gender and communication course, I was challenging Cindy's epistemological expectations in relation to content by stating that in a course on gender and communication, we would consider queer and straight lives. I was also challenging her expectations in relation to what she considered legitimate forms of content, by explicitly letting students know that the course would not attempt to solidify a list of behaviours that are "usual" for men and for women. In terms of content, I was questioning the legitimacy of knowledge that had opted to ignore, in the context of gender and communication, the significance of queer norms and experience. Further, by inserting such content, I questioned the validity of generalizable knowledge as a form of knowing. I was rattling constructions and forms of knowledge in which broad, seemingly universal assertions were legitimate and preferred to lived practice. I was also suggesting that acontextual and generalizable knowledge claims might be internally unsound.

In contrast to Cindy, Allison seemed eager to investigate how knowledge about race and about gender overlapped, and to attend to power and specificity. She commented on her sense of a disconnect from nation a few weeks later in the term than when Cindy made her insertion, and offered her comments following a reading on intersectionality. Addressing this concept, that day's reading stated that "people live multiple, layered identities derived from social relations, history, and the operation of structures of power." An intersectional approach to social issues grapples with both "unique individual experiences" based on one's membership in multiple identity groups, and "historical, social and political contexts." Directly challenging an additive approach, or one that argues that "the combining of identities additively increase[es] one's burden," intersectionality focuses on the ways in which distinct combinations of identity produce qualitatively different experiences (Association for Women's Rights in Development, 2004, p. 2).

Allison considered knowledge that would account for gender and race. Even as she did not risk such consideration with the class as a whole, and offered it in a reflection paper that I read, Allison indicated an openness to both epistemological content and form that had seemed to make Cindy uneasy. As I noted in chapter 1, when I asked students about where they placed queer lives in relation to gender, students stated firmly that "sexual identity shouldn't matter" and that "gays and lesbians are exceptions." What had led Cindy, and at least some of her peers, to believe that our knowledge about gender, about living as men and women, could legitimately exclude specific types of bodies? How had the maintenance of certain conceptual categories become more valuable than the lives of those such categories ignored?

Cindy had most likely come to expect both particular content and forms of knowledge in her courses. She noted her desire for streamlined education precisely at the moment when I stated plainly that queer lives would be part of the gendered subject, which also simultaneously challenged the unquestioned legitimacy of broad generalizations. In a sense, Cindy's epistemological architecture was most aligned with broad generalizations about living as women and as men, particularly when those generalizations did not challenge her world view. It was most likely easy for Cindy to affirm, for example, that women are generally nurturing and that men typically have a hard time communicating their emotions. Yet, I was fundamentally challenging not only Cindy's epistemological content, or the specifics of such generalizations, and the validity of the idea that women as a homogeneous, fixed group are generally more nurturing. I also offered a challenge to Cindy's epistemological architecture and called into question the utility, possibility, and desirability of "usual" behaviours for "men" and "women."

In normalizing specific knowledge content and forms for knowledge, faculty members contribute to students' expectations and influence the ways in which they will be more or less able to move towards democratic practices, the public good, and justice. At a minimum, such movement will require the ability to consider the materiality of all social life, even and especially when such attention to embodied, lived experience challenges conceptual categories that have emptied themselves of the material. Whatever Cindy wanted to believe about gender and communication, individuals had repeatedly removed the queer student banner from its location on campus. Education that habitualizes democratic forms of living will not reject materiality, the negotiation of power, and lived experience. To what extent do most courses reward students for placing a higher value on generalizable content than on the materiality of the social, or the ways in which embodied experience might challenge such content? In many ways, we teach students to dismiss difference, and to conceptually minimize the relevance of power and of competing interests.

At the same time, students are active, resistant, and unruly learners. They do not respond in even or predictable ways to the course content and epistemological possibilities that faculty members offer. Further, students are differently positioned, and they come to university and to the classes that we teach with different knowledges. In the intercultural communication course, for example, Gloria came with knowledge about police violence and about her community's distrust of the police. In the gender and communication course, Allison came with knowledge about how individuals and institutions in Canada had contributed to supporting a disconnect from nation. These knowledges exist and are significant. Faculty members offer epistemological and pedagogical norms that establish some subjects as more valid than others. As one scholar states, the history of knowledge in Western frameworks "has allowed Western man (the gendered term is intentionally used here) to represent his knowledge as the only one capable of achieving a universal consciousness, and to dismiss non-Western knowledge as particularistic and, thus, unable to achieve universality." This, in turn, has led to "a hierarchy of superior and inferior knowledge and, thus, of superior and inferior people" (Grosfoguel, 2007, p. 214). An epistemological insistence on ranking, on "a hierarchy of superior and inferior knowledge," is a dehumanizing and, ultimately, violent act. Faculty members can opt to make epistemological moves that resist such dehumanization and violence. I will next examine the ways in which (1) traditional epistemological norms, (2) epistemological attention to difference, and (3) textbooks support specific epistemological architectures.

Epistemological Approaches to Constituting the Subject

Traditional Epistemologies

Traditional epistemologies have asserted that knowledge is "pure, abstract, rational, universal, dispassionate, and entirely disconnected from the knower" (Simpson, 2003, p. 73). Feminists and others have criticized traditional epistemologies for their insistence on "abstract, rationalistic, and universal" claims that "can be applied to all people in the same way" (p. 74). According to this critique, "the disembodied and unlocated neutrality and objectivity" of Western forms of knowledge is a "myth" (Grosfoguel, 2007, p. 214). While feminist epistemologists have faulted traditional epistemologies for their refusal to substantively consider the significance of women to all social life, postmodernists have challenged essentialized notions of truth and the idea of a "coherent, stable self" (Flax, 1990, p. 30). Even as such critique is widespread, knowledge that is easily generalizable still has considerable power and legitimacy in nearly all disciplines (Lander, 2009).

Two concepts are central to traditional epistemologies. First, these theories of knowing assume that "social and physical relationships everywhere conform to the same principles, and these principles are universally good" (Simpson, 2003, p. 74). As many scholars have pointed out, these principles have consistently been Western and Eurocentric, and have made claims to universality even as they have always been particular (Mignolo, 2009; Smith, 2001). In effect, Western epistemologies have "hid[den] the location of the subject of enunciation" or disembodied the knower (Grosfoguel, 2007, p. 214). Abstract theories, detached from any concrete practice, have become authoritative and naturalized. The force of such theories diminishes the need to ask about their origins, about what the knowledge makers might be assuming, or about the interests that are at stake.

Second, traditional epistemologies claim that "a homogeneous form of reason exists within all humans and this reason is not determined or affected by other (heterogeneous) factors such as desire or historical experience" (Flax, 1990, p. 149). Following directly from the first principle of universality, "By delinking ethnic/racial/gender/sexual epistemic location from the subject that speaks, Western philosophy and sciences are able to produce a myth about a Truthful universal knowledge" (Grosfoguel, 2007, p. 213) in ways that construct the knower and what is known as detached from structures of power. These two assumptions have supported several central tenets of traditional epistemologies, including the ideas that knowledge requires distancing between the knower and known, or "subject" and "object"; that emotions should be entirely absent from all processes of knowing; and that ethics are inappropriate to producing and representing knowledge (Collins, 2000). Again, such epistemological assumptions easily lead to forms of knowing that might reject the material. As soon as knowers begin considering the demands of the social, of a particular and embodied "we," ethics, interests, and power, all components of knowledge that traditional epistemologies have rejected, are active.

In the context of an extensive critique of such scholarly norms in a variety of disciplines, to what extent has this critique substantively altered knowledge representation in pedagogical settings? Many faculty members have a strong grasp of the shortcomings of traditional epistemologies. We might discuss with our students, for example, the idea that reality is socially constructed, or that context is significant to all lived reality. Both of these ideas, at their best, resist broad generalizations and claims detached from specific settings and sets of interests. Yet, in the day-to-day rigours and demands of classroom teaching, particularly in large, lower division undergraduate courses, we repeatedly offer knowledge that is acontextual and generalizable, and that appears to be disinterested. As I discussed in chapters 4 and 5, liberal norms have a close fit with such epistemological priorities, including an interest in generalizable truths and a rejection of interests and of ethics. Traditional epistemologies, in concert with liberal norms, had firmly established the epistemological architecture on which Cindy had come to rely, and to which she turned when I suggested that queer lives might be part of the subject. How do epistemologies leave room for a "we," for forms of sociality that reject the false rhetorical and epistemological constructions of universal, predictable, and disinterested knowledge claims?

Epistemological Approaches to Difference

In addition to (1) students' and faculty members' expectations and (2) traditional theories of knowledge, epistemological approaches to difference constitute a third site of practice in regard to constructions of the subject in any given course. Inasmuch as traditional epistemologies have aimed for universalizable, generalizable, and detached knowledge claims, such epistemologies have, in effect, made difference unknowable, particularly when these differences (in terms of communities, interests, or ideas) challenge dominant norms. Consideration of difference as a category is, at a very basic level, a refusal of conventional forms of knowledge, as any robust attention to difference must reject or at least question the possibility of generalizability. At the same time, it has become increasingly untenable in intellectual discourse to act as if gender, race, sexuality, class, ability, and other markers of difference do not exist. While some scholars have responded to this tension by opting to pursue epistemological frameworks that "de-link" (Mignolo, 2009) as much as possible from Western epistemological norms, the great majority of educators have opted to accept the legitimacy of such norms, even as these educators might simultaneously note the limitations of Western epistemological frameworks. Further, rigorous critique of such limitations, as well as the suggestion of alternate frameworks (i.e., frameworks that aim to do more than identify the limits of Western approaches) rarely make their way into undergraduate classrooms.

constructor of
knowledge to
ignore
diff

One component of the epistemological rationale that may have led to
Cindy's demand for streamlined education is visible in how gender has
been epistemologically constructed, a process that has, in many ways,
ignored differences among women. In the 1960s and 1970s, feminist
scholars in the humanities, social sciences, and natural sciences asserted
that existing scholarship, for the most part, had taken "men, their lives,
and their beliefs as the human norm" (Harding & Hintikka, 1983, p. x).
On the whole, existing knowledge production in North America, at
the time, was carried out by European American men and represented
white men as the norm. In response, as increasing numbers of women
entered faculty positions, feminists and other scholars began to add
women to the practices of knowledge production and representation.
In fields such as history (Kelly-Gadol, 1987), psychology (Sherif, 1987),
sociology (Hartmann, 1987; Smith, 1987), and communication (Wood,
1993), feminist scholars offered challenges to disciplinary knowledge
that ignored or insufficiently explored gender. Increasingly, scholars
began to understand and position women as knowers and as relevant
to intellectual analysis.

At the same time, such incursions into mainstream academic thought
and an interest in academic legitimation required feminist scholars to
consider and be responsive to existing epistemological methods. Likewise, many feminist scholars made claims that generalized gender-based
oppression. On the one hand, feminist scholars criticized generalizable
knowledge as it left out women. At the same time, these same scholars, in
producing knowledge about women, "did not specify to which women
they were referring" (Simpson, 2003, p. 81).

Feminist scholars clearly faced a contradiction in legitimizing knowledge by and about women. They were pointing to the value of specificity
and particularity in a context that required universality and generalizability. Even as many white feminist scholars brought women into
mainstream intellectual discourse, they also, to a large extent, accepted
the terms of that discourse. This ensured that much of the knowledge
about women was generalizable. Scholars in numerous disciplines, and
particularly women of colour, have offered a robust critique of this type
of feminist scholarship (Bernal, 2006). These scholars have urged consideration of a range of socially structured groups, identified by gender,
race, class, sexuality, and ability. This approach is often termed intersectional, and routinely places lived experience at the centre of intellectual
analysis. These scholars have advocated for epistemological norms that
value partiality and that require consideration of context and ethics.

One response to this critique has been to add superficial content about specific groups such as women or people of colour onto existing bodies of knowledge. This can increase the visibility of knowledge about groups that scholars previously ignored. It also potentially sets up a knowledge hierarchy, in which one body of knowledge is perceived as universal and with the most value, and several secondary bodies of knowledge that address non-dominant groups are understood to possess less value and legitimacy. As feminist historian Tessie Liu has commented, "adding diversity in" while simultaneously leaving unchanged epistemological and methodological norms "merely sprinkles color onto a white background" (1994, pp. 571, 572). In contrast, analysing "difference in social structural terms, in terms of interests, of privileges, and of deprivations" (p. 575) draws attention to power and to the reality of interests as embedded in all processes of knowledge production and representation.

While this chapter does not aim to offer an extensive review of traditional epistemologies and epistemological and various disciplinary treatments of difference, this overview points to the ways in which epistemological, intellectual, and disciplinary histories and norms shape curricula and pedagogy, influence what constitutes the subject, and contribute to epistemological architectures. Is "the subject" in a course on gender and communication broad generalizations about "usual" behaviours for men and women? Or is the subject the ways in which individuals and institutions construct spaces for gendered bodies, which are simultaneously straight and queer, raced and classed? What possibilities for defining the subject do traditional epistemologies and approaches to gender offer? Cindy's demand for streamlined education was, given epistemological, disciplinary, and liberal educational norms, very sensible. She had learned that generalizable, acontextual knowledge was to be valued, even as it also, at some level, required her to ignore what was happening on campus and its relationship to knowledge about gender and communication.

It is quite common for disciplinary representations of knowledge to "add on" queer or raced lives to existing curricular content. A text might include a chapter or two on these groups. In the gender course, however, I was stating from the outset that queer lives were not an exception, not to be slotted into a special section of the course. When texts or faculty members do "add on" a chapter or a unit, yet leave the rest of the book or course intact, what do we communicate to students? Fully acknowledging the social, grappling with the ways in which all

public life is constituted by relational negotiations of power, points to
the idea of difference as ontologically and epistemologically constitutive. Why are we willing to leave any lives "behind"? In what ways
does the acceptance of generalizations and of existing forms of knowledge production and representation legitimate and even require the
dismissal of the lives of those in non-dominant groups? How does such
a move differently value, for example, queer and straight bodies? How
do existing epistemologies, which become authoritative in our courses,
render lives that fall outside of or resist universal categories? How do
our own epistemological practices normalize, differentiate, and value
specific assumptions and assertions about reality and social life? In the
next section, I discuss an additional site of knowing for Cindy and her
peers, that of textbooks.

Textbooks as Sites of Knowing

In this chapter, I am centrally concerned with the ways in which
routine approaches to knowledge in the classroom make it more or
less likely that students will have the capacities to grapple with the
demands of public life. If, as I argued in chapter 4, all life is relational,
power matters, inequity exists, and democratic societies require a language and imagination for the public good and for justice, the ways
in which our students learn to take in the "not yet" of knowledge,
particularly of knowledge that has to do with the material and with
embodied experience, is crucial. How do students learn to consider a
"we" and, in particular, a "we" that is varied, at times contradictory,
and burdened with systems of inequity and injustice? In the process
of engaging such a "we," students' abilities to offer broad, acontextual
generalizations that are supposedly "interest free" will have limited
to no utility. In contrast, when students like Cindy, Allison, and their
peers have an understanding of living together well, can take in the
demands of specific situations and of an ungeneralizable materiality,
and address power (all areas I will explore further in chapter 7), they
may be more likely to consider knowledge that can speak to such considerations.

I am interested in textbooks as sites of knowing because of their
prevalence in undergraduate courses. Textbooks are a primary component of students' education. While the centrality of textbooks does vary
in terms of (1) their existence as the only reading material in a course or
as one source among many, (2) the degree to which any given faculty

content in textbooks will bear on how students see

person critiques or challenges the textbook, and (3) the significance of the textbook as the basis for and means of evaluation of student work, textbooks tend to have levels of authority and consistency shared by few other components of students' education. Epistemological content in textbooks will bear on how students see. If textbooks repeatedly construct specific communities as not worth conceptual consideration, and likewise represent dominant groups as a norm, we can expect that many students will, to some extent, adopt and expect this epistemological framework. Such frameworks also indicate what students might do with content that challenges dominant norms, such as content about queer or racialized communities. I am particularly interested in how textbooks deny or support particular epistemological architectures, and in what they teach Cindy and her peers about knowledge that is "not yet." In this section, I examine (1) broad contextual factors for textbooks especially with regard to social and disciplinary norms, (2) the ways in which textbooks represent epistemological frameworks and (3) how textbooks offer attention to what falls outside of the generalizable categories on which most textbooks rely to communicate knowledge.

Given the extensive use of textbooks and the significant role they play in students' education, scholars have produced relatively little work on the epistemological import of textbooks. While critical theorists have offered the most ongoing attention to the role of textbooks over the past two decades (Apple & Christian-Smith, 1991; Aronowitz & Giroux, 1991), this body of work is quite small. Further, while a few studies examine practices specific to textbooks in particular disciplines, a literature search resulted in very little scholarship that examined the epistemological significance of undergraduate textbooks across the social sciences and humanities at a meta-level. Likewise, I found few to no studies that centrally addressed how textbooks construct particular ways of knowing that bear on how students understand the "we" of public life. Most studies were concerned with epistemological content, rather than the forms of knowledge that textbooks affirm and deny. My discussion of textbooks is aimed at drawing attention to their possible consequences for how students understand the social. I have no interest in offering "cause-effect" types of conclusions that make claims to any kind of certainty or predictability. As one of many "sites of knowing" that students routinely encounter in their courses, how do textbooks encourage students to consider the subject and to grapple with knowledge that is "not yet"?

Textbooks and Social and Disciplinary Norms

Scholarship on textbooks has broadly addressed (1) the ways in which textbooks reflect interests and positions (Apple, 1992; Aronowitz & Giroux, 1991) and (2) how textbooks have responded to methodological and epistemological disciplinary shifts (Johnston, 2000). At one level, scholars clearly assert that textbooks reflect political interests, largely sustain dominant norms, and contain an authorial position (Apple, 1992; Ferguson, Collison, Power, & Stevenson, 2009). Even as the authors of textbooks write them to appear as if they represent a body of knowledge that simply exists, wholly separate from the fray of social interactions and intellectual debates in a discipline, scholars have claimed in clear terms that "text[book]s are not simply 'delivery systems' of 'facts.' They are at once the results of political, economic, and cultural activities, battles, and compromises ... They are published within the political and economic constraints of materials, resources, and power" (Apple & Christian-Smith, 1991, pp. 1–2). Textbooks must meet specific contextual demands, including serving as a source of financial gain for the publisher. They also communicate ideological frameworks and references "which provide but do not rigidly determine particular views of the world" (Aronowitz & Giroux, 1991, p. 215). Further, even as textbooks may be updated, "major ideological frameworks do not markedly change" (Apple, 1992, p. 8).

Textbooks contain forms of knowledge representation and delivery that sustain concrete ways of thinking about the social world, and these ways of thinking have links to ideologies. Scholars have pointed out that textbooks may appear to students as if they represent a disembodied package of knowledge that simply exists, seemingly outside of interests, possible partiality or errors, and particular world views. However, all textbooks are written by "real people" (Apple & Christian-Smith, 1991, p. 2), and necessarily "reflect the author's position, even those which seek to write a discipline's history from a non-paradigmatic stance" (Johnston, 2000, p. 274). In sum, textbooks are largely successful in representing existing ideologies, appearing to be interest and even author free, and legitimating significant amounts of content, even as textbooks are always partial and exclusionary artefacts (McDowell, 1994).

Disciplinary shifts, especially those related to epistemology, have posed challenges to the content and format of textbooks. Theories of knowing have changed from emphasizing (or at least assuming) a fixed idea of an acontextual and universal Truth, to a view of knowledge that foregrounds its partiality and contextuality. To what extent do textbooks reflect these epistemological changes, related both to knowledge content and the forms in which knowledge is delivered? Again, given the prevalence of textbooks in undergraduate education, the paucity of studies on these issues is notable. On the whole, the scholarship that does exist asserts that textbooks in specific disciplines "often ... promote monopolistic, authoritative approaches to knowledge" (Johnston, 2000, p. 271). For example, geography is a discipline in which, at the level of knowledge production, "researchers accept the arguments regarding polyphony," and demonstrate "wide ... appreciation of many of the postmodern and poststructuralist arguments regarding the futility of searching for general (grand) theories" (p. 271). While this acceptance might have "had a major impact on research in the discipline, it has had much less on its teaching" (p. 273). Such studies suggest that one cannot assume that scholarly shifts in disciplinary approaches to knowledge over the past couple of decades have substantively altered how textbooks approach and represent such knowledge.

Textbooks and the Communication of Epistemological Norms

Textbooks both (1) present specific content as "natural, fixed, and inevitable" (N. Rice, 2005, p. 407) and (2) have either refused or resisted adaptation to epistemological shifts across the disciplines. In such a context, how might the process of "enculturating students to a particular world-view ... without also reflecting on the epistemologies involved ... be more akin to indoctrination than to democratic education" (Roth, 2001, p. 21)? Or, put another way, how do textbooks set up parameters for defining the subject? Textbooks, especially those that present the knowledge they contain as context-free, universal, and apositional (i.e., not rooted in specific sets of interests, world views, and assumptions) set up these parameters at three levels. First, textbooks and the knowledge they represent operate in relationship to widely accepted social norms. Second, textbooks communicate broad assertions about a specific topic within a disciplinary framework. Finally, textbooks affirm which types or forms of knowledge are legitimate and which are not.

Textbooks and Social Norms. At a very broad level, textbooks in many ways affirm broadly held social norms and resonate with liberal social thought. In brief, "textbooks ... seek to anchor the political and social norms of a society" (Ferguson et al., 2009, p. 897). Further, inasmuch as textbooks naturalize and leave unquestioned much of the content they represent, students are likely to understand textbooks as a kind of benign yet unassailable fact of their education. Rather than engaging in "dialogue and struggle over the meanings and practices of a historical tradition," textbooks tend to support "learning [as] defined primarily through a pedagogy of transmission ... [and of] unrelated catalogues of shared information" (Aronowitz & Giroux, 1991, p. 226). In this sense, textbooks function for students simultaneously as (1) a link between formal educational settings and the world outside of the classroom and (2) a primary source of "structured dispositions that generate patterned ... perceptions and with it the field of possible ... patterned actions" (Roth, 2001, p. 6). As the textbook increasingly occupies this socio-epistemological space, students can then rely on the habitus that textbooks communicate to accept and dismiss a range of subject matter. Inasmuch as textbooks align with liberal social norms, including, as I noted in chapter 4, the beliefs that institutions are beneficent, that knowledge is disinterested, and that the rational individual is the primary starting point for intellectual and ethical analysis, students like Cindy will find a general alignment between textbooks and mainstream ideologies.

 Representation of Content. At a second level, textbooks communicate specific areas of content relevant to a discipline and to a particular course. Textbooks "help set the canons of truthfulness and ... re-create a major reference point for what knowledge, culture, belief, and morality really *are*" (Apple & Christian-Smith, 1991, p. 4; emphasis in original). Even before Cindy and her peers had begun the gender and communication course, they all had specific ideas about how the course might consider, for example, queer and raced lives. Textbooks play a role in constructing such ideas. In one of the few analyses of the ways in which textbooks in a specific discipline communicate particular content, Schwartz-Shea and Yanow (2002) assert in their study of several textbooks covering research methods in political science that "uniformity of philosophical approach ... obtains across all 14 texts" (p. 459). Importantly, through repeated affirmation and normalization of positivist methods, and with little to no thoughtful attention to interpretive epistemological approaches, textbooks "narrow the possible range of subjects that can 'legitimately' (in terms of the discipline) be explored, rather than a research agenda driven by what it is that one wants to know" (2002, p. 477). Students learn that "choos[ing] the interpretation that best rules out alternative explanations" is desirable (p. 474). Likewise, over time, students can rely on textbooks in early courses to assert in subsequent courses that lives falling outside of broad norms are not part of the subject.

Textbooks and Acceptable Forms of Knowledge. A third area in which textbooks communicate appropriate methods for determining the subject is in regard to the ways in which they solidify certain epistemological architectures, or "structures of believability." In other words, textbooks construct for students the possible means through which they might judge knowledge that is "not yet," or knowledge that for them is new, challenging, or outside of "the subject." On the whole, the commonality of generalizable, disinterested concepts in textbooks profoundly affects both what students learn and the capacities they have and do not have for knowledge that insists on different criteria. Cumulatively, if textbooks repeatedly ignore, for example, the ways in which race bears on specific areas of content, it is not surprising that students, too, learn to ignore race, or at least to assume that it is not part of course content.

In a study of textbooks in the discipline of accounting, Ferguson, Collison, Power, and Stevenson (2009) conducted an ideological analysis of six financial accounting textbooks. More specifically, the authors sought to understand how "power is embedded in these texts" (p. 897) and how the books "present a particular worldview whereby the interests of ownership and management are often prioritised" (p. 898). Ferguson et al. conclude that of modes of ideological operation, the most "prevalent ... was that of legitimation" (2009, p. 907). According to Thompson (1990), "relations of domination may be established and sustained ... by being represented as legitimate" (p. 61). Legitimation is accomplished through strategies of rationalization, universalization, and narrativization, or presenting content as naturalized and timeless. These strategies serve to "rationalize social relations" and claim "that institutional relations that serve a few groups are benefiting everyone" (Ferguson et al., 2009, p. 900). Other commonalities across all six textbooks include an absence of attention to ethics and to the "social and political context" (p. 908).

As these authors point out, inasmuch as textbooks "neglect ... to address the social and political aspects of accounting, or issues of power," they "could be accused of maintaining the ideological status quo" (p. 908). Again, if textbooks repeatedly legitimize knowledge as interest-free, generalizable, and outside of ethical concerns, students can then assume that it is fully appropriate to reject knowledge that is explicitly partial and that is transparent regarding its ethical priorities. Rejecting all partial knowledge because one believes such knowledge is structurally illegitimate (i.e., that partial knowledge is not knowledge) necessarily results in refusing consideration of the lives such knowledge addresses.

For faculty members interested in undergraduate education that turns towards a "we" and the material, it is difficult to overestimate the power of textbooks to work against the habits of democratic living. Textbooks accomplish this work through their refusal of the material, and in their profound (yet invisible to many students) affirmation of knowledge that is both context- and interest-free. The lack of studies on the significance of textbooks both within specific disciplines and at a meta-level does point to the impossibility of making any definitive claims regarding the ways in which textbooks set up possibilities for knowing. Yet to wholly refuse consideration of their pedagogical and epistemological significance has highly problematic consequences, and particularly for educators who have even a modest interest in or commitment to education that can speak to difficult social issues. For students like Cindy, textbooks may have had considerable power in her 30 or so courses prior to the gender and communication course. Given the ways in which textbooks affirm existing social norms, frequently make acontextual claims, and legitimize generalizable knowledge, we ought not to be surprised when Cindy or her peers call for streamlined education and demonstrate no apparent hesitation in resisting consideration of queer lives. Textbooks rarely encourage students like Cindy to "place themselves in networks of power in relation to others" (McDowell, 1994, p. 246). Textbooks also send specific messages to students in terms of individuals, communities, and ideas that challenge dominant forms of knowledge. In other words, textbooks teach Cindy and her peers what to do with queer communities in a class on gender and communication. In sum, textbooks both routinely construct disembodied subjects and downplay the importance of materiality and lived experience.

Textbooks and "Different" Subjects

In the gender and communication course, Cindy and Allison were both grappling with how to make sense of the ways in which the category of "gender" sets up possibilities for constructing meaning. How do textbooks, and particularly the forms of epistemological legitimation they affirm, offer possibilities for subjects that fall outside of conceptual norms? What do textbooks do with "difference"? Applying the descriptor of "difference" to certain types of knowledge and bodies is itself an anti-material move. Making a claim of "difference" requires a standard from which to be different, and thus implicitly affirms that the dominant group sets the ontological terms of existence for all other groups. Quite simply, the existence of difference requires the presence of and investment in sameness. For example, when Allison noted her disconnect from nation, specifically experienced through her gendered and racialized body, she refused to label the racialized component of her experience as external to gender. Separating these aspects of her existence would have required a refusal of the material. Using the label of "different" to refer to race when thinking about gender asserts a norm that perceives race to be irrelevant. Marking raced and queer lives as "different," or as somehow peripheral to the experience of gender, points to the limited and, in fact, profoundly flawed constitution of gender that refuses to understand the ordinariness of bodies that are simultaneously constructed along several planes of existence. If we assume the inevitability of positioned bodies, and the existence of power and interests, difference is a given. No body (or community) occupies an undifferentiated space in terms of positionality and power.

The primary frame of reference through which scholars have worked at insisting on epistemologies that engage the fact of difference in the context of textbooks is through an understanding of dominant and subordinate groups (see chapter 4 for discussion of how this book understands these groups). At a broad level, scholars have asserted that positivist and mainstream constructions of knowledge have differently positioned these groups:

> the circle of dominant ideas *does* accumulate the symbolic power to map or classify the world for others; its classifications do not acquire only the constraining power of dominance over other modes of thought but also the initial authority of habit and instinct. It becomes the horizon of the taken-for-granted: what the world is and how it works, for all practical purposes. Ruling ideas may dominate other conceptions of the social world by setting the limit on what will appear as rational, reasonable, credible, indeed sayable or thinkable within the given vocabularies of motive and action available to us. Their dominance lies precisely in the power they

have to contain within their limits, to frame within their circumference of
thought, the reasoning and calculation of other social groups. (Hall, 1988,
p. 44; emphasis in original)

According to Hall, then, dominant epistemologies quite literally determine the terms of subjecthood for subordinate groups. Faculty members and students can then legitimately rely on such terms to ensure
that what "appears sayable or thinkable" falls within dominant norms.

How have textbooks carried out the processes that Hall describes?
For the most part, textbooks determine the "horizon of the taken-for-
granted" in two ways. Textbooks (1) require that the realities, experiences, ontologies, and epistemologies of subordinate groups are made
sense of through dominant frames and (2) "add onto" existing content, or "include" the concerns and priorities of subordinate groups
and thereby leave problematic epistemological frameworks in place.
Concerning the first practice, textbooks routinely "incorporat[e] the
knowledge and perspectives of the less powerful under the umbrella
of the discourse of dominant groups" (Apple, 1992, p. 8). Dominant
discourses thus legitimately deny subjecthood to less powerful groups.
In regard to the second practice, textbooks might include a "small and
often separate section" on "'the contributions of women' and 'minority
groups,' but without any elaboration of the view of the world as seen
from their perspective" (p. 8). Again, when students repeatedly read
textbooks that naturalize both practices, faculty members should not
be surprised that students object to constitutions of the subject that call
into question the assumptions of dominant discourses.

How have textbooks on gender, in particular, addressed queer lives?
A variety of studies have affirmed that textbooks often "problematiz[e]
LGBT issues and marginaliz[e] LGBT identity" (Macgillivray & Jennings, 2008, p. 174; see also Hogben & Waterman, 1997; Simoni, 1996;
and Young & Middleton, 2002).[2] When they do address LGBT issues,
textbooks often offer the most depth to issues such as suicide, AIDS,
and drug abuse. Marginalization, or what the authors of one article on
introductory sociology textbooks refer to as a "lingering heteronormativity" (Suarez & Balaji, 2007, p. 246), occurs when, for example, heterosexual norms are presented as the "ruler" for queer lives. A statement
such as "'gay partnerships are far more like heterosexual relationships
than they are different,' which may appear benign at face value, has the
effect of reinforcing heterosexual relationships as the norm by which to
judge and compare all others" (Macgillivray & Jennings 2008, p. 175). In

sum, such problematization and marginalization will encourage under-standings of queer subjecthood that are wholly contained within and subject to straight norms and expectations. Again, Cindy's demand is quite sensible in such a framework.

Approaches to queer lives in introductory textbooks on gender are instructive. One is increasingly able to find references to, for example, heteronormativity and transgender issues in introductory chapters (see, e.g., Holmes, 2007). Yet, how do textbooks sustain such attention to differently gendered bodies throughout the remainder of the book? In *What Is Gender? Sociological Approaches*, Holmes (2007) does attend to heteronormativity and intersex individuals. Yet, in her chapter on gender and bodies, she makes almost no explicit reference to straight and queer bodies. On the whole, throughout that textbook, straight-ness is assumed, and queerness goes unmentioned. Many textbooks addressing gender might include one chapter on sexuality and make only passing reference to sexuality in the dozen or so additional chap-ters. Introductory psychology textbooks, which students frequently encounter in lower division courses, consider concepts such as con-sciousness, memory, human development, language and thought, and behaviour and biology. Likewise, sociology textbooks in introductory courses often cover areas including the self, identity, socialization, rela-tionships, stratification, and structures. Such concepts serve as chapter topics and conceptual cornerstones in these textbooks. On the whole, attention to context is largely superficial, with dominant norms most often referenced and assumed. In the 500 or more pages in such text-books, queer lives may be briefly referenced a dozen or so times, and never substantively addressed (see, e.g., Weiten & McCann, 2007; New-man, 2008).

Inasmuch as undergraduate education might offer possibilities for students to consider the reality of "too much wrong," textbooks offer students routes to and rewards for the dismissal of lives that disrupt "political assumptions about the social world" and that challenge the "existing social order" (Wachholz & Mullaly, 2001, p. 55). Even as all "text[books] are open to multiple readings" (Apple, 1992, p. 10), textbooks are perhaps the most consistent and familiar resource for students throughout their undergraduate education, and have consid-erable influence in shaping the epistemological architectures on which students come to rely. In terms of considering democratic practices, the public good, and justice, students will need to be able to consider the "creation and recreation of meanings and values" and to participate in the "deliberation of what is important" (Apple & Christian-Smith, 1991, p. 15). How can we ensure that "social transformation" becomes more important than the "preservation of the current relations of production and reproduction" (Wachholz & Mullaly, 2001, p. 56)? How do textbooks place acontextual, generalizable concepts ahead of lives? What do students learn to do with lives that challenge concepts? Finally, how does the dismissal of lives that challenge dominant concepts fit with broader public discourse and ideologies? In the next section, I analyse the ways in which epistemological architectures that privilege concepts at the expense of lives can lead to what I call epistemological neoliberalism, or practices of knowing that profoundly narrow the space for what it means to be human.

The Logic of an "I": Epistemological Neoliberalism

Students routinely consider the fit of an "I" with a "we," or the intersection of the self with what Dewey has called the practices of "associated living" (1998, p. 390). The first part of this chapter examined the ways in which routine and consequential sites of knowing inform how students work out the fit of an "I" with a "we," and the means through which students and faculty members identify and practise ethical and relational loyalties and allegiances. These sites of knowing – student and faculty member expectations, traditional theories of knowledge, epistemological approaches to difference, and textbooks – are, for the most part, located and negotiated within formal pedagogical settings. How might broad ideologies of consumerism and individual gain, and even more specifically economic and ideological forms of neoliberalism, work as additional sites of knowing for students and faculty members? I claim in the second part of this chapter that neoliberalism, in its relentless interest in "simplification" and efficiency (Couldry, 2010, p. 6), works in concert with traditional epistemologies and desires in the interests of streamlined education. Further, "the *embedding* of neoliberalism as rationality in everyday social organization and imagination" (p. 5; emphasis in original) ensures that justifications for streamlined rationalities exist in multiple locations; are easy for students and faculty members to access, whether or not we do so consciously; and encourage the dismissal of lives that do not fit dominant norms. After providing a brief overview of neoliberalism and neoliberal ideology, I will discuss neoliberal epistemologies and the ways in which they act against possibilities for considering democratic practices, the public good, and justice.

Neoliberalism: An Overview

Neolib
def

Neoliberalism, often recognized as the "economic variant" of liberal-ism (Brown, 2005, p. 39), "insists that there is no other valid principle of human organization than market functioning" (Couldry, 2010, p. 11). Operating "across the whole of social life" (p. 12), neoliberalism is an ideological and political project that narrows understandings of what it means to be human and the possibilities for community (Brown, 2005; Duggan, 2003; Miller & Rose, 2008). At the level of socio-economic pol-icy, neoliberalism is maintained by institutions and those with power "act[ing] primarily in the direct interests of Western creditors and corporations, transferring wealth from the globe's poorest to its rich-est locations" (Duggan, 2003, p. 11). "Borrow[ing] and appropriat[ing] extensively from classic liberal ideas" (Hall, 2012, p. 15), neoliberalism asserts that market-based ideals will ensure the maximum creation of wealth and, in turn, a high quality of life for all. Below, I comment briefly on the history and scope of neoliberalism, and then examine neoliberal links to constituting the subject and engaging the material.

The concepts of "'neoliberalism proper'" and "'neoliberal doctrine'" shed light on the broad scope of neoliberal practice (Couldry, 2010, p. 5). Neoliberalism proper refers to economic theory and principles formu-lated in the 1980s to 2000s that "install market functioning as the domi-nant reference-point of economics and ... [the] political and social order as well" (p. 5). This theory expressly attends to the ways in which the economy ought to relate to society. It relies on thinkers such as Ludwig von Mises, Friedrich von Hayak, and Milton Friedman, and claims that "individual liberty and freedom can best be protected and achieved by an institutional structure, made up of strong property rights, free markets, and free trade" (Harvey, 2011, p. 43). Neoliberalism proper, or the economic theory on which practices of neoliberalism are based, has strong ties to liberalism and its emphasis on the individual. Indeed, inasmuch as economists such as von Mises emphasized the "harmony of rightly understood interests of individuals" (1983, p. 182; see also Hall, 2012), neoliberal economics is aligned with central components of liberalism.

These ties between neoliberalism and social and political liberal-ism have supported the primary components of neoliberal doctrine,

particularly in the past two to three decades. Neoliberal doctrine refers
to the ways in which the economic principles of neoliberalism have
become the "working doctrine of many contemporary democracies"
(Couldry, 2010, p. 5). Central to the implementation of neoliberal economic theory across the social landscape has been the general acceptance of the idea that neoliberalism, as an economic set of principles,
ought to be applied to all forms of social organization and public life.
Thus, going well beyond the bounds of the economy, neoliberalism and
market competition have become a desirable and appropriate framework for any and all arenas of social interaction, including government,
public policy, the family, education, and the individual. In other words,
neoliberal "ideas have long been inscribed in social practices and institutions, and sedimented into the 'habitus' of everyday life, common
sense and popular consciousness – 'traces without an inventory'" (Hall,
2012, p. 15; see also Foucault, 2008). In this sense, individuals are readily
able to agree with the idea that government "must work for the game of
market competition" (Burchell, 1996, p. 27). Such a profound prioritization of individual economic gain and market-based logics, applied to
all areas of social life, necessarily has ontological and epistemological
implications.

Neoliberalism asserts a set of values that prioritizes efficiency, sameness, and private gain. The implementation of these values has had
disastrous economic consequences, particularly for poor and working-
class people across the globe (Coronil, 2000). Working at ideological
and social levels, neoliberalism supports the logic of an "I," reduces
the space for a "we," and appears to many a desirable logic even as
it destroys possibilities for the public good. As a framework through
which students and faculty members might approach and imagine the
social, neoliberalism bears on undergraduate education. It serves as
an important "site of knowing," and works alongside other sources of
knowing to shape epistemological architectures. In particular, I understand neoliberal ideologies to play a role in constituting the subject
and denying the material in three ways, through (1) an overwhelming
focus on privatization and personal responsibility, (2) the destruction of
a notion of the public, and (3) a domestification of difference.

Even as corporations rely heavily on the state "openly respond[ing]
to needs of the market" (Brown, 2005, p. 41), neoliberalism insists on
"radical individualists" (Grossberg, 2005, p. 112), privatization, and
personal responsibility. Individuals are constructed as "entrepreneurial actors in every sphere of life" (Brown, 2005, p. 42). Ideas including

"*competition, self-esteem,* and *independence*" (Duggan, 2003, p. 14; emphasis in original) become ideological touchstones for practices of agency. In such a world, "the model neoliberal citizen is one who strategizes for her- or himself among various social, political, and economic options, not one who strives with others to alter or organize these options" (Brown, 2005, p. 43). This focus on the individual and personal responsibility works directly against any notion of ethical relationality. It manufactures what Zygmunt Bauman has termed, in a discussion of social responsibility and morality, the "social production of distance" (1989, p. 192). Any move towards considering one's implicatedness in social life is countered by a logic of "others do not have any obligatory responsibilities for helping us, and we have none toward them" (Young, 2011, p. 11). Neoliberalism ensures that such rationalities appear sensible.

A second logic through which neoliberalism refuses relationality and the material is through the systematic obliteration of any notion of a public. Apart from the existence of markets, or as a means to individualized gain and fulfilment, neoliberalism normalizes the idea that "there is … *no meaning* to the notion of public or social goals" (Couldry, 2010, p. 5; emphasis in original). Thus, while neoliberalism's move to "transform … global cultures into 'market cultures'" (Duggan, 2003, p. 12) might be read as support for and excitement about diverse cultural groups, such a move is, in fact, a reprioritization of economic gain that will benefit, at least in substantive terms, only a very small group of individuals. In another erasure of the public and the existence of differences within that public, "equality" is framed as access to or acceptance in "a few conservatizing institutions" (Duggan, 2002, p. 190). Inasmuch as a "fully realized neoliberal citizenry would be the opposite of public-minded" (Brown, 2005, p. 43), it becomes nearly impossible to imagine public life as constituted by individuals and groups who participate in social practices that involve irrevocably overlapping interests. In sum, neoliberalism "leaves us with an account of the social that lacks any of the features normally associated with public life" (Couldry, 2010, p. 29). Neoliberal ideologies render a sense of the public unimaginable.

Finally, a third area in which neoliberalism guarantees the erasure of a relational subject is through its refusal of difference, and particularly of ontologies and world views that contradict the logics of rationality, efficiency, and competition. Through its focus on individual advancement and privatized longings, neoliberalism systematically constructs the "right" kind of advancement and longings, organized around "individualised, competitive solutions" (Hall, 2012, p. 16). The parameters of acceptability are narrow and restrictive, even as these parameters might be masked by the illusion of choice or a range of consumer options (in the context of products, travel, leisure, etc., accessible to those with money) (Coronil, 2000; Duggan, 2003; Storper, 2000). Two significant moves in this sociocultural framework are particularly relevant to constituting the subject. First, neoliberalism in tandem with "commodity advertising and consumption regimes" constructs a world in which "individuals come to reconceptualize themselves in terms of their own will to be healthy, to enjoy a maximized normality" (Miller & Rose, 2008, p. 211).[3] In this sense, neoliberal institutions and ideologies define success and even regulate acceptance by insisting on a specific way of being human, one that is consistent with the discourse and practices of privatization (Brown, 2005; Duggan, 2003).

A second move within a neoliberal sociocultural framework is the connection of equality, sameness, and recognition. In considering the subjecthood of, for example, queer communities, this connection implies that queer people ought to seek "incorporation into the mainstream" (Richardson, 2005, p. 519). Equality ought to be measured by the extent to which queer communities "have the same values, aspirations, and lifestyles as most heterosexuals and desire nothing more than to be fully integrated into society as it is" (ibid.). Neoliberalism reserves the right to construct all subjects within one very narrow framework (which has been and is oppressive to specific groups). Any resistance to or questioning of this framework is profoundly problematic, and always worthy of censure and dismissal. Equality is not measured by access to institutional power or the ability to make decisions about the communities in which one lives (Brown, 2005; Young, 1990), but rather by the level of recognition (within a dominant framework, and on dominant terms) marginalized groups have achieved (Duggan, 2002; Engel, 2007; Loutzenheiser & MacIntosh, 2004; Richardson, 2005; for a critique of the idea of recognition, see also Coulthard 2007). In such a framework, queer communities and all other groups that in any way transgress neoliberal norms receive a place at the table only through rigorous mechanisms of objectification.

At the level of policy and practice, neoliberal economics increasingly bear on trade, labour, markets, and global exchange networks. In a very concrete example, in reference to the story I told at the start of this chapter about the firing of teacher Brooke Harris by the administrators of the Pontiac Academy of Excellence, neoliberalism systematically isolates workers from any kind of safety net and possibilities for formal grievance procedures in the context of their workplace. Once the administration dismissed Harris, as an "at-will employee" Harris was not able to challenge their decision. At an ideological and discursive level, neoliberalism has gone far beyond the workings of markets, and acts as a form of "institutionalized culture" that "shapes the *organization of space*" (Couldry, 2010 p. 12; emphasis in original) and the "very scaffolding of our political imaginations"(Massey, 2012, p. 99). The logics of neoliberalism, including its focus on the "I," individual gain and fulfilment, self-sufficiency, and what might be termed an anti-social responsibility, are discursively easy to access, often appearing as common sense and even mundane (Massey, 2012).

Further, logics that resist neoliberalism, that emphasize shared responsibility, the public good, and the notion of a "we" based on ideas other than profit and competition are, to a large extent, available yet much harder earned and realized. When harm done against the queer community at my institution entered the classroom space, the future Cindy was able to imagine seemed to offer no room (in any form) to queer lives. Given that our students live surrounded by repeated affirmation of neoliberal ideologies, to what do our students turn in imagining a just and equitable future? Neoliberal ideologies routinely reiterate a desire for a "streamlined" public. Neoliberal longings, expectations organized around "usual" behaviours for men and women, epistemologies in which disembodied generalizations are the most legitimate form of knowing, and textbooks that normalize such generalizations: how do all of these come together to form what might be called epistemological neoliberalism?

Epistemological Neoliberalism

Neoliberalism, as an ideology focused on a privatized "I," is a way of seeing the world that is readily accessible to all of us in the classroom. Neoliberalism and parallel logics of agency "sustain [themselves] by becoming an intimate part of the action frameworks of individuals, how they see themselves and define their interests, how they approach the world" (Storper, 2000, p. 392). Few students are able to wholly ignore the practices of consumerism as a kind of "template or model for the way in which citizens of contemporary Western societies have come to view all their activities" or to resist "consumerism [as] a kind of default philosophy for all modern life" (Campbell, 2004, pp. 41–42). Traditional epistemologies, as well as epistemological approaches to gender, insistently cast queers as others, and define the bounds of acceptability as those that fall in line with straight experiences and expectations. Such regulation of what it means to be human bears on race and ethnicity as well. Cindy was, in effect, asking for an educational framework in which she could narrow or enlarge the space for the subject, depending on what made sense to her. Eliminating queers from the subject, inasmuch as queer lives transgressed straight norms, made sense. Such individualized expressions of agency are, indeed, a form of neoliberalism. Inhabiting the role of regulator in this way would have also made it possible for Cindy to reject Allison's experience and sense-making frameworks. Neoliberalism insists on an architecture of seeing that refuses the existence of a transgressive public.

Epistemological neoliberalism can be defined as structures of knowing that construct and maintain the desirability of frameworks for self and other that endorse a sterilized and often falsely rendered normality, ignore and/or downplay power, and prioritize detached concepts over the material conditions of how people live. Cindy felt what appeared to be an habitualized entitlement in casting out any lives or questions that did not keep her own sense of herself intact. For Cindy, we simply did not need to address living queer or the significance of sexuality in straight lives. In naming the existence of epistemological neoliberalism, I am asserting the inescapable interplay of our ideological allegiances and how and what we know. Neoliberalism, and its relentless attachments to privatization and the destruction of an ethical and relational public, is epistemologically significant. Epistemological neoliberalism elevates notions of self and community in ways that judge dominant cultural practices to be of more value than the practices of subordinate groups. It is bold, as when my students resisted consideration of the relevance of sexuality in their own lives. Epistemological neoliberalism is also subtle, as when prevailing pedagogical moves continue to opt for oversimplification, generalizations, and the split between knowing and doing.

Epistemological neoliberalism constructs the social and the subject in very specific ways. At the level of the social, epistemological neoliberalism prioritizes pedagogical content that easily conforms to the logic of an "I." Examples of such content include course material that fits with getting ahead in the workplace, that does not disturb widely accepted social norms, and that serves to simplify rather than grapple with the world outside of the classroom. This kind of course material can legitimize the narrowing of our obligations to consider social issues and can dismiss the importance of equity to democratic societies. Epistemological neoliberalism imagines a very specific response to what Comaroff and Comaroff (2000) call "the most fundamental question of all: In what consists the social?" (p. 333). In the case of the first course on gender, Cindy defined the social as not encompassing queer lives. In the second course on gender and communication that I reference in chapter 1, Allison asserted a different sense of the social, one that could encompass relational constructions of the self.

In sum, epistemological neoliberalism rests on a privatized and narrow constitution of both the social and the subject. As one author points out, "in education the problem becomes how one comes to think, along with others, the very structures of signification in avowing and disavowing forms of sociality and their grounds of possibility" (Britzman, 1998, p. 55). Neoliberalism bears on the "structures of signification" we invoke. In this sense, Cindy could rely on her own investments in epistemological neoliberalism to simply dismiss my attention to queer lives. Such dismissal renders profoundly irrelevant the existence of heteronormative violence, the ways in which dominant legal and other structures ignore queers, and the routine valuing of straight over anything outside of heteronormative norms. This has significant consequences, for not only the immediate course content that students must examine, but also for the very ways in which they conceive of their relational responsibilities. In this sense, epistemological neoliberalism shapes the imaginaries for self and other from within which our students will act in the communities in which they live. What is the relationship of neoliberalism, our attention to concepts – a central component of any course – and our students' imaginations for the social, for their construction of the "I" and the "we"? Examining the epistemological undercurrents of the pedagogical relationship of lives and concepts will ideally offer increased clarity to how we imagine self and other and consider a transgressive public.

Concepts can be loosely defined as a set of ideas that have explanatory power. Most if not all disciplines, in the context of undergraduate education, assert a set of learning objectives, and identify and then attend to areas of content that ought to constitute the curriculum and have a direct relationship to those objectives. In the humanities and social sciences, concepts rest on explanatory grammars that instructors and students articulate and apply to a variety of contexts. In communication, for example, in an interpersonal communication course, concepts typically include the self, perception, listening, conflict, and relationships. Instructors and texts frequently break down concepts into identifiable blocks. Attention to conflict in the context of an interpersonal communication course, for example, examines definitions of conflict, types of conflict, and conflict management styles. Even as most educators understand the shortcomings of concepts, the ways in which they cannot speak to every variety of lived experience, we are centrally attuned to how to "cover" concepts central to our disciplines and particular to a course. Such concepts often serve as a kind of structural backdrop for our work as educators.

Concrete pedagogical and epistemological practices within neoliberal and dominant epistemological frameworks support the construction of a privatized sociality and narrow subjects. One of these practices is the elevation of concepts over lives. Such elevation allows for the logical dismissal of lives that transgress concepts. Indeed, to maintain the integrity of concepts, such prioritization necessitates this dismissal. Cindy's and Allison's comments draw attention to the relationship of lives and concepts. When I asked students how their constructions of gender, which for the most part assumed an all-encompassing straightness, considered or excluded the undeniable existence of queer lives, many students acted swiftly and decisively to assert that my questions were the problem, not their understanding of concepts. In this sense, the elevation of acontextual concepts, inasmuch as these concepts exclude lives, is a way of denying transgressive publics. The primacy of concepts exacts a dismissal of lives that transgress and renders such lives unknowable in three ways.

First, instructors present concepts that are prominent in many undergraduate classrooms as detached, generalizable ideas. The primary work of these concepts is to explain or address phenomena in our day-to-day lives from a disciplinary perspective. Concepts most often do this work from a position of authority that seemingly transcends context. In this sense, concepts (1) assert their own "subjecthood" (such as in the earlier examples in an interpersonal communication course: identity, perception, conflict) and (2) impose a set of ethical obligations on any content or experience that enters the classroom. In effect, the primacy of concepts can ensure that their logics set the bounds and content of the subject. At the same time, concepts are most often built on a set of dominant norms and thus fit most closely (i.e., have the most effective explanatory power) with the knowledge and world views of those in dominant groups. Thus when we discussed how gender is learned, students could easily leave out sexuality. There was simply no need to consider queer lives or the ways in which heteronormativity might be harmful. Here is where the epistemological primacy of concepts begins to do harm: in their displacement of lives as the subject.

 The assertion of concepts as the epistemological cornerstone by which all else ought to be measured has a strong fit with neoliberalism's emphasis on the desirability of normalization and the elimination of complexity. The orientation to a privatized "I" rather than a richly social "we," alongside a logic of "'self-care' – [one's] ability to provide for their own ends and service their own ambitions" (Brown 2005, p. 42), parallels a pedagogical focus on concepts that do not need to account for non-dominant lives. Further, as one author points out, the "private world" on which neoliberalism insists "appears as an imaginary construction, not a historical reality … [a] rhetorical universe" (Duggan, 2003, p. 13). Cindy's preference for "streamlined" education, an education in which queer lives could be judged as not worth knowing, was also an investment in an "imaginary construction" and not a "historical reality" (p. 13). A few months earlier, individuals had removed a banner on our campus naming the existence of the queer student group on campus. We had briefly discussed this removal in class. The fact of the banner and its removal both affirm the relevance of queer lives in Cindy's educational environment. In an expectation of streamlined education, concepts can serve to substantively refuse the materiality of the worlds in which we live. They can, quite literally, and in profoundly significant ways, change the subject.

Second, this articulation of conceptual universes that have more to do with rhetoric than reality contributes to an epistemological infrastructure that has tiered slots for dominant and subordinate knowledge. Concepts that affirm dominant epistemological logics go unchallenged, while ideas that in any way trouble taken-for-granted norms are ignored or dismissed. At a minimum, such transgressive knowledge – the idea, for example, that my students' lives might be about straight and queer realities as much as they were about being men and being women – is knowledge to be refuted rather than considered. In other words, our pedagogical moves, inasmuch as we place concepts ahead of lives, prescribe normalcy through whom we construct as "entitled to an everyday" (Britzman, 1998, p. 55). Cindy's gendered reality was deserving of a very public "everyday." The lived reality of being queer was not.

In a neoliberal framework, this slotting of dominant and subordinate lives occurs through the building of a "national mainstream" that necessarily "shrink[s] gay public spheres." Equality is represented as

"access" to mainstream institutions (Duggan, 2003, 51). In a pedagogical sense, then, the first move of epistemological neoliberalism is to
assert concepts as primary. The second move is to assign particular concepts to specific places within an epistemological architecture that normalizes and hierarchicalizes dominant and subordinate constructions
of the social. In offering our affective and cognitive loyalties to a set of
concepts, instructors and students can legitimately render unknowable
the "everyday" of lives that transgress dominant norms.

Finally, a third consequence of placing concepts in the centre of our
epistemological frameworks is that the work and scope of knowledge
both shift so that knowledge acts as a kind of armour, a defence system put in place to protect a privileged world view. Allison was using
knowledge to better understand her experience, and to find links
between discipline-relevant concepts and her life. In this sense, the
work of knowledge was to illuminate. Knowledge's scope was partial,
in that it did not need to speak in the same way to all situations (Collins,
1998, 2000). In contrast, Cindy used knowledge to protect, and assumed
its scope to be universal. Do we use knowledge to deny questions of
power, location, and specificity, or to understand how the relational
demands of various publics pose ethical and ontological questions?
Knowledge that seeks to deny questions of power and the "everyday"
of non-dominant groups renders ignorance desirable because of what
it protects (see Britzman, 1998).

For Cindy, and perhaps others, this ignorance was, indeed, preferred
because it did protect, left the architecture noted above in place. Such
uses of "knowledge" have a strong fit with a neoliberal politics of normalization and, in turn, act to contain all forms of difference. This containment informs the production of what one author terms *acceptably
visible* forms of existence (Richardson, 2005, p. 524; emphasis in original). Transgression must be domesticated. Queer lives must fit within
Cindy's notion of streamlined, perhaps another expression of Richardson's acceptable visibility. In this sense, knowledge becomes a fixing,
a pinning of what makes sense to a body of what we call knowledge,
regardless of how such pinning harms. As stated earlier, my concern
here is not so much Cindy's move to protect, but the ways in which
institutional norms and faculty members' practices render such moves
possible, desirable, necessary, and ultimately, invisible in their normalcy. How had all of us at my institution taught Cindy that it was
entirely appropriate to drop out peoples' lives to keep a set of concepts
intact?

Such dropping out is a kind of privatization, a move that insists on an "I" or a "mine" rather than on a "we" or an "ours." Cindy's comment sought to line up the course and the educational process with her idea of gender and communication. Allison's statement was also an assertion of her world view, but in a way that evoked a relationality that sought to understand troubled positionalities rather than exclude them from the subject altogether. Neoliberal logic is intertwined with these epistemological expectations. It favours a privatized rationality that is not ethically bound to consider the lives it leaves behind. Neoliberal logic succeeds through the efficiency of narrowing considerations of what it means to be human and live together well. Epistemological neoliberalism insists on concepts as the determinants for the ways in which we see our lives in relation to others. Such epistemologies privilege knowledge as a mastery of concepts instead of knowledge as a grappling with a set of lived, embodied relationships.

Transgressing Epistemological Neoliberalism: Imagining the Social

Cindy and Allison both made claims on the work of education, communicated a set of expectations for the obligations to which knowledge might best respond. Educators in university contexts continue to construct pedagogical and disciplinary spaces that variously turn towards and refuse transgressive publics. As faculty members, whose lives do we welcome? How do we reaffirm a familiar yet stifling set of falsely constructed norms, and walk into the embodied space of an unruly public? How did Allison and Cindy pursue the subject, construct their "everyday"? When I asked about the relevance of sexuality in the students' lives, Cindy turned towards an educational and epistemological framework that could legitimately reject my constitution of the subject. If the class was supposed to be streamlined, we would then retreat to an imagined world in which sexuality did not exist. The "everyday" of queer lives – coming out, the pleasures of meeting other queer students, lack of visibility on campus, introducing one's same-sex partner to a best friend and feeling that friend's unexpected support, the removal of a banner put up by the queer student group on campus and my university's lack of response – could not be present. In contrast, Allison turned towards her "everyday" – the ways in which individuals and institutions let her know she did not belong to the nation-state of Canada as a racialized woman. As faculty members, we act to transgress neoliberal epistemologies and imagine the social when we (1) insist that the barriers to and practices of living together well constitute the subject and (2) pursue knowledge that is in conversation with material expressions of the social.

Many educators might agree that the primary ethical obligation of the disciplines and of our work as educators is to offer an attentiveness to living together well with at least minimal attention to power and equity issues. Yet faculty members often perform a crucial sleight of hand in this attentiveness: "living together well" often prioritizes ideas about living together well rather than the material practices of living together well. In brief, this privileges living together well as process and downplays the relevance of consequences and outcomes. Faculty members teach as if ideas about living together well, including ideas that drop out the "everyday" of transgressive publics, are a sufficient organizing framework for constitution of the subject. While courses might touch on, for example, "race" or even "racial inequality," subjects such as state-sanctioned violence against Black and Indigenous communities, disproportionate graduation rates by race, and other forms of racial inequity are simply not present as subject matter. Placing lived practice, and not only ideas about that practice, at the centre of disciplinary constitutions of the subject would significantly shift most curricular content. Education that has any significance for life outside of the classroom, that can intelligently critique how we live, must minimally consider the existence of inequity, the fact of a complicated and conflicting public, and a construction of the social organized around agency, institutional constraints on that agency, and power. Cindy was fixing her knowledge around an idea about living together well – the idea that if we close off discussion of queer lives, her world view would remain intact. Yet, centring lived experience – the undeniable existence of straight norms and queer lives, the embodied intersections of gender, race, and class – differently constructs the subject.

When Allison wrote in her response that she felt "no connection or loyalty to this country because they clearly feel none towards me," she was, in effect, refusing pedagogical content built around ideas about her life. These ideas had largely denied her the possibility to carefully consider the ways in which the nation-state of Canada, and those living in this country, had rejected or distorted her participation and constrained forms of agency available to her. Through her response, she acted to centre her lived experience, and then to link this experience with the concept of intersectionality. Reconstituting the disciplinary, curricular, and pedagogical subject to focus on the material realities of how people live centres relationships of power and insists on subjects as "sites of affective investment in which power is distributed, transmitted, between and among those who are constituted through belonging" (Rowe, 2008, 3).

Starting with people's lives allows students and instructors to consider the complex and inescapable relationality that grounds our lives together. Starting with lives requires a constitution of the subject that reminds us that all lives matter, all the time, and demands an approach to the subject that refuses the violence of course content that cannot hold lives that fall outside of conventional epistemological norms (Britzman, 1995; Simpson, 2007). If instructors shape course content by centring material relationships of power and how people are living together well or not, concepts must serve to illuminate these relationships, rather than demanding the reduction, simplification, or misrepresentation of relationships to fit the concepts. Such reduction is the insistent logic of neoliberalism, and one that has no place in higher education.

Pursuing knowledge that is in conversation with a notion of a public, and with the practices of sociality, requires an examination of multiple constitutions of the "we." Further, the ethical parameters of the "we," however expressed, are most appropriately informed by democratic values and the ability to determine the conditions of one's actions (Young, 1990), rather than the considerations of privatized economic gain. Cindy acted to refuse the "we" of straight and queer lives, lived together. To respond to such refusals, faculty members must have our own language for the social, and be able to remind ourselves and our students that the work of education is to turn towards and not away from materiality and complexity. Rather than taking Cindy up in the tight space of her refusal, it is crucial to reassert a broader framework, to offer a language for the social and the importance of a "we," and to openly name the inhumane logics of a privatized "I." In this sense, knowledge is the "dialogic of implication, not the problem of application" (Britzman, 1995, p. 163). Knowledge becomes most useful when it leads to a rigorous consideration of our implicatedness in specific relations of power, and of how we might construct various publics so that justice is possible and even likely. When we understand knowledge as an object to be "applied," we are already retreating from the inevitability of interests. Knowledge that works as implication and not application requires a simultaneous undoing (i.e., identifying and critiquing epistemological practices that harm) and doing (i.e., reimagining possibilities for a different future) (Simpson, 2014). We must insist on the work of the "we."

Neoliberal longings are rarely, if ever, absent from the classroom. Increasingly, the logic of privatized well-being and the normalization of expedient and often violent ontological prescriptions are discursively and materially available to our students. In a variety of public arenas, "citizens discuss one thing and one thing only: who gets what for the pursuit of individual life-projects" (Beiner, 1992, p. 101). Such logics and priorities are epistemologically employed, used by ourselves and our students to construct and maintain narrow disciplinary priorities and possibilities. How do we all constitute the subject in any given course? What are we teaching Cindy, Allison, and other students to expect? Where and how do we make room for lives, for the effects of power, for the pressing and urgent consequences of inequity? How do we as faculty members constitute the subject, streamline queer subjecthood right out of the public space of the classroom, or allow for narratives of nation that dare to contradict the myth of Canadian multiculturalism and name the existence of systemic racism across North America? Streamlined education disallows a notion of a public. In epistemologically constructing rooms that assign different values to different groups of humans, it does harm. To transgress neoliberal epistemologies, faculty members must insist on a reimagined materiality, on epistemologies that are centred in how we live, and that refuse conceptual containment. We must insist on the inhumanity of streamlined ontologies and epistemologies, and on the very humanity of a transgressive public.

7 The Work of the "We": Democracy's Agenda and Curricular and Pedagogical Possibilities

In the winter of 2010, I taught a 400-level course on persuasion. Early in the semester, I asked the students how they understood the term "public good." I am interested in students becoming familiar with constructions of and orientations towards a "we" that have connections with understandings of the "public good." In the persuasion course, students are in many ways acquainted with the course topic and routinely active in processes of persuasion: they take in and adopt social norms, evaluate messages, and act to convince their peers. Particularly in a course on persuasion, an area of study with roots in rhetoric and public dialogue, questions about who and what persuasion ought to be for are relevant and immediate. Inasmuch as I hope that we will consider how we are ethically implicated, we will explore what such implication looks like. In relation to any course, I am interested in asking: What does [title of course] have to do with the practices of living together well or not? How does [course title] foreground or make less visible a particular "we"?

In the persuasion course, I will explicitly link our consideration of images, media, and the psychological and social aspects of persuasion to material practices, drawing on examples from students' lives and from a range of social interactions that are centrally tied to how we live together well or not. Persuasion is a process centrally linked to affective and cognitive identifications, and the students easily reference persuasive interactions in their own lives: talking friends into seeing a movie, convincing a co-worker to cover their shift, explaining to their parents their choice of a major, talking with a partner about whether a joke told by a mutual acquaintance is sexist or not. In discussing the "public good" in a course on persuasion, I am encouraging the students to position all persuasive processes, including the ones in which they are implicated, in relation to the effects of those processes. If we begin to have a language for the public good, an understanding of what it entails, we can start to consider and identify the ethical contours of persuasion. While I will give the students a few ideas on how they might understand the term "public good," I am equally concerned with "waking up" their own routes for doing and caring. I hope that through considering the term "public good," they might wrestle with their own sense of the relationship between an "I" and a "we."

When I asked students in the course on persuasion about the idea of the public good, they seemed to have little understanding of the term. Students can experience years of formal education and never learn about or discuss the public good. In the persuasion class, when I realized that the notion of the public good was largely outside of what was familiar, I backed up. I asked them to start with the word public. "What does public mean? How do you understand this term?" Initially, they seemed slightly surprised, as if I had asked a strange question. At the same time, they seemed willing to consider it. After a minute or two, one student raised the example of Facebook, and the ability to post large numbers of photographs that anyone with a Facebook account could view. I am not a Facebook user, and never have been. I had the sense that posting photographs on Facebook did not have strong parallels with my understanding of the public good. Yet, in regard to Facebook, most if not all of the students were frequent users, and invested. Following the initial comment about photographs on Facebook, there was a slight buzz of conversation, relieved smiles: this, they could talk about, and with a sense of authority and familiarity.

"How does that work?" I asked the students. "Do all of you make your pictures public?" "No way!" one student laughs in response. "You can check a box, decide who can see which pictures," another explains. "What is 'public' about that?" I asked. "I don't know … just that it's open to everybody, I guess, that any part of the public can see my photos." "Doesn't that feel kind of weird – letting all those people see your pictures?" For about 20 minutes, I received a sophisticated and informed lesson not only about Facebook, but more importantly, about how the students' use of it was shaping their conception of the term "public". The students talked with each other, disagreed, asked questions, considered their own ways into both Facebook and the term public. Some students laughed about posting hundreds of photos, and making them available to any Facebook user. They seemed pleased with the basic possibility of this. Other students responded, "What's the good in that? Why do you really want everyone looking at your private life?" As the conversation went on, with no involvement or direction from me, students moved into more challenging questions.

"So what's useful about posting all those pictures? Do you think you have deeper relationships with people? 'Friending' everyone – what's that about? I don't really talk about anything serious on Facebook."

"Yeah, that's true."

"I've used Facebook to organize in resistance to the G20 and related issues. It makes it easy to connect and get out information about demonstrations and meetings."

As the discussion went on, the students made clear, for all of us in the room, that Facebook was active in terms of contributing to their notion of the term public. For the most part, the individual user was the "I," and the "we" was most often a disembodied, loose, and changing group of individuals. On the whole, connections among users existed largely on the surface and rarely with any concrete sense of embeddedness or meaning, beyond pursuing numerous points of fleeting contact. Interactions were by necessity with a highly mediated "other," brief, unrooted, and in some cases recurring. There seemed to be an initial realization among students that the understanding of "public" that Facebook generally encouraged – which largely revolved around, especially in relation to posting photos, drawing attention to the self in the interests of endlessly re-centring that self – might, in fact, be limited and even problematic. In that 20 minutes of conversation, the students had enacted a small shift. Through focused and explicit attention to the construction of a "we," there was now additional attention to the "so what?" of that we. Students were beginning to consider the ways in which Facebook activities were situated in a broader context, always evoking questions of an "I" and a "we." We were now attuned to questions of a "public."

Like the Persuasion course, Public Communication is also a class that easily invokes questions about the term public. I taught this 200-level course in the fall of 2009. On the first day of class, I showed an interview that Bill Moyers conducted with Frances Moore Lappé in 2005, in which Lappé discussed agency and democracy, and referred to the "good life." As in the Persuasion course, I would also ask the students in the Public Communication course to reflect on how they were envisioning the "I" and the "we," the relationship of self and other. I wanted us to have a language that named where we were with these types of questions and that also left room for imagining movement to a different place.

Before we watched the interview, I said to the students, "Lappé will refer to the term 'the good life.' What is this for you?" The students needed little time to consider, and they had the specifics. "A good job." "A house and two vacations a year." "A family." "I want to earn enough to buy an island so I can take my family there." This last response, from one of the more intellectually astute individuals in the course, took me aback. Even as he smiled when answering, it also seemed that the student was serious about his response. When there was a pause, I asked, "Is that it? Any more ideas about the good life? Or have you covered it?"

In response to this second set of questions, the students were not as quick. They seemed to offer more thought to the issues we had raised, and to enter the conversation at a deeper level. "Sometimes I wonder: is a good job really enough? Is having a lot of money really going to make me happy?" "The good life – it seems like that should have something to do with what I care about, what is meaningful, but I don't really go there. I'm not sure why." I asked, "Where do you learn about the good life? What has informed your ideas?" Several students mentioned their parents, and the pressures to pursue a certain career, with little to no consideration of what they cared about or wanted to explore. There was struggle: "I know my parents want the best for me, but I'm not sure that what they have in mind is what I want." "The 'good life' – it could mean doing something important, relevant – but it also means earning enough money, finding a good job." They talked about relation-ships and meaning, a desire for material comfort and when this desire becomes excessive. I felt a kind of fragility in this particular discussion. The issue and our conversation had evoked a sense of intimacy in the room. Already on the first day of class, we had moved very close to something that touched on issues close to our skin, if often under the surface. Such a basic question – what is the good life? – yet so layered with silences, ambiguity, and significance.

Finally, I was with two young women on a Saturday afternoon in August 2012. One of the women had taken several courses with me and graduated a year earlier. The second woman was entering her third year of university and would take a course with me in the fall. I asked the student about her fall schedule. The woman who had graduated commented, "I'll miss that." When she didn't say more, I asked her, "What's the 'that'? What exactly will you miss?" "The 'that'– well – in a few courses, maybe four or five, I was able to connect my internal experiences with theoretical ideas." She went on:

> Connecting the internal and the external – I could bring in my own experience of racism, I knew that it was important, I could stop keeping it under tabs ... Most often, you listen to your professor, cater to the professor ... [In those four or five courses] I learned that my voice is important, that it has weight to it ... I learned I have power and can use it. If there's no space for racism, you can't talk about that experience. But talking about it is how I come to understand – if you come at theory through experience, you know how it feels ... It has a realness to it.

What do we allow to be real? How do students enter their own agency, give voice to an "I" and develop a sense of the "we"? In democratic societies, what are the costs of turning away from notions of various publics, of skirting around understandings of a good that goes beyond individual and economic gain, of establishing a distance from issues that disturb and unsettle? As the young Asian Canadian woman stated above, what does it mean to link internal experience with theoretical ideas?

Throughout this book, I have stressed the importance of subject matter that is turned towards the material and that engages the ways in which power acts on bodies. Cindy calling for streamlined education. Allison noting her disconnect from nation. Amadou Diallo, Trayvon Martin, Frank Paul – all are dead. There are disproportionate graduation rates by race. Individuals and institutions remove queer lives and communities from public spaces. Educators shape expectations and contribute to notions of what is possible and desirable. We grapple with the charge of being a moral dictator, and the ethical intricacies of keeping promises. We are embedded, ethically and relationally implicated. We think, feel, care. What do we do with this thinking, feeling, and caring? What is the work of the "we"? When it comes to moving from too much wrong to less wrong to justice, what is possible in pedagogical settings, and how do we inhabit these possibilities?

In this chapter, I am centrally concerned with imagining avenues for pedagogy and approaches to the subject that lead students away from expecting streamlined education. In earlier chapters, I offered a broad critique of existing orientations and practices related to undergraduate education and constructions of the subject. I have asserted that liberal frameworks often obscure understandings of the "we" that will support consideration of democratic practices, the public good, and justice. This chapter provides a rationale for an alternate orientation to undergraduate education. I consider classroom practices that start with transparent attention to the reality of too much wrong and to the challenges of implication and interests. While I do discuss how instructors might approach such challenges, consider the ethics of a "we," this is not a "how to" chapter, a kind of manual for next steps. Faculty members who consciously inhabit a different set of starting points from those offered by liberal understandings of undergraduate education are themselves best situated to consider the significance and implications of such starting points. One can move from too much wrong to less wrong to justice in a variety of ways. Further, faculty members will necessarily move forward in direct relationship to the particular histories and trajectories of their departments and disciplines, and of their institutions and professional circles.

In the first section of this chapter, I respond to the central questions I considered in chapter 2: What are the obligations of higher education to public life? What are the aims of undergraduate education? In the chapter's second section, I address how educators interested in attending to democratic practices, the public good, and justice might approach the subject, which I understand as the practices of living together well. Also in the second section, I examine the role of the disciplines given my understanding of the subject. In the third and final section, I address what I have called throughout the book "the work of the we," particularly in relation to curriculum and pedagogy. How might instructors approach curriculum and pedagogy when the practices of living together well are the subject? In sum, the aim of this chapter is to suggest a different logic for considering undergraduate education, one that moves students away from streamlined notions of the subject. I am interested in curricular and pedagogical approaches that shift the landscape for considering the subject, so that a regard for democratic practices, the public good, and justice, for ethical investments and interests, are where we begin and what we stay turned towards, always.

Higher Education's Obligations to Public Life and the Aims of Undergraduate Education

In chapter 2, I offered an identification and analysis of how scholars have addressed higher education's obligation to respond to social needs, and of the ends of undergraduate education. In brief, I asserted that while scholarship has addressed how higher education might respond to social concerns, nearly all of this scholarship, particularly that from a liberal perspective, has been overly general and either explicitly or implicitly detached from concrete interests. I also made the claim that this scholarship is not robust enough to contribute to careful considerations of justice. This lack of clarity and concreteness related to higher education's obligations to social life has, in turn, weakened the ability of faculty members to consider the ends of undergraduate education. Ultimately, the work of faculty members will be strengthened by a cohesive and carefully constructed rationale linking the responsibilities that higher education has to the social and the ends of undergraduate education. The former ought to centrally inform the latter. Further, such rationales must not remain at the level of the conceptual, detached from actual practice and the demands of public life. They must make a commitment to addressing the material, or how people live with the reality of injustice and with possibilities for justice.

Higher Education's Obligations to Public Life

Institutions of higher education in North America have an obligation to centrally inhabit ethical, ontological, and epistemological frameworks that acknowledge our relational embeddedness, the significance of power, the inevitability of interests and consequences, and the importance of justice in contexts in which individuals and institutions claim democratic aspirations. In other words, questions of ethics must be understood as integral and foundational to all academic work. In many cases, ethics is "added onto" content that purportedly exists outside of ethics. For example, in teaching a course on persuasion, faculty members and students might consider ethics in week 10 of a 10–12-week course. The textbook on which an instructor might rely in such a course might address attitudes, cognitive dissonance, audience, and persuasive effects, and, outside of a chapter or section, offer little to no attention to ethics. Such an approach to any given course topic communicates that detaching ethical concerns from any number of concepts and issues is possible and desirable. The pairing of liberal scholarship's reluctance and even refusal to address interests, and powerful Western ontological and epistemological dichotomies, including the separation of interests and ideas, has significant consequences.[1] Defining social needs with no explicit attention to ethics is highly acceptable, even sensible for many educators. However, if as I claimed in chapter 4, faculty members begin with the assumption that we are embedded, such an approach is neither possible nor desirable.

In practice, all faculty members and our students inhabit an ethical and relational universe. We define, identify, accept, reject, support, resist, and prioritize social needs from within a set of affective, cognitive, ethical, and relational investments. When we teach a course, we decide to affirm or reject disciplinary assumptions, and we always in some way endorse or resist existing social practices and norms. In simple terms, to state that "higher education ought to consider social needs with attention to ethical priorities," which implies that social needs exist separately from ethics, is wholly out of step with what it means to be human and with how we live. The process of identifying and responding to social needs is itself inherently ethical. Once students and faculty members learn about the existence of disproportionate graduation rates by race, how do we respond? What is the urgency of this need in relation to other needs? Such decisions are ethical, and suggest a course of action that will affect the well-being of various communities. Attempting to see (1) social needs and (2) ethical priorities as discrete concerns might be possible at a conceptual level, but this way of seeing has no correspondence to practice and to how power acts on bodies.

In societies that profess an allegiance to democratic priorities, institutions of higher education have an obligation to (1) grapple with the material expressions of democratic practices, the public good, and justice and what these demand of us in ethical terms and (2) to approach social needs and concerns from this ethical understanding and with a focus on material practices. Individuals and communities cannot fix, predict, or homogenize the ways in which ethical investments lead to the realization of democratic practices, the public good, and justice. Claiming that institutions of higher education ought to consider what it means to live together well related to democratic practices, the public good, and justice does not necessitate any one response. The processes that lead to the realization of the public good and justice will be varied. Further, the ways in which institutions, faculty members, and students will pursue such questions and the responses to them will be closely linked to contextual demands, the specifics of particular institutions, and social issues that emerge from within specific communities. Those in institutions of higher education will address questions of ethics and social needs at multiple levels, such as institutional, faculty/college/school, and departmental; and across numerous groups and interests, including, for example, the classroom, community organizations, public-serving institutions, social services, and industry.

Consideration of the practices of living together well, with attention to democratic practices, the public good, and justice, will require ongoing dialogue and decisions, as well as multiple and complex expressions of individual and institutional agency. For example, institutions such as my own have invested considerable resources into a large cooperative education program and have likewise entered into working relationships with organizations in the tar sands and other industries. Students like Chris Lok, as discussed in chapter 2, can opt to complete a co-op term with an oil company in Cold Lake, Alberta. When considering higher education's obligations to public life, certain questions are useful: How do the tar sands support and/or constrain democratic practices, the public good, and justice? What are the multiple interests at stake? What are the consequences of the tar sands for various communities, such as the owners of tar sands companies, seasonal employees, and local residents? How do practices in the tar sands sustain oppressive practices against Indigenous communities? How is the environment effected, in the short and long term? Questions of ethics and democratic practices are embedded with such concerns. With regard to effects on the environment and on specific communities, what does the public good look like? Which practices will move us from too much wrong to less wrong to justice?

This grappling will inevitably be messy, complicated, and time-consuming. It will require open acknowledgment of the four parameters of the social that I outlined in chapter 4. Such careful and transparent attention to the ethical demands of democratic practices, the public good, and justice in connection with concrete settings and issues can inform how institutions and faculty members work out their consideration of and response to social needs. Dialogues that can fully attend to ethical orientations and agency in relation to democratic practices, the public good, and justice, and the obligations that institutions of higher education, and those in them, have in relation to these orientations and agency will require persistence and patience. Educators will need to insist on attention to the material and to lived reality, and to guard against a retreat into the purely conceptual. As articulated in chapter 4, in the movement between ethical priorities and the obligations that higher education has to public life, there must be an insistence on naming what is, always in material terms and related to how power acts on bodies; and to imagining what might be, in regard to practices that move us towards justice in particular settings.

Ends of Undergraduate Education

Claiming that institutions of higher education (1) have an obligation to grapple with the material expressions of democratic practices, the public good, and justice and what those demand of us in ethical terms and (2) ought to approach social needs and concerns from this ethical understanding has direct implications for considering the ends and aims of undergraduate education. As I asserted in chapter 2, higher education scholarship, particularly that from a liberal perspective, evidences a lack of clarity regarding the ends of undergraduate education. Even as many scholars address intellectual, professional, and civic ends, they rarely offer in-depth attention to the relationship of all three and what these ends have to do with higher education's social contract with public life. In addition, with the exception of work authored by critical scholars, scholarship considering the three ends often does so with no consideration of material practices and ethical priorities in democratic societies.

If universities are obligated to ethically consider democratic practices, the public good, and justice, and to respond to social needs from such a framework, then undergraduate education must perform at least three tasks. First, undergraduate education must cultivate a sense of both agency and implicatedness in students. Second, students must develop the ontological and epistemological capacities that support consideration of relationships and power. Finally, undergraduate education must encourage an imagination for the public good.

Agency and Implicatedness

A strong sense of agency and implicatedness are at the heart of the practices of, in Dewey's terms, "associated living" (1998, p. 390). Agency, at a very basic level, "is the power to *do* something" (Nealon & Searls Giroux, 2012, p. 255; emphasis in original). While some students may come to higher education with a strong sense of their own possibilities to effect change, others enter courses with a less active regard for the consequentiality and significance of their own choices and practices. When my students talked about their uses of Facebook, they were, in effect, identifying their own practices of agency, cognitively and affectively "showing up" for the significance of their lives and actions. When I asked about what such uses of agency had to do with a "we," I was encouraging them to consider extending their grasp of agency, what it means in relation to broader issues. As my former student expressed in thinking about her education, "I learned that my voice is important, that it has weight to it ... I learned I have power and can use it." Entering into a sense of the "weight" of one's existence is a crucial component of agency. Further, agency itself is bound up with one's positioned and relational access to different forms of power and one's affective and cognitive loyalties. Institutions both constrain and make possible specific performances of agency.

Educators can encourage students to link their own implicatedness and commitments with course content. Agency, or inhabiting various uses of power, necessarily invokes a "we": "I will use this power to these ends in this context." Agency and implicatedness are inseparable. Implicatedness involves the understanding that all of us are situated within a web of relationships and power. Understanding one's implicatedness requires an ongoing regard for the various "we's" in which one is situated. Students live in a "we" at home, at school, and at work; and with family and friends. Before one can grapple with the ethical demands of democratic practices, the public good, and justice, and consider social needs from this ethical framework, one must have at least an initial sense that one can and does act, can "respond to" and "change" (Nealon & Searls Giroux, 2012, p. 255) the contexts in which we live.

Ontology, Epistemology, Relationships, and Power

A second component of the aims of undergraduate education given the above-stated obligations is support for the ontological and epistemological capacities to consider relationships and power.

Ontological Capacities

Ontology in very basic terms is the study of what it is to be human. Democratic forms of living require that our understandings of being human acknowledge the embeddedness I addressed in chapter 4. Rather than understanding the self as an independent, free-standing "I," democratic practices require an understanding that one's "autonomy is defined in relation to the social" (Macdonald, 2008, p. 350). In concrete terms, the capacity to consider relationships and power is most possible when students and faculty members start from the assumption that to be human is to be embedded, practice a willingness to critically analyse one's location, and routinely inhabit the demands and pleasures of a "we."

Orienting oneself towards notions of autonomy grounded in the social, particularly in formal educational settings and concerning course subject matter, may be new for many students and for faculty members. At the same time, most if not all students will be familiar with settings in which a "we" is prominent and insistent. These settings may be, for example, with parents, siblings, or friends. They may be in the context of faith-based commitments, or experiences with an athletic team or through ongoing involvement with another group or organization. As I was attempting to do in both the Persuasion and Public Communication courses, constructing oneself within a "we" in whatever settings one inhabits is crucial. Rejecting a "we," or opting for an impoverished understanding of our ongoing sociality, will constrain possibilities for democratic practices.

Second, once students begin considering their relationships to a "we" in a variety of settings and contexts, this might support becoming adept in practices of reflexivity, of understanding the particularities of one's own positionality and location. Reflexivity demands a sense of how one inhabits locations of both power and oppression, and of how one's own relationship to practices of power and domination bears on the lives of others. In the persuasion class, in our discussion of Facebook, I had first encouraged the students to consider the term "public," or how they entered the question of the "we." They identified Facebook as an active and familiar "we" for themselves. Then I asked them to explore: How do you approach the "we" of Facebook? How are you an "I" within the parameters of constructing meaning that Facebook offers? Already, even in such a basic example, they are considering relationships and power, and how they are engaging both.

A third element of the ontological component of analysing relationships and power is what historian Elsa Barkley Brown has called "pivoting the centre" (1990, p. 10). Pivoting the centre offers a way forward from reflexivity. It concerns the "how" of considering one's fit with others. As Brown asserts in response to the issue of how people can overcome "years of notions of what is normative," pivoting the centre requires that one is able to believe "in the possibility of a variety of experiences, a variety of ways of understanding the world, a variety of frameworks of operation, without imposing consciously or unconsciously a notion of the norm" (p. 10). It is not only about one's capacity for intellectual analysis. Brown states that students (and others) do not need to "feel what it is like" to be someone other than who they are or to be someone else in terms of gender, sexuality, race, or class. Instead, pivoting the centre is a process of centring an experience that is different from their own and evaluating that experience "by its own standards without need of comparison" (p. 10).

Crucial to Brown's articulation of pivoting the centre is the idea of a "variety of frameworks of operation." Pivoting the centre requires an acknowledgment of multiple world views and value systems, and it also makes demands on how we listen. It requires what students may often feel as an "illogical ... openness" (Simpson, 2008, p. 186) and dialogue invested in just forms of living (Simpson, 2003). "Pivoting the centre" is, in ontological terms, a way to be with others that both takes into account the power of dominant norms yet simultaneously insists that it is possible to set up modes of living and relating that engage more just forms of subjectivity (see also Macdonald, 2008).

Epistemological Capacities

Ontological capacities, or the ways we approach being human, have a direct relationship to epistemological practices. We are human knowers. That is, we perform all knowing from particular ways of being human. The above three ontological practices – identifying the "we," practising reflexivity, and pivoting the centre – will directly support specific approaches to knowing that can, in turn, sustain the capacities for consideration of relationships and power. Two epistemological activities central to analysis of relationships and power include naming and imagining.

Naming involves assessing and articulating the ways in which power, at individual and institutional levels, acts on bodies. What we see when a white man hisses at boys of colour in a library computer room, and in regard to disporportionate graduation rates by race, the deaths of Amadou Diallo and Frank Paul, and the removal of queer lives from public spaces all require concrete forms of naming, which lead to specific practices of knowing. They are ways of knowing that are grounded in how people live; in the daily, pressing, and routine violence of oppression and domination; and in the profound dehumanization that such oppression and domination require.

A second epistemological activity critical to analyses of relationships and power is imagining – the commitment to know that a different future is possible. Imagining is the work of refusing the inevitability of injustice, of "expos[ing] what lies under the skin" of democratic hopes and a longing for justice (Simpson 2010b, p. 203). Imagining a different future is only possible when accompanied by careful attention to power. Moving from too much wrong to less wrong to justice requires understanding power and how it is constituted both in existing practices of injustice and in moving towards justice. In this way, the work of naming and imagining, or moving towards justice, occurs within the complex negotiation of institutional forces and individual agency. Institutions necessarily shape possibilities for agency.

Considering the Public Good

Finally, in addition to the aims of instilling a sense of agency and implicatedness, and supporting ontological and epistemological capacities for the consideration of relationships and power, undergraduate education must repeatedly turn towards dimensions of the public good across disciplines and courses. Inasmuch as higher education is obligated to consider social needs within an ethical framework rooted in democratic practices, the public good, and justice, students must understand what these concepts mean, at discursive and material levels. The way in which we understand and prioritize social needs, and the placement of some in the foreground and others in the background, have ties to deeply rooted affective and cognitive investments. In societies that profess commitments to democratic values, such ties must orient themselves towards the public good. Further, as I have stated earlier in the book, healthy democracies and a realization of the public good cannot occur alongside routine and institutionally supported practices of injustice. In sum, students must develop an awareness of and regard for the public good, and they must be able to articulate its absence, promise, and contours in a range of settings and in relationship to multiple social issues.

These three aims – instilling a sense of agency, the ontological and epistemological capacities to consider relationships and power, and an imagination for the public good – have a connection to the discussion of objectives in chapter 2. In particular, I addressed liberal scholarship's consideration of three types of educational outcomes, including civic, professional, and intellectual. As I pointed out in chapter 2, while literature addresses each of these types of aims and what they involve, in-depth consideration of the relationship of all three is more difficult to find.[2] At a minimum, the separation into three discrete categories of intellectual, civic, and professional implies that one must choose. This separation also suggests that these aims might be in opposition to each other. Setting up (either implicitly or explicitly) these three aims as discrete entities, and fundamentally separate, largely rests on the dichotomies I addressed in chapter 4, and furthers the intellectually unsound premise that one can separate theory and practice.

A recent report by the National Task Force on Civic Learning and Democratic Engagement addresses the problems with what the authors of the report call a "zero-sum choice between the fullest preparation for economic success and education for citizenship." As this report asserts, employers themselves have pointed out that positioning "informed democratic citizenship" and preparation for the workplace and career opportunities as opposing choices is a problematic way of understanding educational outcomes. Indeed, the report claims that "there is a civic dimension to every field of study ... and to every workplace." Employees in the technical professions, industries, and service fields will routinely face ethical and social responsibilities. Indeed, "The nation – and the world – have experienced disastrous results when civic consequences are ignored and only economic profit is considered" (2012, p. 10).

In North America, we never live outside of democratic contradictions and aspirations. The above excerpt draws attention to the presence of "ethical and social responsibilities" across contexts. The above claim implies that it is not only students in particular fields, such as those in education or social work, who will necessarily engage in public citizenship. Rather, all work is interested, and must therefore be intentional about turning towards public concerns. Reducing ends to a "zero-sum choice" – that is, civic, intellectual, or professional, but never two or three working together – in effect, misrepresents and oversimplifies each of these ends. In practice, it is nearly impossible, let alone desirable, to fully unravel the ways they are interrelated.

A parallel thread of the argument that insists on or suggests a separation between civic, professional, and intellectual ends is the distinction between the ethical aspects of educational practices and education that focuses on functional or instrumental outcomes. In the former view, education ought to consider questions of meaning, the constitution of equitable communities, and social challenges. In an instrumental or functional view, education turns itself towards the specific "functions" that those who are educated might perform. Such a view has clear alignment with a focus on professional or workplace ends that are seemingly divorced from ethics or questions of social relevance.

Indeed, any educator might approach the Persuasion class I referred to earlier from a supposedly primarily functional perspective. A faculty person might foreground specific presentational or argumentative skills suitable for an individual working in public relations. In another example, from a functional perspective, in a school of education, "reading specialists" might be particularly attuned to "technical advancement[s]" in the field of reading, to those techniques that purportedly advance children's capacities to read. From an educational framework that considers ethics, those same specialists "should have the ability to understand and appreciate why millions of children who by virtue of their race, ethnicity, gender, and class have not benefited from these technical advancements and remain illiterate or semiliterate" (Macedo, 1998, p. xiii). While it may be possible, particularly in mainstream educational contexts, to maintain such distinctions in discussions that remain at an abstract level, they are far more difficult to sustain when faculty members and students consider lived practice, and attend to how various acts hurt and help different communities.

At one level, frameworks for education that in any way assume a firm and non-porous line between ethics and functions, the uses of knowledge and skills and the skills themselves, rest on dichotomies that are in opposition to what it means to be human. Such dichotomies, as I addressed in chapter 5, may hold up rhetorically or discursively, yet are highly inadequate for considering how power works on bodies, how we live with and respond to complicated social issues, and how education has consequences for how we live. At a second level, as I asserted in chapter 4, we are enmeshed. We are always and everywhere ethically implicated. If I teach a Persuasion course and focus nearly entirely on presentation, argumentative, and public speaking skills, with little or no attention to the consequences of how students use such skills, this focus is ethically invested. Focusing on technical capacities with no consideration of how students will use those capacities is, on the whole, ethically supportive of existing norms and power relations. All teaching is ethically implicated, regardless of levels of ethical transparency, and whether or not that education implicitly endorses or persistently resists the status quo. Resistance to that status quo might involve reading specialists "mak[ing] linkages between their self-contained technical reading methods and the social and political realities that generate unacceptably high failure reading rates among certain groups of students" (Macedo, 1998, p. xiii). Endorsement of the status quo might mean that educators address reading methods with no attention to the "social and political realities" that bear on different groups. Both approaches are ethical and functional.

In sum, approaching the ends of undergraduate education as if civic, professional, and intellectual ends are mutually exclusive or discrete is both intellectually unsound and out of step with both how students learn and with how we live. If faculty members assume (1) that we are all ethically implicated, (2) that students will act or perform agency in a range of settings, and (3) that in societies that profess allegiance to democratic values and practices, one must have at least some awareness of the public good and of those democratic values and practices. Understanding civic, professional, and intellectual ends as always intersecting is both intellectually sound and pedagogically promising. When I teach the Persuasion class, for example, I am fully committed to strengthening the students' capacities for strategic and effective persuasive skills. In an assignment the students work on in groups over the course of the term, they are responsible for audience analysis, identification of what is at stake for whom, articulation of persuasive messages and strategies, and assessment of decision making and power structures in relationship to their persuasive goals. They also have a 30-minute meeting with an individual or individuals in a position of power (e.g., student government officer, regional planner, city council person) in which they participate in a process of persuasion based on the above tasks.

In one respect, all of these tasks are functional. The students will ideally complete this assignment and the course with increased persuasive skills which they will then apply in a range of contexts. Further, they may use these skills to ends I might consider undemocratic. As I point out to the students in the classes I teach, the above capacities will make them more attractive to employers in nearly all settings, whether corporate, social or public service, activist, educational, or industry-related.

At the same time, in the persuasion and other classes that I teach, we also address the uses of such skills, and their relationship to disciplinary frameworks for communication and rhetoric. In terms of uses, the readings, assignments, lectures, and course discussions will ask students to grapple with persuasion in democratic contexts, with what the public good looks like, with what justice requires, and with how multiple forms of persuasion might hinder or advance democratic practices. Based in disciplinary and scholarly work, students learn to understand psychological and social aspects of persuasion; how images bear on how we think, feel, and act; and the reception of and contributions to persuasive messages in corporate, public, political, and popular settings. In every class meeting and through assignments, I ask students to consider: How are you persuaded? How do you persuade? What do you accept as a given, and how is this persuasion? With what values, norms, and aspirations do you identify, and why? What is the significance of persuasion to how we live, particularly in democratic contexts where the public good and justice ought to be on our radar? Acting on an attentiveness to workplace and economic concerns does not require that one jettison democratic values, or privilege a marketplace or neoliberal logic.

In sum, all education, and the ways in which our students will use what they have learned, is complex. Encouraging students to grapple with democratic practices, the public good, and justice in no way requires that educators prescribe a fixed way of thinking or a specific political agenda. Offering students an understanding of implication, and teaching so that they can inhabit that implicatedness through the very day-to-day content of their courses, can open up possibilities for living well together. Considering disciplinary concepts and course-related capacities in relation to democratic practices and how we are living well together or not should not be a strange, problematic, or unfamiliar framework for pursuing educational content and questions of the subject, particularly in societies that have some allegiance to democratic values. Attending to the three aims articulated earlier – encouraging in students (1) a sense of agency and implicatedness, (2) the ontological and epistemological capacities to consider relationships and power, and (3) an imagination for the public good – will ideally be understood as quite ordinary.

Further, rather than opting for a "zero-sum choice" (National Task Force on Civic Learning and Democratic Engagement, 2012, p. 10) in terms of civic, intellectual, and professional ends, we can educate students who might then graduate with a deeper sense of their own power to consider and effect change, to feel and think their way through complicated social issues in dialogue with others, to carry with them a conceptual language and set of analytical tools gained within a particular discipline, and to grapple with power and with how the public good and justice can be realized. Such an approach refuses to simplify the lives and potential contributions of our students or the world in which they live. Such an approach refuses the costs and consequences of streamlined education. Such an approach may make it possible to acknowledge that we live with shards, flying; to name injustice and imagine justice; and to see ourselves into a different world.

What Is the Subject? The Practices of Living Together Well

Throughout this book, I have repeatedly asked, what is the subject? Certainly, both Cindy and Allison's comments were assertions about the subject and represent claims on what a course such as Gender, Communication, and Culture ought to address. What is the subject? Numerous points of entry into this question exist in academic contexts. Students, faculty members, and administrators routinely attend to this question. Further, departments, faculties, schools, disciplinary and professional associations, and campus centres (such as those facilitating civic engagement and service-learning efforts) also carefully and methodically construct areas of content that constitute "the subject." At very broad levels, university mission statements often make explicit or implicit references to what constitutes the subject for all students at that institution. For example, my institution states a commitment to "preparing students to be global citizens" (see University of Waterloo, "Informing the University Plan") as well as to ensuring that "all graduates possess" certain "distinguishing characteristics," which include "well-honed problem-solving and critical thinking skills" ("The University Plan"). Such references will, ideally, inform what happens at more concrete levels of curriculum and instruction.

I understand the subject to be the practices of living together well. In societies that profess an allegiance to democratic values, the meaning of "well" is grounded in understandings of the public good and justice. The subject is primarily about practice, about the material, and about how power works on bodies. Committing oneself, or a course, to the study of the practices of living together well requires a repeated turning towards the reality of too much wrong, towards the pressing and urgent consequences of individuals and institutions using power to do violence and dehumanize, and towards the possibilities for all of us to live together well. It requires, as Young (1990) discusses in her work on justice, the act of listening – to students like Gloria, naming the Black community's distrust of the police; to those asking about the deaths of men like Frank Paul and Amadou Diallo; and to those who draw attention to the removal of the banner of the queer student group on my campus. It requires, as Grande points out in her discussion of democracy, a critique of "the historic, economic, and material conditions of 'difference'" (2004, p. 34).

In order to stay turned towards the practices of living together well, it is especially useful to habitualize consideration of and regard for three areas of focus. More than discrete steps or linear parts of an equation, these three areas must consistently remain in the frame, and be in the foreground of all instances of considering the subject. Through identification of the material, analysis of the social, and an imagination for the ethical, undergraduate education is more likely to support movement from too much wrong to less wrong to justice. Identification of the material invokes an active concern for and realistic assessment of practices of injustice, of the ordinariness and extent of too much wrong. It assumes that inequity exists, that it is systemic, and that it disproportionately harms communities that exist in a subordinate relationship to dominant groups, based on race, gender, sexuality, and socio-economic class. It explicitly refuses the liberal notion of a "common vulnerability" (Nussbaum, 1997, p. 91), as the practices of the material wholly discredit such a claim. Contrary to Nussbaum's assertion that "being prosperous or powerful does not remove one from the ranks of needy humanity" (p. 91), my life will never be at risk in the ways that the lives of Diallo, Martin, and Paul were. Living in a white body ensures levels of protection that systems do not afford those in communities of colour.

Identification of the material might begin with a consideration of concrete locations in which students and faculty members are implicated, such as campus life and local communities, and then move outward towards regional, provincial and state, and national and international contexts. Indeed, one can, in very specific settings, find a myriad of levels of implication. In order to identify the material in ways that fully consider the devastating consequences of too much wrong, students and faculty members must pursue a seeing and knowing that do not flinch, and that return to and remain with stories that disturb, unsettle, and contradict. For those faculty members and students who have made affective, cognitive, and indeed professional investments in a denial of the material and the day-to-day practices of injustice, such identification may well require a profound reconstitution of how one sees and knows.

In addition to this identification of the material, a second area of focus that must remain in the foreground is an analysis of the social or, more particularly, an ongoing examination of the workings of power and agency at individual and institutional levels. Movement closer to or further from the practices of living together well always occurs through the negotiation of power. In simple terms, power is the ability to make decisions about how we live together; it concerns the capacity to determine the "conditions of one's actions" (Young, 1990, p. 37). Power is individual and institutional, acts as a "productive network ... much more than a repressing force" (Foucault, 1980, p. 119), and relies on deep-seated ideologies and norms. The practices of living together well will require an identification of the material in ways that name the workings of power. In regard to the deaths of men like Frank Paul and Amadou Diallo and boys like Trayvon Martin, policing and criminal justice systems in North America demonstrate lower levels of regard for the bodies of people of colour than for white bodies. In regard to disproportionate graduation rates by race, educational institutions and those working in them privilege white students and their families and communities. In regard to the removal of the banner of the queer student group on my campus, to my knowledge, no campus body of which I am aware has unambiguously and in a public forum stated that such removal is wrong and unjust. In most cases, a retreat from power will also ensure a retreat from the material.

Analyses of power are also critical to effecting change, to moving from too much wrong to less wrong to justice. Likewise, such analyses have a direct link to the third element of considering the practices of living together well, which is an imagination for ethical practices grounded in notions of the public good and justice. Identification of the material and analyses of power must be linked to an imagination for the public good and justice. We cannot move towards that which we do not hold in our imaginations (Anzaldúa, 1999; Lorde, 1984). Imagining a particular future, beginning to articulate what it might require for men like Amadou Diallo and Frank Paul and boys like Trayvon Martin to live, is necessary for change. While the work of such imagining is not predictable, homogeneous, or uniform, it does reach for a vision of the good life in which "developing and exercising one's capacities and expressing one's experience ... [and] participating in determining one's action and the conditions of one's action" (Young, 1990, p. 37) are routine and equitable across groups. Such imagining, with students, is both intellectually demanding and an act of profound hopefulness.

In identifying the material, analysing power, and imagining the public good, what is the role of the disciplines? How do disciplines, constituted by areas of content that maintain distinctness and that overlap, fit with an understanding of the subject as the practices of living together well that I have suggested above? At their best, disciplines will offer a concrete conceptual language for analysis in regard to these practices and to the material, social, and ethical. Ideally, disciplinary knowledge offers a set of theories and ideas that might illuminate such identification, analysis, and imagination.

In the discipline of communication, a common and easily accessible definition of communication as an intellectual area of work is "the shared process of making meaning." Further exploration of this definition invites consideration of what constitutes meaning and according to whom, how meaning is made, and how such processes are shared. Areas of study in the field of communication include the media and culture industries; ideologies and how they are communicated and received; the psychological and social aspects of interpersonal, workplace, and organizational communication; communication, difference, and social inequity; and communication in various aspects of public life. Definitions of disciplines, their broad orientational frameworks, the components of these frameworks, and the conceptual languages and areas of study that have developed within them offer a set of tools that can aid in identification, analysis, and imagination in the interests of the practices of living together well.

At the same time, the ways in which disciplines and their analytical languages work as resources must be secondary to identification of the material, analyses of the social, and imagination for the ethical and the public good. Disciplines are tools, not ends. As such, educators might work at shaping the tools to fit the ends. Nearly all of us, as faculty members, do our work within disciplinary constraints and possibilities, at both institutional and departmental levels, and within professional associations and bodies (related to journals, conferences, etc.). Educators can and do continue to rely on disciplines and their related conceptual tools to support practices of injustice. The central tenets and parameters of disciplines change in relation to the work faculty members do within disciplinary infrastructures. Disciplines continue to construct and maintain a range of ways of ignoring the material and reasserting acontextual concepts. Scholars can and do support disciplinary practices that have high levels of alignment with the neoliberal ideologies and conventional forms of epistemology examined in chapter 6. At the same time, faculty members on the whole, especially those with tenure, have fairly high degrees of agency within disciplinary frameworks.

Given this agency, we might opt to pursue the practices of living together well with our primary allegiances directed towards the realization of the public good rather than to disciplinary priorities that are in opposition to the practices of living together well. When disciplinary commitments and norms in any way encourage or expect us to deny the material, to minimize power, and to reject the inevitability of ethical interests and the centrality of the public good to our work as faculty members, we might then ask: who and what ends are such disciplines serving? Likewise, when our disciplines urge that we simplify the complexity of public life in order to keep a set of concepts intact, or to protect a certain way of seeing and knowing, a regard for the public good requires that we name how such disciplinary practices are doing harm.

In sum, the practices of living together well, and the related work of naming injustice and imagining justice, at material and discursive levels, constitute the subject of undergraduate education. This subject has a direct fit with higher education's obligation to public life and with the three aims of undergraduate education articulated earlier in this chapter. As faculty members, all of our work requires us to act on our ethical investments, to engage a set of affective and cognitive commitments as we move toward one type of future and not another. In pursuing the practices of living together well, in naming injustice and imagining justice, our loyalties must be to these ends rather than to a fixed set of disciplinary norms grounded in dominant ontologies and epistemologies. We can opt to work from within our disciplines and critique them when they impede pursuit of the public good and of justice. In the next section, I will examine "the work of the we" in curricular and pedagogical contexts.

"The Work of the We": The Practices of Living Together Well in Curricular and Pedagogical Contexts

Throughout this book, I have asserted that all education is directed at constituting self and other, at inhabiting various forms of a "we." Students enter a course, and the "work of the we" is immediate. They walk into the classroom, look around, and identify who is familiar. They will sit at a desk and, depending on the physical set-up of the classroom, immediately look at the backs of heads or into the faces of their peers. Students will engage in forms of social interaction that are deep and with a sense of curiosity, or that are fleeting and reserved. Educators, as well, in preparing for and teaching the course, have faced and will continue to face questions of the "we." This will occur in regard to course content and format. Which subjects will we address, and whose lives (implicitly and explicitly) will be in the foreground? What will assignments require students to consider and do, together and/or alone? Once students bring in unexpected content, questions, and examples, what do we do with these?

In a week from now, as I am working on this chapter, my colleagues and I will begin another fall term. I will teach an introductory Intercultural Communication course, which I have taught 20 times before. Even as I am familiar with this course, with my conceptual framework for the topic, and with how students often approach the course, I am once again reworking the group project assignment. I find it difficult in a 12-week term, in a 200-level course, to construct meaningful group work, that which offers depth and identifiable outcomes in relation to both areas of content and intellectual practices I would like the students to strengthen. I also aim for group project assignments that give the students a high degree of agency in identifying and shaping the topics they will address. A week before the term begins, I decide that the group project is too important to drop. I struggle with familiar questions: What are the primary objectives of the assignment? How can I achieve depth in both content and process, without overwhelming the students? The group project is one assignment among several in this course; how does this assignment fit with other work in the course? As faculty members, we have agency. We invite students into particular ways of constructing the social. We can opt to turn towards complexity, risk the messiness of refusing streamlined education and engaging with, as I said in chapter 6, the very humanity of a transgressive public.

I have also asserted throughout this book that in societies with any form of allegiance to democratic values, the "work of the we" must have connections to the public good and to justice. The subject, then, becomes a matter of the practices of living together well. It becomes not only a conversation about the good life, as my students began to have on the first day of that Public Communication course I mentioned at the start of this chapter, but also about the processes and realization of inhabiting such a life. As I see a white man attempting to dehumanize four boys of colour, hear about the deaths of men such as Frank Paul and Amadou Diallo, listen to my students talk about the removal of the banner of the queer student group on campus, I turn towards the lived reality of too much wrong. The desire to inhabit a life where less wrong exists and where justice is a possibility is a longing. We reveal the most about ourselves in the ways that we turn towards too much wrong.

Curricular Conversations

All curricular and pedagogical practices are ways of inhabiting a specific and located "we," positioning ourselves among others, leaning towards one vision of the future and away from other visions. I wonder what might be possible in any given department if a group of faculty members considered the question of the "we," did so in ways that valued transparency and a range of viewpoints, and simultaneously grappled with a rigorous consideration of the public good and justice. This, perhaps, is one place for departments to begin. Inasmuch as all departmental curriculum minimally represents the intellectual scaffolding within that department, the conceptual architecture on which faculty members hope students will rely in and outside of the classroom, curriculum itself is a way of imagining the "work of the we." Educators might ask, together: How has our discipline confronted or not the practices of living together well? How has it solidified the problematic dualisms addressed in chapter 5? How do our disciplinary norms constrain or make possible consideration of the material, the social, and the ethical? How might we rely on disciplinary efforts, whether mainstream or critical, to carry us into questions of the "we" and of the material realities of too much wrong and into possibilities for less wrong and for justice?

Further, departments might consider: What is distinctive about our department, at this institution, and within the context of our discipline? Given our department's historical and intellectual trajectories, how are we positioned to consider questions of the material, social, and ethical? How are we positioned to ignore such questions? Faculty members in a department might ask: What is our history with turning towards the public good and the social, and towards democratic practices and justice, in material and concrete ways? How do our existing affective and cognitive investments, as individual faculty members and as departments, bear on and constrain our capacities for attending to the material? Faculty members might begin with the assumption of implication rather than in a mode of application. How are we already embedded in particular ways in our institutions and communities? What does it mean, particularly at public institutions, as a primary space of educational practice, to be embedded? When we hear a lecture one night addressing colonialism in Canada, and then turn on our computers to see pictures of the tar sands as a co-op site for our institution, how do we move within that reality?

Obviously, such conversations will not be easy, straightforward, convenient, or necessarily rewarded. Individuals and institutions will often ensure that such dialogues are difficult, discouraged, inconvenient, and circumvented. They will also be time-consuming and intellectually and affectively demanding. The pace and progress of such conversations may feel uneven, inconsistent, and elusive. Some faculty members in the department may act in opposition to such conversations. Rather than discuss these questions with half or more of the members of one's faculty, it may be that one finds only one or two colleagues who are interested. One's ability to centre these questions within a department will depend on one's power and will occur with respect to factors such as length of time at the institution and one's terms of employment (contract, tenured, untenured, etc.). Such conversations are often more likely when one has an active professional relationship with one's departmental colleagues, which takes time. To move such conversations forward in any significant and systemic sense, faculty members and departments will need to be strategic, always.

Departments, faculties, programs, and schools construct the primary structural backdrop that will guide the education of our students. Such structures will shape what students understand as important, possible, and desirable. These structures will give students clues: for example, streamlined education is acceptable, noting a disconnect from nation is not. At the level of departments (and other structures set up to govern undergraduate education), curriculum is the primary resource we as faculty members have. It will have significant consequences for our students' education. Further, even as many faculty members might opt to maintain a firm distance from such departmental conversations and the questions I raised above, we are all responsible for the curriculum in our departments. The choice to not participate in such conversations does not negate our role and the fact of our implication.

In sum, curriculum is a central departmental resource when considering higher education's obligations to public life and the primary response in regard to the aims and consequences of undergraduate education. Curriculum is the avenue through which structural bodies such as departments demonstrate their commitments to questions of the "we," to the practices of living together well, and to the demands of the material, the social, and the ethical in democratic societies. Departments might consider links and gaps between their own intellectual and curricular priorities and the strengths and limitations of their disciplines. They might be explicit and transparent about their own implication, about the ways in which curriculum represents a map of a department's caring and lays down the routes on which the students will travel. What can a curriculum offer a world in which there is too much wrong? How does it reflect the hopes that lie under our skin, the ways in which we will imagine a different world with our students?

Pedagogical Possibilities

As I discussed at the start of this chapter, in the courses that I teach, I am explicitly concerned with my students' understandings of an "I" and "we" throughout the term. For at least the past few years, I have attended to the fact that we are living in a society that aspires to democratic forms of public life, and with my students I have considered what this means in relation to course subject matter. When I started teaching, although I was fairly aware of my own ethical interests, which were turned towards democratic practices, the public good, and justice, I did not address these specifically with students. Over time, though, it became clear that my students and I could not avoid ethical choices and the fact of implication. We routinely came up against questions of the material. In many ways, students had a language for ethical support of existing disciplinary and social norms. Indeed, to a certain extent, university courses had provided them with and strengthened this language. If queer lives complicated the subject of gender, it was quite acceptable to simply eliminate these lives from our discussion of gender. To many of the students, existing norms seemed more a given than constructed. Within a normative ethical framework, eliminating queer communities from the subject was necessary and inevitable rather than a choice. Likewise, considering queer subjects was problematic. In such a context, students might read any explicit attention to the public good or justice as extraneous to course subject matter and, therefore, itself a problem.

Concerning ethical commitments, then, I faced at least two issues. First, students had come to understand specific aspects of communication (and, in turn, content in communication courses) as natural, or as "the way things are." While students might have perceived these aspects to be primarily conceptual, they were also, in fact, ethical and material. For example, nearly all communication textbooks approach interpersonal communication in ways that foreground and centre the individual. Even as the social is considered, the individual is primary. As noted earlier in this book, such an approach has limitations and makes it difficult to consider a public or the social. This conceptual approach has ethical consequences, in that it, for example, prioritizes consideration of the individual over analyses of power. Such an approach might make it seem acceptable to drop queer lives and communities from the subject. In the course on gender and communication, students could resist considering the connection of queer or raced communities to gender. This rejection of certain communities from the subject areas of undergraduate courses is an ethical act. Thus, students had an ethical approach, yet did not read it as such.

Second, students understood ethical considerations of the social or of democratic practices, the public good, and justice as extraneous to the work we ought to be doing in the classroom. As we made our way through course content and disciplinary concepts, and considered ideas central to course subject matter in relation to life outside the classroom, our lack of a common language for starting points for agency became problematic. It was as if we were irrevocably attached to a set of relational realities in our everyday lives – living with the fact of others, the backdrop of democratic values and aspirations, and the reality of too much wrong – yet, in the classroom, we could act as if these realities did not exist. I wanted to normalize attention to the ethical dimensions of the "we" and offer a transparency to the inevitability of ethical uses of agency and power. Further, I wanted to do so with explicit attention to democratic values, as these ought to shape public life in North America.

I started thinking through, with my students, the significance of these values and ethical uses of agency in connection with various course topics. "How do you benefit from living in a democratic society?" "How do you contribute to a democratic society?" "Make a list of what you have done in the last week that is related to your role as a citizen." "Make a list of what you have done in the last week that is related to your role as a consumer." "What does democracy have to do with [course title]?" I introduced brief readings on democracy in the first week or two of the term, gradually making explicit the democratic ethical parameters that shaped, at least in part, our work together over the term. In sum, I brought to the fore questions of a "we," rather than acting as if these questions were not present.

This was new, for my students and for myself. I moved forward with these questions and readings persistently yet cautiously, trying to gauge their effects in the process and consequences of learning. These readings encouraged students to consider widely accepted democratic values (Minow, 2002), what Frances Moore Lappé calls "strong democracy" (2005), the notion of "our presence in the world as ethical" (Freire, 1998, p. 57), and the significance of the ability to "manipulate social relations" (Dewey, 1927, p. 169; see also Maracle, 2005). These readings were not lengthy or prescriptive. They were primarily a means of exploring the ground from and context within which we were all doing the work of learning.

Such readings and conversations, grappling with the language of the relationship of self to other, is a crucial component of the "work of the we." Further, settings that link what happens in the classroom with the demands of public life require a language. If institutions of higher education in North America have an obligation to centrally inhabit ethical, ontological, and epistemological frameworks that consider the public good and justice, pedagogical content and practice must also inhabit such frameworks. Inasmuch as undergraduate education aims to encourage capacities for agency, consideration of relationships and power, and an imagination for the public good, courses must begin to make visible understandings of democratic practices, the public good, and justice. I have found that students are very receptive to such readings and conversations. As evidenced by the discussion I addressed at the start of this chapter, with respect to the meanings students attached to the word "public" and their struggles with what "the good life" entails, they understand the inevitability of ethical implication. They are living with that implication every day, working through its demands.

Pedagogy, in any given course, can be approached as a negotiation of two components, both situated directly within the topic for a specific course. These components include (1) disciplinary norms, priorities, and resources and (2) the material, the social, and the ethical. Constructing a course with these two components in the foreground can inform all aspects of that course: readings, assignments, use of in-class time, group and individual work, lectures, and the means of evaluation and assessment. Further, the method by which faculty members and students move through course content is the ongoing process of naming what is and imagining what might be different. In constructing a course, faculty members might consider the following: How does this course have an immediate relationship to routine practices and to everyday negotiations of power? From a disciplinary perspective and my own experience teaching this course, what are the four or five key concepts with which I want students to be familiar when they complete the course? How do these concepts play out in public life? As faculty members, we can both start from and work within an explicit and active regard for the practices of living together well, and consider how our work with our students might strengthen that regard.

A regard for the challenges of justice, for the significance of a white man's hissing at four boys of colour in a library computer room, has shaped the scope and content of this book. Even as book titles are most often finalized shortly before publication, my experience has been that colleagues and friends often ask "What will the title be?" when the book is merely a notion, a murky fog of questions and unsharpened assumptions one wants to address in print. One word that has always been attached to this book, from its inception through its actual writing, is the word longing. The experience of longing – something deeply felt, much more than rational, and in this context an unapologetic commitment to higher education's role in constructing more just practices of living together. Sitting in that library computer room, longing for a space where a white man's dehumanization of boys of colour is not routine; living with Cindy's demand for streamlined education and Allison's disconnect from nation, longing for educational conversations that turn towards complexity and open up space for what it means to be human: What are we up to? How do we inhabit the contours of our caring?

We live in a world of too much wrong. We live with state-sanctioned violence against communities of colour, disproportionate graduation rates by race, the removal of queer lives from public spaces. We live in the midst of large scale and particular inequities, visited on bodies, that harm individuals and communities. What stories do you see, hear, tell? Moving from too much wrong to less wrong to justice. The possibilities that emerge when we understand the subject as the practices of living together well. The world that we might imagine when we turn toward the reality of shards, flying. What hopes live under your skin? Turning towards injustice and longing for justice. Which promises will you keep, and with whom? Education can be a story that gets under our skin, that pulls at our commitments, that reminds us that our choices matter. In a world in which systemic inequity persists, I long to move from too much wrong to less wrong to justice. This is where my heart lives, where the pulse of this book resides. Naming injustice and imagining justice. What do you see? Where will you begin?

Notes

1. Higher Education and Democracy's Agenda

1 I use the term queer throughout the book to "refer to any sexual or gender expressions or identities that do not conform to the heteronormative and either/or gender frameworks ... Queer theory helps us to deconstruct and confound normative categories of sexuality and gender by" addressing lives and experiences that refuse these binaries (Haskell & Burtch, 2010, p. 10).

2 Throughout this book, I address post-secondary education in North America. I am centrally concerned with colleges and universities in the United States and with universities in Canada.

3 Literature on civic engagement and service learning does, in many ways, consider democratic practices. I would assert that this literature is not primarily directed at articulating a rationale linking democracy, higher education, engagement, and the public good, but that it is centrally focused on the curricular, administrative, pedagogical, and institutional demands involved in service learning and civic engagement efforts. See chapter 3 for further discussion.

4 I will discuss each of these traditions in more depth in chapter 3. Both have a variety of expressions. It is perhaps useful to state here that by critical, I am referring to work that has theoretical affinities with the Frankfurt School, which initially developed in the 1930s in Germany. This group of theorists shared a "belief that injustice and subjugation shaped the lived world" (Kincheloe 2008, p. 46). Critical work as I define it in this book includes scholarship that explicitly attends to the material conditions of how people live, power, and change. I agree with Patricia Hill Collins, who states that "what makes critical social theory 'critical' is its commitment to justice" (1998, p. xiv). Critical in this book does not refer to postmodernist scholarship.

5 My primary focus in this book is undergraduate education, in part because as a faculty member, I have worked most extensively with undergraduate students and programs. At the same time, the analysis I present explores the starting points, assumptions, and possibilities for a range of educational practices in institutions of higher learning. I do not aim to be prescriptive or definitive. Approaches to undergraduate education necessarily intersect with teaching graduate students.

6 Deliberative democracy has, over the past decade, received considerable scholarly attention (Fishkin, 2009; Gutman & Thompson, 2004; Kahane et al., 2010; Nabatdni et al., 2012; Thomas, 2010). Addressing the contextual considerations for dialogue in democratic societies, and ideal processes for and objectives of such dialogues, work on deliberative democracy is particularly attentive to collective decision-making processes that prioritize access, multiple forms of argument and deliberation, relational considerations, and possibilities for shared control (Chappell, 2012). On the whole, work on deliberative democracy is centrally concerned with the conditions for public dialogues, and the means by which such dialogues might be achieved. Most literature on deliberative democracy is less concerned with the realization of equity. Within this literature, an implicit reliance on liberal norms often results in a lack of in-depth attention to inequitable power dynamics and existing forms of injustice and their consequences.

2. Higher Education and the Social Contract

1 The format for my university's homepage, including the text stating that "Everything you discover at Waterloo belongs to you," was replaced by a different format after the picture with Chris Lok appeared.

2 The queer student group on campus was from September 2009 to December 2011 named the Queer and Questioning Community Centre. In December 2011, the organization was renamed the Glow Centre for Sexual and Gender Diversity.

3 I searched the existing online archives of the student paper (not complete for the dates in question), and emailed the newspaper to ask about coverage of the removal of the banner. I did not find, nor was I made aware of, any coverage of the removal of the banner.

4 I will further explore these two areas of scholarship in chapters 3 and 4.

5 It is not the purpose of this chapter or book to offer an in-depth discussion of the history and philosophy of liberal education. For attention to these areas, see, e.g., Kimball (1995), Rothblatt (1993), and Shapiro (2005).

6 Not all scholars I cite in this section identify themselves as "critical." Further, there are scholars who embrace one area of critical theory yet eschew others. For example, various scholars critique market logic and its effects on higher education, yet simultaneously support the idea of disinterested scholarship (Axelrod, 2000; Woodhouse, 2001). Throughout this book, I use the term critical to refer to scholars who explicitly "use inquiry as a means for challenging forms of oppression and marginality that limit full and equitable participation in public life" (Torres & Rhoads, 2006, p. 6).

7 I am in agreement with those scholars who understand politics as a reliance on various forms of power to exercise agency within institutional and contextual constraints and norms. In simple terms, politics is the negotiation of the social, and in this sense is ontologically significant, and, as such, clearly part of all public life, including the various activities in higher education.

3. Civic Engagement and Service Learning

1 It is possible to find scholarship in which authors put "race – specifically, African American identity – at the center of analyzing town/gown relationships" (Evans, 2009, p. xi; see also Calderón, 2007; Evans, Taylor, Dunlap, & Miller, 2009). Such work is useful in terms of considering service learning as rooted in, e.g., African American history, communities, and pursuit of social change. At the same time, the lack of race analysis within much mainstream service learning scholarship (i.e., especially that pursued by primarily white educators) persists.

2 Ongoing conversations I have with civic engagement scholars have confirmed that these scholars do have an awareness of deeply entrenched injustice in North America, and the oppression of groups based on race, gender, class, and other positionalities. Yet, on the whole, the scholarship does not reflect this awareness.

3 See chapter 1 for additional attention to the problems with inclusion.

4. "What Do You Think? 41 Bullets?"

1 It is worth noting that the Sanford Police Department, which has jurisdiction where Zimmerman killed Martin, employs a Neighborhood Watch organizer.

2 In making more visible the ways in which forms of scholarship and approaches to knowledge and curriculum shape what students learn, it is

instructive to broadly consider liberal and critical approaches to education. As with any body of intellectual work and practice, there are tensions and differences within each of these bodies of work. Further, the ways in which faculty members draw on either or both frameworks is not impermeable. As a critical scholar, I may at times invoke liberal norms. Likewise, liberal scholars may articulate critical priorities. My aim is not to offer definitive, fixed, or exhaustive definitions or analyses of either body or both bodies of work. Rather, I am interested in contributing to a discourse in which educators, in our research and teaching, might be more attuned to the ways in which our educational assumptions shape our educational practices. See chapter 1, n4, for a brief definition of my use of the word "critical."

6. Epistemological Architectures

1 I want to affirm that, in terms of considering gender, epistemology, and queer lives, there are many ways to approach these subjects. Queer theory (Barnard, 2004; Sedgwick, 1990; Sullivan, 2003) has raised many of these issues. I do not aim in this book to offer an exhaustive analysis of these questions and issues from the particularity of gender and queer theory. Rather, I am using the course on Gender and Communication, and the epistemological questions that Cindy's and Allison's insertions raise, as a way of opening up certain sets of questions which have relevance to a range of courses and subjects.
2 LGBT refers to lesbian, gay, bisexual, and transgender.
3 Miller and Rose's statement refers to specific moves in the 1980s. I want to emphasize their reference to normality, and would argue that the desire for normality as a way of being is, in many ways, steadily increasing.

7. The Work of the "We"

1 The reluctance of liberal scholars to explicitly address interests and power is not consistent, in terms of frequency or depth, and it would be risky to make definitive claims. Many liberal scholars might, for example, affirm the significance of context, agree that power is significant to how we live, and claim that most, if not all educational work is interested in some particular set of priorities. At the same time, such assertions, made by liberal scholars in unambiguous, bold, and public ways, are rare. Further, my experience of public attention to educational investments and interests (at conferences, meetings, etc.) is that liberal scholars might affirm such commitments in the abstract, but demonstrate a caution or refusal to commit to concrete

investments. As demonstrated by Bok, liberal scholars are more comfortable addressing "promises" and other ethical interests at a broad, conceptual level, than at the level of an embodied materiality.

2 To some extent, faculty members may find it helpful to consider each of these objectives (civic, professional, and intellectual) as offering discrete types of competencies. My primary critique with the discussion of these aims is that there is little scholarship offering a broad rationale for how, in the work of teaching, it is to some extent impossible to consistently and effectively separate these aims. The work we do with students most often pursues all three aims in overlapping ways.

References

Abel, Charles Frederick, and Arthur J. Sementelli. 2004. *Evolutionary Critical Theory and Its Role in Public Affairs*. Armonk, NY: M.E. Sharpe.

Alanís, Jaime. 2006. "How Much Are You Willing to Risk? How Far Are You Willing to Go?" *Cultural Studies Critical Methodologies* 6 (1): 166–184. http://dx.doi.org/10.1177/1532708605282816.

Alexander, Bryant Keith. 1999. "Performing Culture in the Classroom: An Instructional (Auto)ethnography." *Text and Performance Quarterly* 19 (4): 307–331. http://dx.doi.org/10.1080/10462939909366272.

Alexander, Thomas M. 1987. *John Dewey's Theory of Art, Experience, and Nature*. Albany: State University of New York Press.

Alfred, Taiaiake. 1999. *Peace Power Righteousness: An Indigenous Manifesto*. Don Mills, ON: Oxford University Press.

Alfred, Taiaiake, and Jeff Corntassel. 2005. "Being Indigenous: Resurgences against Contemporary Colonialism." *Government and Opposition* 40 (4): 597–614. http://dx.doi.org/10.1111/j.1477-7053.2005.00166.x.

Allen, M. 1993. "Critical and Tradition Science: Implications for Communication Research." *Western Journal of Communication* 57: 200–208.

American Association of State Colleges and Universities. 2002. *Stepping Forward as Stewards of Place: A Guide for Leading Public Engagement at State Colleges and Universities*. Washington, DC: Author.

Anzaldúa, Gloria E. 1999. *Borderlands/La Frontera: The New Mestiza*. San Francisco: Aunt Lute Books.

Apple, Michael W. 1992. "The Text and Cultural Politics." *Educational Researcher* 21 (7): 4–19. http://dx.doi.org/10.3102/0013189X021007004.

Apple, Michael W., and Linda K. Christian-Smith. 1991. "The Politics of the Textbook." In *The Politics of the Textbook*, ed. Michael W. Apple and Linda K. Christian-Smith, 1–21. New York: Routledge.

Armaline, William T., David Silfen Glasberg, and Bandana Purkayastha, eds. 2011. *Human Rights in Our Own Backyard: Injustice and Resistance in the United States*. Philadelphia: University of Pennsylvania Press.

Aronowitz, Stanley. 2001. *The Last Good Job in America*. Lanham, MD: Rowman & Littlefield.

Aronowitz, Stanley. 2005. "Higher Education as a Public Good." In *Critical Social Issues in American Education*, ed. H. Svi Shapiro and David E. Purpel, 109–121. Mahwah, NJ: Lawrence Erlbaum.

Aronowitz, Stanley. 2006. *Left Turn: Forging a New Political Future*. Boulder, CO: Paradigm.

Aronowitz, Stanley. 2008. *Against Schooling: For an Education that Matters*. Boulder, CO: Paradigm.

Aronowitz, Stanley, and Henry A. Giroux. 1991. "Textual Authority, Culture, and the Politics of Literacy." In *The Politics of the Textbook*, ed. Michael W. Apple and Linda K. Christian-Smith, 213–241. New York: Routledge.

Association for Women's Rights in Development. 2004. "Intersectionality: A Tool for Gender and Economic Justice." *Women's Rights and Economic Change* 9 (Aug.): 1–8.

Axelrod, Paul. 2000. "What Is to Be Done? Envisioning the University's Future." In *The Corporate Campus: Commercialization and the Dangers to Canada's Colleges and Universities*, ed. James L. Turk, 201–208. Toronto: Lorimer.

Axelrod, Paul. 2002. *Values in Conflict: The University, the Marketplace, and the Trials of Liberal Education*. Montreal and Kingston: McGill-Queen's University Press.

Axelrod, Paul, Paul Anisef, and Zeng Lin. 2001. "Against All Odds? The Enduring Value of Liberal Education in Universities, Professions, and the Labour Market." *Canadian Journal of Higher Education* 31 (2): 47–78.

Barker, Derek. 2004. "The Scholarship of Engagement: A Taxonomy of Five Emerging Practices." *Journal of Higher Education Outreach and Engagement* 9 (2): 123–137.

Barker, Derek, and David W. Brown. 2009. *A Different Kind of Politics: Readings on the Role of Higher Education in Democracy*. Dayton, OH: Kettering Foundation.

Barnard, Ian. 2004. *Queer Race: Cultural Interventions in the Racial Politics of Queer Theory*. New York: Peter Lang.

Battistoni, Richard M., and William E. Hudson. 1997. *Practicing Democracy: Concepts and Models of Service-Learning in Political Science*. Washington, DC: American Association of Higher Education.

Bauer, Greta, Rob Travers, Rebecca Hammond, Michelle Boyce, and Scott Anderson. 2007. *Trans PULSE Report on Phase I & Plans for Phases II and III*. Toronto: Trans PULSE Project.

Bauman, Zygmunt. 1989. *Modernity and the Holocaust*. Cambridge: Polity.

Bauman, Zygmunt. 2011. *Collateral Damage: Social Inequalities in a Global Age*. Cambridge: Polity.

Beiner, Ronald. 1992. *What's the Matter with Liberalism?* Berkeley: University of California Press.

Bell, Richard H. 1998. *Simone Weil: The Way of Justice as Compassion*. Lanham, MD: Rowman & Littlefield.

Berger, Ben. 2009. "Political Theory, Political Science, and the End of Civic Engagement." *Perspectives on Politics* 7 (2): 335–350. http://dx.doi.org/10.1017/S153759270909080X.

Bernal, Dolores Delgado. 2006. *Chicana/Latina Education in Everyday Life: Feminista Perspectives on Pedagogy and Epistemology*. Albany: State University of New York Press.

Bernecker, Sven, and Duncan Pritchard. 2011. *The Routledge Companion to Epistemology*. New York: Routledge.

Biesta, Gert. 2006. *Beyond Learning: Democratic Education for a Human Future*. Boulder, CO: Paradigm.

Bjarnason, Sylvia, and Patrick Coldstream. 2003. *The Idea of Engagement: Universities in Society*. London: Association of Commonwealth Universities.

Blewett, Lori. "Communication and Gender: Tentative Syllabus." Accessed 11 May 2009. http://academic.evergreen.edu/curricular/commgender/syllabus.htm.

Bloom, Allan. 1987. *The Closing of the American Mind: How Higher Education Has Failed Democracy and Impoverished the Souls of Today's Students*. New York: Simon & Schuster.

Bok, Derek Curtis. 1982. *Beyond the Ivory Tower: Social Responsibilities in the Modern University*. Boston: Harvard University Press.

Bok, Derek Curtis. 2003. *Universities in the Marketplace: The Commercialization of Higher Education*. Princeton, NJ: Princeton University Press.

Bok, Derek Curtis. 2006. *Our Underachieving Colleges: A Candid Look at How Much Students Learn and Why They Should Be Learning More*. Princeton, NJ: Princeton University Press.

Bonilla-Silva, Eduardo. 2010. *Racism without Racists: Colour-Blind Racism and the Persistence of Inequality in North America*. Lanham, MD: Rowman & Littlefield.

Bowen, Howard R. 1977. *Investment in Learning*. San Francisco: Jossey-Bass.

Boyer, Ernst L. 1990. *Scholarship Reconsidered: Priorities of the Professoriate*. Princeton, NJ: Princeton University Press.

Boyer, Ernst L. 1996. "From Scholarship Reconsidered to Scholarship Assessed." *Quest* 48 (2): 129–139. http://dx.doi.org/10.1080/00336297.1996.10484184.

Boyte, Harry C. 2008."Public Work: Civic Populism versus Technocracy in Higher Education." In *Agent of Democracy: Higher Education and the HEX Journey*, ed. David W. Brown and Deborah Witte, 81–102. Dayton, OH: Kettering Foundation.

Boyte, Harry C., and James Farr. 1997. "The Work of Citizenship and the Problem of Service-Learning." In *Experiencing Citizenship*, ed. Richard Battistoni and William Hudson, 1–12. Washington, DC: American Association of Higher Education.

Brabant, Margaret, and Arthur Hochman. 2004. "What Are Schools For? Crossing Institutional Boundaries for the Sake of Learning." *Educational Studies* 36 (2): 159–177. http://dx.doi.org/10.1207/s15326993es3602_4.

Brabant, Margaret, and Donald Braid. 2009. "The Devil Is in the Details: Defining Civic Engagement." *Journal of Higher Education Outreach and Engagement* 13 (2): 59–87.

Bringle, Robert G., Julie A. Hatcher, and Patti H. Clayton. 2006. "The Scholarship of Civic Engagement: Defining, Documenting and Evaluating Faculty Work." In *To Improve the Academy*, ed. Douglas Reimondo Robertson and Linda Burzotta Nilson, 257–279. Bolton, MA: Anker.

Brint, Steven, Mark Riddle, Lori Turk-Bicakci, and Charles S. Levy. 2005. "From the Liberal to the Practical Arts in American Colleges and Universities: Organizational Analysis and Curricular Change." *Journal of Higher Education* 76 (2): 151–180. http://dx.doi.org/10.1353/jhe.2005.0011.

Britzman, Deborah P. 1995. "Is There a Queer Pedagogy? Or, Stop Reading Straight." *Educational Theory* 45 (2): 151–165. http://dx.doi.org/10.1111/j.1741-5446.1995.00151.x.

Britzman, Deborah P. 1998. "Queer Pedagogy and Its Strange Techniques." In *Inside the Academy and Out: Lesbian/Gay/Queer Studies and Social Action*, ed. Janice Lynn Ristock and Catherine G. Taylor, 49–71. Toronto: University of Toronto Press.

Brown, Elsa Barkley. 1990. "African American Women's Quilting: A Framework for Conceptualizing and Teaching African American Women's History." In *Black Women in America: Social Science Perspectives*, ed. Micheline R. Malson, Elisabeth Mudimbe-Boyi, Jean F. O'Barr, and Mary Wyer, 9–18. Chicago: University of Chicago Press.

Brown, Wendy. 2005. *Edgework: Critical Essays on Knowledge and Politics*. Princeton, NJ: Princeton University Press.

Burchell, Graham. 1996. "Liberal Government and Techniques of the Self." In *Foucault and Political Reason*, ed. Andrew Barry, Thomas Osborne, and Nikolas Rose, 19–36. London: UCL Press.

Burkhardt, Mary Jane, Barbara Holland, Stephen L. Percy, and Nancy Zimpher. 2004. *Calling the Question: Is Higher Education Ready to Commit to*

Community Engagement? Milwaukee: University of Wisconsin-Milwaukee.

Calderón, José Z. 2007. *Race, Poverty, and Social Justice: Multidisciplinary Perspectives through Service Learning.* Sterling, VA: Stylus.

Campbell, Colin. 2004. "I Shop therefore I Know that I Am." In *Elusive Consumption,* ed. Karin M. Ekström and Helene Brembeck, 27–44. Oxford: Berg.

Cannon, Martin John, and Lina Sunseri, eds. 2011. *Racism, Colonialism, and Indigeneity in Canada: A Reader.* Don Mills, ON: Oxford University Press.

Carleton, Sean. 2011. "Colonizing Minds: Public Education, the 'Textbook Indian,' and Settler Colonialism in British Columbia, 1920–1970." *BC Studies* 169: 101–130, 175.

Center for Constitutional Rights a. "*Daniels et al. v. City of New York.*" Web page accessed 2 Aug. 2012. http://ccrjustice.org/ourcases/past-cases/daniels,-et-al.-v.-city-new-york.

Centre for Constitutional Rights b. "*Floyd et al. v. City of New York et al.*" Web page accessed 2 Aug. 2012. http://ccrjustice.org/floyd.

Chambers, Tony C. 2005. "The Special Role of Higher Education in Society: As a Public Good for the Public Good." In *Higher Education for the Public Good: Emerging Voices from a National Movement,* ed. Adrianna J. Kezar, Tony C. Chambers, and John C. Burkhardt, 3–22. San Francisco: Jossey-Bass.

Chappell, Zsuzsanna. 2012. *Deliberative Democracy: A Critical Introduction.* New York: Palgrave Macmillan.

City of New York Police Department. n.d. "Mission, Home." Accessed 20 May 2013. http://www.nyc.gov/html/nypd/html/administration/mission.shtml.

Colby, Anne, Elizabeth Beaumont, Thomas Ehrlich, and Josh Corngold. 2007. *Educating for Democracy: Preparing Undergraduates for Responsible Political Engagement.* San Francisco: Jossey-Bass.

Colby, Anne, Thomas Ehrlich, Elizabeth Beaumont, Jennifer Rosner, and Jason Stephens. 2000. "Higher Education and the Development of Civic Responsibility." In *Civic Responsibility and Higher Education,* ed. Thomas Ehrlich, xxi–xliii. Phoenix, AZ: American Council on Education and Onyx Press.

Collins, Patricia Hill. 1998. *Fighting Words: Black Women and the Search for Justice.* Minneapolis: University of Minnesota Press.

Collins, Patricia Hill. 2000. *Black Feminist Thought: Knowledge, Consciousness, and the Politics of Empowerment.* 2nd ed. New York: Routledge.

Comaroff, Jean, and John L. Comaroff. 2000. "Millennial Capitalism: First Thoughts on a Second Coming." *Public Culture* 12 (2): 291–343. http://dx.doi.org/10.1215/08992363-12-2-291.

Coronil, Fernando. 2000. "Towards a Critique of Globalcentrism: Speculations on Capitalism's Nature." *Public Culture* 12 (2): 351–374. http://dx.doi.org/10.1215/08992363-12-2-351.

Coté, James E., and Anton Allahar. 2007. *Ivory Tower Blues: A University System in Crisis*. Toronto: University of Toronto Press.

Coté, Mark, Richard J.F. Day, and Greig de Peuter. 2007. *Utopian Pedagogy: Radical Experiments against Neoliberal Globalization*. Toronto: University of Toronto Press.

Couldry, Nick. 2010. *Why Voice Matters: Culture and Politics after Neoliberalism*. Los Angeles: Sage.

Coulthard, Glen S. 2007. "Subjects of Empire: Indigenous Peoples and the 'Politics of Recognition' in Canada." *Contemporary Political Theory* 6 (4): 437–460. http://dx.doi.org/10.1057/palgrave.cpt.9300307.

Cox, E. Sam, and Wendy L. Geiger. 2011. Communication Activism: A Service-Learning Project with Hateful/Harmful Speech. Paper presented at the annual meeting of the National Communication Association, New Orleans, LA.

Crenshaw, Kimberle. 1995. *Critical Race Theory: The Key Writings That Formed the Movement*. New York: New Press.

Cruz, Cindy. 2001. "Toward an Epistemology of a Brown Body." *Qualitative Studies in Education* 14 (5): 657–669. http://dx.doi.org/10.1080/09518390110059874.

Dallmayr, Fred. 2011. "Liberal Democracy and Its Critics: Some Voices from East and West." In *Democratic Culture: Historical and Philosophical Essays*, ed. Akeel Bilgrami, 1–22. New Delhi: Routledge.

Danelzik, Mathis. 2008. "Does Non-dualism Imply an Approach to Power? Non-dualizing Epistemology and the Political." *Constructivist Foundations* 3 (3): 214–220.

Daniels, Ronald J., and Michael J. Trebilcock. 2005. "Towards a New Compact for University Education in Ontario." In *Taking Public Universities Seriously*, ed. Frank Iacobucci and Carolyn J. Tuohy, 87–118. Toronto: University of Toronto Press.

Darder, Antonia. 2011. *A Dissident Voice: Essays on Culture, Pedagogy, and Power*. New York: Peter Lang.

Dauphinee, Elizabeth. 2010. "The Ethics of Autoethnography." *Review of International Studies* 36 (03): 799–818. http://dx.doi.org/10.1017/S0260210510000690.

Davidson, Richard J. 2000. "Cognitive Neuroscience Needs Affective Neuroscience (and Vice Versa)." *Brain and Cognition* 42 (1): 89–92. http://dx.doi.org/10.1006/brcg.1999.1170.

Dei, George J. Sefa. 2000. "Recasting Anti-Racism and the Axis of Difference: Beyond the Question of Theory." *Race, Gender & Class* 7 (2): 38–56.

Dei, George J. Sefa. 2008. "Schooling as Community: Race, Schooling and the Education of African Youth." *Journal of Black Studies* 38 (3): 346–366.

Delgado, Richard, and Jean Stefancic. 2005. The Role of Critical Race Theory in Understanding Race, Crime, and Justice Issues. Paper presented at the John Jay College of Criminal Justice, New York, Dec.

Delgado, Richard, and Jean Stefancic. 2013. *Critical Race Theory: The Cutting Edge*. 3rd ed. Philadelphia, PA: Temple University Press.

Della Porta, Donatella, and Dieter Rucht. 2013a. "Power and Democracy in Social Movements: An Introduction." In *Meeting Democracy: Power and Deliberation in Global Justice Movements*, ed. Donatella della Porta and Dieter Rucht, 1–22. Cambridge: Cambridge University Press. http://dx.doi.org/10.1017/CBO9781139236034.002.

Della Porta, Donatella, and Dieter Rucht. 2013b. "Power and Democracy: Concluding Remarks." In *Meeting Democracy: Power and Deliberation in Global Justice Movements*, ed. Donatella della Porta and Dieter Rucht, 214–235. Cambridge: Cambridge University Press. http://dx.doi.org/10.1017/CBO9781139236034.010.

Democracy Now. 2012. "Despite Praise & Permission, Detroit Teacher Fired for Helping Students' Trayvon Martin Fundraiser." 13 Apr. http://www.democracynow.org/2012/4/13/despite_praise_permission_detroit_schoolteacher_brooke.

Dewey, John. 1927. *The Public and Its Problems*. Denver, CO: Allan Swallow.

Dewey, John. 1978. *The Middle Works of John Dewey*, vol. 5, *Ethics*. Edited by Jo Ann Boydston. Carbondale: Southern Illinois University Press.

Dewey, John. 1993. *The Political Writings of John Dewey*. Edited by Debra Morris and Ian Shapiro. Indianapolis, IN: Hackett.

Dewey, John. 1998. *The Essential Dewey*. Edited by Larry Hickman and Thomas M. Alexander. Bloomington, IN: Indiana University Press.

Dolcos, Florin, Alexandru D. Iordan, and Sanda Dolcos. 2011. "Neural Correlates of Emotion-Cognition Interactions: A Review of Evidence from Brain Imaging Investigations." *Journal of Cognitive Psychology* 23 (6): 669–694. http://dx.doi.org/10.1080/20445911.2011.594433.

Drolet, Marie, and Karen Mumford. 2012. "The Gender Pay Gap for Private-Sector Employees in Canada and Britain." *British Journal of Industrial Relations* 50 (3): 529–553. http://dx.doi.org/10.1111/j.1467-8543.2011.00868.x.

Dryzek, John S. 2000. *Deliberative Democracy and Beyond: Liberals, Critics, Contestations*. Oxford: Oxford University Press.

Dugan, Máire A. 2004. *Power Inequities*. Edited by Heidi Burgess and Guy Burgess. Accessed 4 June 2012. http://www.beyondintractability.org/bi-essay/power-inequities.

Duggan, Lisa. 2002. "The New Homonormativity: The Sexual Politics of Neoliberalism." In *Materializing Democracy: Toward a Revitalized Cultural Politics*, ed. Russ Castronovo and Dana D. Nelson, pp. 175–194. Durham, NC: Duke University Press. http://dx.doi.org/10.1215/9780822383901-007.

Duggan, Lisa. 2003. *The Twilight of Equality? Neoliberalism, Cultural Politics, and the Attack on Democracy*. Boston: Beacon.

Dunne, L. 2009. "Discourses of Inclusion: A Critique." *Power and Education* 1 (1): 42–56. http://dx.doi.org/10.2304/power.2009.1.1.42.

Dyson, Michael Eric. 2005. "Some of Us Are." In *First Class, But the Plane Is in Trouble*. Washington, DC: Presentation, Unvarnished Truth Awards.

Dzur, Albert W. 2008. *Democratic Professionalism: Citizen Participation and the Reconstruction of Professional Ethics, Identity, and Practice*. University Park: Pennsylvania State University Press.

Earnheardt, Alan. "Gender Communication Syllabus, Youngstown State University." Accessed 5 Aug. 2013. http://web.ysu.edu/gen/fpa_generated_bin/documents/basic_module/3750.pdf.

Eckert, Penelope, and Sally McConnell-Ginet. 2003. *Language and Gender*. Cambridge: Cambridge University Press. http://dx.doi.org/10.1017/CBO9780511791147.

Edmonds, Penelope. 2010. "Unpacking Settler Colonialism's Urban Strategies: Indigenous Peoples in Victoria, British Columbia, and the Transition to a Settler-Colonial City." *Urban History Review/Revue d'histoire urbaine* 38 (2): 4–20, 88. http://dx.doi.org/10.7202/039671ar.

Ehrlich, Thomas. 1995. "Taking Service Seriously." *American Association of Higher Education Bulletin* 47 (7): 8–10.

Ellis, Carolyn, Tony E. Adams, and Arthur P. Bochner. 2011. "Autoethnography: An Overview." *Forum: Qualitative Social Research* 12, no. 1: n.p. http://www.qualitative-research.net/index.php/fqs/article/view/1589/3095.

Endres, Benjamin. 2002. "Critical Pedagogy and Liberal Education: Reconciling Tradition, Critique, and Democracy." *Philosophy of Education Yearbook*, 59–68.

Engel, Antke. 2007. "Challenging the Heteronormativity of Tolerance Pluralism: Articulations of Non-Normative Sexualities." *Redescriptions: Yearbook of Political Thought and Conceptual History* 11: 78–98.

Engell, James, and Anthony Dangerfield. 2005. *Saving Higher Education in the Age of Money*. Charlottesville, VA: University of Virginia Press.

Evans, Stephanie Y. 2009. "Preface: Using History, Experience, and Theory to Balance Relationships in Community Engagement." In *African Americans and Community Engagement in Higher Education: Community Service, Service-Learning, and Community-Based Research*, ed. Stephanie Y. Evans, Colette M. Taylor, Michelle R. Dunlap, and DeMond S. Miller, xi–xx. Albany: State University of New York Press.

Evans, Stephanie Y., Colette M. Taylor, Michelle R. Dunlap, and S. Miller DeMond, eds. 2009. *African Americans and Community Engagement in Higher Education: Community Service, Service-Learning, and Community-Based Research*. Albany: State University of New York Press.

Exley, Robert J. 2004. "A Critique of the Civic Engagement Model." In *Service-Learning: History, Theory, and Issues*, ed. Bruce W. Speck and Sherry Lee Hoppe, 85–97. Westport, CT: Praeger.

Fabian, Johannes. 1983. *Time and the Other: How Anthropology Makes Its Object*. New York: Columbia University Press.

Fallis, George. 2007. *Multiversities, Ideas, and Democracy*. Toronto: University of Toronto Press.

Ferguson, John, David Collison, David Power, and Lorna Stevenson. 2009. "Constructing Meaning in the Service of Power: An Analysis of the Typical Modes of Ideology in Accounting Textbooks." *Critical Perspectives on Accounting* 20 (8): 896–909. http://dx.doi.org/10.1016/j.cpa.2009.02.002.

Findlay, Allan, Russell King, Alexandra Stam, and Enric Ruiz-Gelices. 2006. "Ever Reluctant Europeans: The Changing Geographies of UK Students Studying and Working Abroad." *European Urban and Regional Studies* 13 (4): 291–318. http://dx.doi.org/10.1177/0969776406065429.

Fish, Stanley. 2008. *Save the World on Your Own Time*. Oxford: Oxford University Press.

Fishkin, James S. 2009. *When the People Speak: Deliberative Democracy and Public Consultation*. Oxford: Oxford University Press.

Flax, Jane. 1990. *Thinking Fragments: Psychoanalysis, Feminism, and Postmodernism in the Contemporary West*. Berkeley: University of California Press.

Fleras, Augie. 2011. *The Media Gaze: Representations of Diversities in Canada*. Vancouver: UBC Press.

Foss, Sonja K. 2009. "Course Syllabus of CMMU4265." Accessed 11 May 2009. http://www.sonjafoss.com/html/syllabi.html.

Foucault, Michel. 1980. *Power/Knowledge*. New York: Pantheon.

Foucault, Michel. 1997. "What Is Enlightenment?" In *The Politics of Truth*. Edited by Sylvère Lotringer, 101–134. Los Angeles: Semiotext(e).

Foucault, Michel. 2008. *The Birth of Biopolitics*. Basingstoke: Palgrave. http://dx.doi.org/10.1057/9780230594180.

Freeman, Victoria. 2010. "'Toronto Has No History!' Indigeneity, Settler Colonialism, and Historical Memory in Canada's Largest City." *Urban History Review/ Revue d'histoire urbaine* 38 (2): 21–35, 88. http://dx.doi.org/10.7202/039672ar.

Freire, Paulo. 1998. *Pedagogy of Freedom: Ethics, Democracy, and Civic Courage.* Lanham, MD: Rowman & Littlefield.

Freire, Paulo. 2001. "Reading the World and Reading the Word: An Interview with Paulo Freire." In *Philosophy of Education: Introductory Readings,* ed. William Hare and John P. Portelli, 142–152. Calgary: Detselig. (Reprinted from *Language Arts,* 1985).

Giroux, Henry A. 2002a. "Educated Hope in an Age of Privatized Visions." *Cultural Studies/Critical Methodologies* 2 (1): 93–112. http://dx.doi.org/10.1177/153270860200200111.

Giroux, Henry A. 2002b. "Neoliberalism, Corporate Culture, and the Promise of Higher Education: The University as a Democratic Public Sphere." *Harvard Educational Review* 72 (4): 424–463.

Giroux, Henry A. 2002c. "The Corporate War against Higher Education." *Henry A. Giroux.* http://www.henryagiroux.com/online_articles/corporate_war.htm.

Giroux, Henry A. 2003. *Public Spaces, Private Lives: Beyond the Culture of Cynicism.* Lanham, MD: Rowman and Littlefield.

Giroux, Henry A. 2005a. "Critical Pedagogy and the Challenge of Neoliberalism." *Chinese Cross Currents* 2 (3): 128–150.

Giroux, Henry A. 2005b. "Globalizing Dissent and Rradicalizing Democray: Politics, Pedagogy, and the Responsibility of Critical Intellectuals." In *Radical Relevance: Toward a Scholarship of the Whole Left,* ed. Laura Gray-Rosendale and Steven Rosendale, 141–159. Albany: SUNY Press.

Giroux, Henry A. 2005c. "Resisting Market Fundamentalism and the New Authoritarianism: A New Task for Cultural Studies?" *JAC* 25 (1): 1–29.

Giroux, Henry A. 2005d."The Politics of Public Pedagogy." In *If Classrooms Matter: Place, Pedagogy and Politics,* ed. Jeffrey Di Leo et al., 15–36. New York: Routledge.

Giroux, Henry A. 2005e. "Translating the Future: Speaking to the Next Generation of Youth." *Review of Education, Pedagogy & Cultural Studies* 27 (3): 213–218. http://dx.doi.org/10.1080/10714410500228876.

Giroux, Henry A. 2007a. "Introduction: Democracy, Education, and the Politics of Critical Pedagogy." In *Critical Pedagogy: Where Are We Now?* ed. Peter McLaren and Joe L. Kincheloe, 1–6. New York: Peter Lang.

Giroux, Henry A. 2007b. "Utopian Thinking in Dangerous Times: Critical Pedagogy and the Project of Educated Hope." In *Utopian Pedagogy: Radical Experiments against Neoliberal Globalization,* ed. M. Coté, R.J.F. Day, and G. de Peuter, 25–42. Toronto: University of Toronto Press.

Giroux, Henry A., and Susan Searls Giroux. 2004. *Take Back Higher Education: Race, Youth, and the Crisis of Democracy in the Post-Civil Rights Era*. New York: Palgrave Macmillan. http://dx.doi.org/10.1057/9781403982667.

Goldberg, David Theo. 1993. "Modernity, Race, and Morality." *Cultural Critique* 24 (24): 193–227. http://dx.doi.org/10.2307/1354133.

Gomberg-Muñoz, Ruth. 2012. "Inequality in a 'Postracial' Era." *Du Bois Review* 9 (02): 339–353. http://dx.doi.org/10.1017/S1742058X11000579.

Grande, Sandy. 2004. *Red Pedagogy: Native American Social and Political Thought*. Lanham, MD: Rowman & Littlefield.

Grant, Karen R. 2002. "A Conversation on the Future of the Academy with James Turk, PhD, Executive Director, Canadian Association of University Teachers." *Canadian Review of Sociology and Anthropology/La Revue canadienne de sociologie et d'anthropologie* 39 (3): 261–74. http://dx.doi.org/10.1111/j.1755-618X.2002.tb00620.x.

Gray, Jeremy R., Todd S. Braver, and Marcus E. Raichle. 2002. "Integration of Emotion and Cognition in the Lateral Prefrontal Cortex." *Proceedings of the National Academy of Sciences of the United States of America* 99 (6): 4115–4120. http://dx.doi.org/10.1073/pnas.062381899.

Grosfoguel, Ramón. 2007. "The Epistemic Decolonial Turn: Beyond Political Economy Paradigms." *Cultural Studies* 21 (2): 211–223. http://dx.doi.org/10.1080/09502380601162514.

Grossberg, Lawrence. 2005. *Caught in the Crossfire*. Boulder, CO: Paradigm.

Gurin, Patricia. 1999. "Expert Report of Patricia Gurin, *Gratz, et al.* v. *Bollinger, et al.*, No. 97-75321(E.D. Mich.) *Grutter, et al.* v. *Bollinger, et al.*, No. 97-75928 (E.D. Mich.)"

Gutman, Amy, and Dennis F. Thompson. 2004. *Why Deliberative Democracy?* Princeton, NJ: Princeton University Press.

Hackney, S. 1994. "The Roles and Responsibilities of Urban Universities in Their Communities: Five University Presidents Call for Action." *Universities and Community Schools* 1/2: 9–11.

Haggett, Scott, 2012. "Imperial Launches C$2 Billion Oil Sands Expansion." *Reuters Canada*, 3 Feb. Accessed 1 May 2014. http://ca.reuters.com/article/domesticNews/idCATRE81218720120203

Hall, Stuart. 1988. "The Toad in the Garden: Thatcherism among the Theorists." In *Marxism and the Interpretation of Culture*, ed. Cary Nelson and Lawrence Grossberg, 35–57. Urbana: University of Illinois Press.

Hall, Stuart. 2012. "The Neoliberal Revolution." In "The Neoliberal Crisis," ed. Jonathan Rutherford and Sally Davison. *Soundings: A Journal of Politics and Culture*, 8–26.

Hansen, David T., ed. 2006. *John Dewey and Our Educational Prospect: A Critical Engagement with Dewey's Democracy and Education*. Albany,: SUNY Press.

Harding, Sandra, and Merrill B. Hintikka. 1983. "Introduction." In *Discovering Reality: Feminist Perspectives on Epistemology, Metaphysics, Methodology, and Philosophy of Science*, ed. Sandra Harding and Merrill B. Hintikka, ix–xix. Boston: Reidel.

Harding, Sandra, and Merrill B. Hintikka, eds. 2003. *Discovering Reality: Feminist Perspectives on Epistemology, Metaphysics, Methodology, and Philosophy of Science*. 2nd ed. Dordrecht: Kluwer Academic. http://dx.doi .org/10.1007/978-94-010-0101-4.

Hartley, Matthew. 2009. "Reclaiming the Democratic Purpose of American Higher Education: Tracing the Trajectory of the Civic Engagement Movement." *Learning and Teaching* 2 (3): 11–30. http://dx.doi.org/10.3167/ latiss.2009.020302.

Hartley, Matthew. 2011. "Idealism and Compromise and the Civic Engagement Movement." In *To Serve a Larger Purpose: Engagement for Democracy and the Transformation of Higher Education*, ed. John Saltmarsh and Matthew Hartley, 27-48. Philadelphia, PA: Temple University Press.

Hartmann, Heidi. 1987. "The Family as the Locus of Gender, Class, and Political Struggle: The Example of Housework." In *Feminism and Methodology*, ed. Sandra Harding, 109–134. Bloomington, IN: Indiana University Press.

Harvey, David. 2011. "The Rise of Neoliberalism and the Riddle of Capital." In *Capital and Its Discontents: Conversations with Radical Thinkers in a Time of Tumult*, ed. Sasha Lilley, 43–77. Winnipeg: Fernwood.

Haskell, Rebecca, and Brian Burtch. 2010. *Get that Freak: Homophobia and Transphobia in High School*. Halifax: Fernwood.

Hauerwas, Stanley. 2007. *The State of the University: Academic Knowledges and the Knowledge of God*. Malden, MA: Blackwell. http://dx.doi. org/10.1002/9780470692516.

Hausmann, Ricardo, Laura D. Tyson, and Saadia Zahidi. 2011. *The Global Gender Gap Report 2011*. Geneva: Word Economic Forum.

Hendricks, Vincent F., and Duncan Pritchard. 2008. *New Waves in Epistemology*. Basingstoke: Palgrave Macmillan.

Henry, Frances, and Carol Tator. 2009. *The Colour of Democracy*. Scarborough, ON: Racism in Canadian Society.

Hill, Darryl B., and Martin E. Morf. 2000. "Undoing Theory/Practice Dualism: Joint Action and Knowing from Within." *Journal of Theoretical and Philosophical Psychology* 20 (2): 208–224. http://dx.doi.org/10.1037/ h0091210.

Hironimus-Wendt, Robert J., and Larry Lovell-Troy. 1999. "Grounding Service Learning in Social Theory." *Teaching Sociology* 27 (4): 360–372. http://dx.doi .org/10.2307/1319042.

Hogben, Matthew, and Caroline K. Waterman. 1997. "Are All of Your Students Represented in Their Textbooks? A Content Analysis of Coverage of Diversity Issues in Introductory Psychology Textbooks." *Teaching of Psychology* 24 (2): 95–100. http://dx.doi.org/10.1207/s15328023top2402_3.

Hokowhitu, Brendan. 2009. "Indigenous Existentialism and the Body." *Cultic Studies Review* 15 (2): 101–118.

Hollenbach, David. 2002. *The Common Good and Christian Ethics*. Cambridge: Cambridge University Press. http://dx.doi.org/10.1017/CBO9780511606380.

Hollis, Shirley A. 2004. "Blaming Me, Blaming You: Assessing Service Learning and Participants' Tendency to Blame the Victim." *Sociological Spectrum* 24 (5): 575–600. http://dx.doi.org/10.1080/02732170490448829.

Holmes, Mary. 2007. *What Is Gender? Sociological Approaches*. London: Sage.

Hoppe, Sherry L. 2004. "A Synthesis of the Theoretical Stances." In *Service-Learning: History, Theory, and Issues*, ed. Bruce W. Speck and Sherry L. Hoppe, 137–149. Westport, CT: Praeger.

Houghton, Luke. 2009. "Generalization and Systemic Epistemology: Why Should It Make Sense?" *Systems Research and Behavioral Science* 26 (1): 99–108. http://dx.doi.org/10.1002/sres.929.

Hubbard, Tasha, dir. 2004. *Two Worlds Colliding*. Produced by the National Film Board.

Huemer, Michael, and Robert Audi. 2002. *Epistemology: Contemporary Readings*. London: Routledge.

Jacoby, Barbara. 1996. *Service Learning in Higher Education: Concepts and Practices*. San Francisco: Jossey-Bass.

Jaggar, Alison M., and Susan R. Bordo. 1992. *Gender/Body/Knowledge: Feminist Reconstructions of Being and Knowing*. New Brunswick, NJ: Rutgers University Press.

James, Royson. 2007. "Black Schools in Focus." *Toronto Star*, 18 Nov. http://www.thestar.com/news/gta/2007/11/18/black_schools_in_focus.html.

Jenkins, Laura. 2005. "Corporeal Ontology: Beyond Mind-Body Dualism?" *Politics* 25 (1): 1–11. http://dx.doi.org/10.1111/j.1467-9256.2005.00223.x.

Jiwani, Yasmin, and Mary Lynn Young. 2006. "Missing and Murdered Women: Reproducing Marginality in News Discourse." *Canadian Journal of Communications*, Special Issue on Sexuality, 895–917.

Johnston, Ron. 2000. "Authors, Editors and Authority in the Postmodern Academy." *Antipode* 32 (3): 271–291.

Jones, James M. 1997. *Prejudice and Racism*. New York: McGraw-Hill.

Kahn, Hilary E. 2011. "Overcoming the Challenges of International Service Learning: A Visual Approach to Sharing Authority, Community

Development, and Global Learning." In *International Service Learning: Conceptual Frameworks and Research*, ed. Robert G. Bringle, Julie A. Hatcher, and Steven G. Jones, 113–124. Sterling, VA: Stylus.

Kahane, David J., Daniel Weinstock, Dominique Leydet, and Melissa Williams, eds. 2010. *Deliberative Democracy in Practice*. Vancouver: UBC Press.

Kellner, Douglas. 2000. "Globalization and New Social Movements: Lessons for Critical Theory and Pedagogy." In *Globalization and Education: Critical Perspectives*, ed. Nicholas C. Burbules and Alberto Torres, 299–321. New York: Routledge.

Kelly-Gadol, Joan. 1987. "The Social Relation of the Sexes: Methodological Implications of Women's History." In *Feminism and Methodology*, ed. Sandra G. Harding, 15–28. Bloomington: Indiana University Press.

Kennerly, Rebecca M. 2011. *Service Learning, Intercultural Communication, and Advanced Video Praxis: Developing a Sustainable Program of Community Activism with/in a Mexican Migrant Community*. Paper presented at the annual meeting of the National Communication Association, New Orleans.

Kezar, Adrianna J. 2005. "Creating Dialogue: A New Charter and Vision of the Public Good." In *Higher Education for the Public Good: Emerging Voices from a National Movement*, ed. John Burkhardt and Adrianna J. Kezar, 317–325. San Francisco: Jossey-Bass.

Kezar, Adrianna J. 2008. "Universities in the Marketplace, and: Academic Capitalism, and: Remaking the American University: Market Smart and Mission Centered (review)." *Journal of Higher Education* 79 (4): 473–481.

Kezar, Adrianna, and Robert A. Rhoads. 2001. "The Dynamic Tensions of Service Learning in Higher Education: A Philosophical Perspective." *Journal of Higher Education* 72 (2): 148–171. http://dx.doi.org/10.2307/2649320.

Kezar, Anthony, C. Chambers, and John C. Burkhardt. 2005. *Higher Education for the Public Good: Emerging Voices from a National Movement*. San Francisco: Jossey-Bass.

Kimball, Bruce A. 1995. *Orators and Philosophers: A History of the Idea of Liberal Education*. New York: College Entrance Examination Board.

Kincheloe, Joe L. 2008. *Critical Pedagogy Primer*. New York: Peter Lang. http://dx.doi.org/10.1007/978-1-4020-8224-5.

Klugman, Jeni. 2011. *Human Development Reports: United Nations Development Programme*. New York: Palgrave Macmillan.

Koliba, Christopher, KerryAnn O'Meara, and Robert Seidel. 2000. "Social Justice Principles for Experiential Education." *National Society for Experiential Education Quarterly* 26 (1): 27–29.

Krebs, Andreas. 2011. "Reproducing Colonialism: Subject Formation and Talk Radio in English Canada." *Canadian Journal of Political Science* 44 (2): 317–339. http://dx.doi.org/10.1017/S0008423911000163.

Lander, Edgardo. 2009. "Eurocentrism, Modern Knowledges and the 'Natural' Order of Global Capital." *Kult* 6: 40–64.

Lappé, Frances Moore. 2005. *Democracy's Edge: Choosing to Save Our Country by Bringing Democracy to Life.* San Francisco: Jossey-Bass.

La Prairie, Carol. 2002. "Aboriginal Over-Representation in the Criminal Justice System: A Tale of Nine Cities." *Canadian Journal of Criminology* 44 (2): 181–208.

Lawrence, Bonita. 2008. "Colonialism, War, and Imperialism." Panel participant, Researchers and Academics of Colour for Equity Conference, Ryerson University, Toronto.

Lee, Damien. 2011. "Windigo Faces: Environmental Non-Governmental Organizations Serving Canadian Colonialism." *Canadian Journal of Native Studies* 31 (2): 133–153, 188.

Lewis, Tammy L. 2004. "Service Learning for Social Change: Lessons from a Liberal Arts College." *Teaching Sociology* 32 (1): 94–108. http://dx.doi.org/10 .1177/0092055X0403200109.

Ling, L.H.M. 2000. "Hegemonic Liberalism: Martha Nussbaum, Jörg Haider, and the Struggle for Late Modernity." Paper presented at the International Studies Association, 14–18 Mar. Accessed 15 Oct. 2012. http://www.geocities .co.jp/CollegeLife-Club/5676/Hegemonic-Liberalism.

Lips, Hilary M. 2013. "The Gender Pay Gap: Challenging the Rationalizations, Perceived Equity, Discrmination, and the Limits of Human Capital Models." *Sex Roles* 68 (3–4): 169–185. http://dx.doi.org/10.1007/s11199-012-0165-z.

Liu, Tessie. 1994. "Teaching the Differences among Women from a Historical Perspective: Rethinking Race and Gender as Social Categories." In *Unequal Sisters: A Multicultural Reader in U.S. Women's History*, ed. Vicki L. Ruiz and Ellen Carol Dubois, 571–583. New York: Routledge.

London, Scott. 2003. *Higher Education for the Public Good: A Report from the National Leadership Dialogues.* Ann Arbor, MI: National Forum on Higher Education for the Public Good.

Lorde, Audre. 1984. *Sister Outsider: Essays and Speeches.* Berkeley: Crossing Press.

Loutzenheiser, Lisa W., and Lori B. MacIntosh. 2004. "Sexualities, Citizenships and Education." *Theory into Practice* 43 (2): 151–159. http://dx.doi. org/10.1207/s15430421tip4302_9.

Lund, Darren E., and Paul R. Carr. 2008a. "Antiracist Education." In *Encyclopedia of the Social and Cultural Foundations of Education*, ed. Eugene F. Provenzo, Jr, 48–52. Thousand Oaks, CA: Sage.

Lund, Darren E., and Paul R. Carr. 2008b. "Scanning Democracy." Introduction in *Doing Democracy: Striving for Political Literacy and Social Justice*, ed. Darren E. Lund and Paul R. Carr, 1–29. New York: Peter Lang.

Lynd, Robert S. 1939. *Knowledge for What? The Place of Social Science in American Culture.* New York: Grove.

Macdonald, Gaynor. 2008. "Difference or Disappearance: The Politics of Indigenous Inclusion in the Liberal State." *Anthropologica* 50: 341–358.

Macedo, Donaldo. 1998. "Foreword." In *Pedagogy of Freedom: Ethics, Democracy, and Civic Courage*, by Paulo Freire, xi–xxxii. Lanham, MD: Rowman & Littlefield.

Macgillivray, Ian K., and Todd Jennings. 2008. "A Content Analysis Exploring Lesbian, Gay, Bisexual, and Transgender Topics in Foundations of Education Textbooks." *Journal of Teacher Education* 59 (2): 170–188. http://dx.doi.org/10.1177/0022487107313160.

Mack, Johnny. 2010. "Hoquotist: Reorienting through Storied Practice." In *Storied Communities: Narratives of Contact and Arrival in Constituting Political Community*, ed. Jeremy H.A. Webber, Hester Lessard, and Rebecca Johnson, 287–307. Vancouver: UBC Press.

Mackey, Eva. 2002. *The House of Difference: Cultural Politics and National Identity in Canada*. Toronto: University of Toronto Press.

Magnusson, Jamie. 2000. "Examining Higher Education and Citizenship in a Global Context of Neoliberal Restructuring." *Canadian Ethnic Studies* 32: 72–88.

Maracle, Lee. 2005. "Some Words on Study as a Process of Discovery." Presentation given at TransCanada: Literature, Institutions, Vancouver.

Marketwired, "Premium Petroleum Corp. Increases Lands Position to 11,520 Acres." Accessed 1 May 2014. http://www.marketwired.com/press-release/Premium-Petroleum-Corp-Increases-Lands-Position-to-11520-Acres-PINK-SHEETS-PPTL-771517.htm.

Martínez Alemán, Ana M., and Katya Salkever. 2001. "Multiculturalism and the Mission of Liberal Education." *Journal of General Education* 50 (2): 102–139. http://dx.doi.org/10.1353/jge.2001.0013.

Marullo, Sam, and Bob Edwards. 2000. "From Charity to Justice: The Potential of University-Community Collaboration for Social Change." *American Behavioral Scientist* 43 (5): 895–912. http://dx.doi.org/10.1177/00027640021955540.

Massey, Doreen. 2012. "The Political Struggle Ahead." In "The Neoliberal Crisis," ed. Jonathan Rutherford and Sally Davison, *Soundings: A Journal of Politics and Culture*, 70–82.

Matsuda, Mari J., Charles R. Lawrence, III, Richard Delgado, and Kimberlè Williams Crenshaw. 1993. "Introduction." In *Words that Wound: Critical Race Theory, Assaultive Speech, and the First Amendment*, ed. Mari J. Matsuda, Charles R. Lawrence, III, Richard Delgado, and Kimberlè Williams Crenshaw, 1–15. Boulder, CO: Westview.

Mbembe, Achille. 2001. *On the Postcolony*. Berkeley: University of California Press.

McClay, Wilfred M. 1998. "Communitarianism and the Federal Idea." In *Community and Political Thought Today*, ed. Peter Augustine Lawle and Dale D. McConkey, 101–107. Westport, CT: Praeger.

McDowell, Linda. 1994. "Polyphony and Pedagogic Authority." *Area* 26: 221–248.

Meshulam, Meir, Eyal Winter, Gershon Ben-Shakhar, and Itzhak Aharon. 2012. "Rational Emotions." *Social Neuroscience* 7 (1): 11–17. http://dx.doi.org/10.1080/17470919.2011.559124.

Mignolo, Walter D. 2009. "Epistemic Disobedience, Independent Thought and De-Colonial Freedom." *Theory, Culture & Society* 26 (7–8): 159–181.

Miller, Peter, and Nikolas Rose. 2008. *Governing the Present: Administering Economic, Social and Personal Life*. Cambridge, MA: Polity.

Mills, C. Wright. 1959. *The Sociological Imagination*. London: Oxford University Press.

Minnich, Elizabeth Kamarck. 1997. "The American Tradition of Aspirational Democracy." In *Education and Democracy: Re-imagining Liberal Learning in America*, ed. Robert Orrill, 175–205. New York: College Entrance Examination Board.

Minow, Martha. 2002. *Partners Not Rivals: Privatization and the Public Good*. Boston: Beacon.

Mohamedou, Mohammad-Mahmoud. 2000. *The Persistence and Mutation of Racism*. Versoix: International Council on Human Rights Policy.

Mohanty, Chandra Talpade. 2003. *Feminism without Borders: Decolonizing Theory, Practicing Solidarity*. Durham, NC: Duke University Press. http://dx.doi.org/10.1215/9780822384649.

Monsebraaten, Laurie. 2013. "Ontario's Gender Pay Gap Inspires Call for Equal Pay Day." *Toronto Star*, 18 Apr.

Moore, James, Ryan Walker, and Ian Skelton. 2011. "Challenging the New Canadian Myth: Colonialism, Post-Colonialism, and Urban Aboriginal Policy in Thompson and Brandon, Manitoba." *Canadian Journal of Native Studies* 31 (1): 17–42.

Morrow, Raymond A. 2006. "Foreword." In *The University, State, and Market: The Political Economy of Globalization in the Americas*, ed. Robert Rhoads and Carlos Torres, xvii–xxxiii. Stanford, CA: Stanford University Press.

Morton, Keith, and John Saltmarsh. 1997. "Addams, Day, and Dewey: The Emergence of Community Service in American Culture." *Michigan Journal of Community Service Learning* 4 (1): 137–149.

Moya, Paula M.L. 2002. *Learning from Experience: Minority Identities, Multicultural Struggles*. Berkeley: University of California Press.

Murakawa, Naomi, and Katherine Beckett. 2010. "The Penology of Racial Innocence: The Erasure of Racism in the Study and Practice of Punishment."

Law & Society Review 44 (3–4): 695–730. http://dx.doi.org/10.1111/j.1540 -5893.2010.00420.x.

Murphy, Christina. 2004. "A Critique of the Communitarian Model." In *Service Learning: History, Theory, and Issues,* ed. Bruce W. Speck and Sherry L. Hoppe, 119–135. Westport, CT: Praeger.

Nabatdni, Tina, and John Gastil, G. Michael Weiksner, and Matt Leighninger. (Eds.). 2012. *Democracy in Motion: Evaluating the Practice and Impact of Deliberative Civic Engagement.* Oxford: Oxford University Press.

National Commission on Civic Renewal. 1997. *A Nation of Spectators: How Civic Disengagement Weakens America and What We Can Do about It.* College Park, MD: Author.

National Task Force on Civic Learning and Democratic Engagement. 2012. *A Crucible Moment: College Learning and Democracy's Future.* Washington, DC: Association of American Colleges and Universities.

Nealon, Jeffrey, and Susan Searls Giroux. 2012. *The Theory Toolbox: Critical Concepts for the Humanities, Arts, and Social Sciences.* Lanham, MD: Rowman & Littlefield.

Newman, David M. 2008. *Sociology: Exploring the Architecture of Everyday Life.* Los Angeles: Pine Forge Press.

Newman, Frank. 1985. *Higher Education and the American Resurgence: A Carnegie Foundation Special Report.* Princeton, NJ: Princeton University Press.

Newman, Frank, and Lara K. Couturier. 2002. *Trading Public Good in the Higher Education Market.* London: Observatory on Borderless Higher Education.

Newman, John Henry. 1888. *The Idea of a University.* London: Green, & Co.

Nixon, Jon. 2011. *Higher Education and the Public Good: Imagining the University.* New York: Continuum.

Nussbaum, Martha C. 1997. *Cultivating Humanity: A Classical Defense of Reform in Liberal Education.* Cambridge, MA: Harvard University Press.

Nussbaum, Martha C. 2010. *Not for Profit: Why Democracy Needs the Humanities.* Princeton, NJ: Princeton University Press.

Owusu-Bempah, Akwasi. 2013. "Why We Should Worry about Who's Going to Jail: Blacks and Aboriginals Are Overrepresented in the Ontario Correctional System – and It Matters." *Toronto Star,* 2 Mar.

Pagano, Jo Anne. 1999. "Critical Education and the Liberal Arts." In *Critical Theories in Education: Changing Terrains of Knowledge and Politics,* ed. Thomas Popkewitz and Lynn Fendler, 229–247. New York: Routledge.

Parenti, Michael. 2008. *Democracy for the Few.* Boston: Thomson-Wadsworth.

Pascarella, Ernest T., and Patrick T. Terenzini. 2005. *How College Affects Students: A Third Decade of Research,* vol. 2. San Francisco: Jossey-Bass.

Pastor, Michael J. 2002. "A Tragedy and a Crime? Amadou Diallo, Specific Intent, and the Federal Prosecution of Civil Rights Violations." *Legislation and Public Policy* 6: 171–205.

Pedwell, Terry. 2013. "Canada Is Failing Aboriginal Peoples Who Wind Up Behind Bars, Report Says." *Canadian Press*, 7 Mar.

Peters, Scott J. 2004. "Educating the Civic Professional: Reconfigurations and Resistances." *Michigan Journal of Community Service Learning* 11 (1): 47–58.

Piper, Martha C. 2003. "Building a Civil Society: A New Role for the Human Sciences." *Canadian Journal of Higher Education* 33: 113–130.

Pocklington, Thomas C, and Allan Tupper. 2002. *No Place to Learn: Why Universities Aren't Working*. Vancouver: UBC Press.

Polster, Claire. 2002. "A Break from the Past: Impacts and Implications of the Canada Foundation for Innovation and the Canada Research Chairs Initiatives." *Canadian Review of Sociology and Anthropology/ La Revue canadienne de sociologie et d'anthropologie* 39 (3): 275–299.

Polster, Claire. 2004. "Canadian University Research Policy at the Turn of the Century: Continuity and Change in the Social Relations of Academic Research." *Studies in Political Economy* 71/72: 177–199.

Polster, Claire. 2006. "Alternatives to Private Ownership." Paper prepared for Canadian Association of University Teachers conference" Controlling Intellectual Property – The Academic Community and the Future of Knowledge," Ottawa.

Polster, Claire. 2007. "The Nature and Implications of the Growing Importance of Research Grants to Canadian Universities and Academics." *Higher Education* 53 (5): 599–622. http://dx.doi.org/10.1007/s10734-005-1118-z.

Preece, Julia. 2001. "Challenging the Discourses of Inclusion and Exclusion with Off Limits Curricula." *Studies in the Education of Adults* 33 (2): 201–216.

Ray, Sangeeta. 2003. "Against Earnestness: The Place of Performance in Feminist Theory." *Studies in Practical Philosophy* 3 (1): 68–79. http://dx.doi .org/10.5840/studpracphil2003314.

Razack, Sherene. 1998. *Looking White People in the Eye: Gender, Race, and Culture in Courtrooms and Classrooms*. Toronto: University of Toronto Press.

Razack, Sherene. 2008. Opening plenary, "Theorizing Race," at conference "Theorizing Anti-Racism: Critical Race and Anticolonial Studies," Toronto, 14 Nov.

Razack, Sherene, Malinda Sharon Smith, and Sunera Thobani. 2010. *States of Race: Critical Race Feminism for the 21st Century*. Toronto: Between the Lines.

Readings, Bill. 1997. *The University in Ruins*. Cambridge, MA: Harvard University Press.

Rhoads, Robert A., and Carlos Alberto Torres. 2006. *The University, State, and Market: The Political Economy of Globalization in the Americas*. Palo Alto, CA: Stanford University Press.

Rice, Nancy. 2005. "Guardians of Tradition: Presentations of Inclusion in Three Introductory Special Education Textbooks." *International Journal of Inclusive Education* 9 (4): 405–429. http://dx.doi.org/10.1080/13603110500147179.

Rice, R. Eugene. 2005. "'Scholarship Reconsidered': History and Context." In *Faculty Priorities Reconsidered: Rewarding Multiple Forms of Scholarship*, ed. KerryAnn O'Meara and R. Eugene Rice, 17–31. San Francisco: Jossey-Bass.

Richardson, D. (2005). "Desiring Sameness? The Rise of a Neoliberal Politics of Normalisation." *Antipode* 37: 515–535.

Richardson, Troy, and Sofia Villenas. 2000. "'Other' Encounters: Dances with Whiteness in Multicultural Education." *Educational Theory* 50 (2): 255–273. http://dx.doi.org/10.1111/j.1741-5446.2000.00255.x.

Roberts, J. Timmons, & Bradley C. Parks. 2007. *A Climate of Injustice: Global Inequality, North-South Politics, and Climate Policy.* Cambridge, MA: MIT Press.

Rocheleau, Jordy. 2004. "Theoretical Roots of Service-Learning: Progressive Education and the Development of Citizenship." In *Service-Learning: History, Theory, and Issues*, ed. Bruce W. Speck and Sherry Lee Hoppe, 3–21. Westport, CT: Praeger.

Rocque, Michael, and Raymond Paternoster. 2011. "Understanding the Antecedents of the 'School-to-Jail' Link: The Relationship between Race and School Discipline." *Journal of Criminal Law & Criminology* 101: 633–665.

Rooke, C. 2003. "The Engagement of Self and Other: Liberal Education and Its Contributions to the Public Good." In *The Idea of Engagement: Universities in Society*, ed. Svana Bjarnason and Patrick Coldstream, 228–250. London: Association of Commonwealth Universities.

Roth, Wolff-Michael. 2001. "'Enculturation': Acquisition of Conceptual Blind Spots and Epistemological Prejudices." *British Educational Research Journal* 27 (1): 5–27.

Rothblatt, Sheldon. 1993. "The Limbs of Osiris: Liberal Education in the English-Speaking World." In *The European and American University since 1800: Historical and Sociological Essays*, ed. Sheldon Rothblatt and Bjorn Wittrock, 19–73. Cambridge: Cambridge University Press. http://dx.doi.org/10.1017/CBO9780511720925.002.

Rowe, Aimee Carrillo. 2008. *Power Lines: On the Subject of Feminist Alliances.* Durham, NC: Duke University Press. http://dx.doi.org/10.1215/9780822389200.

Ruitenberg, Claudia W. 2009. "Educating Political Adversaries: Chantal Mouffe and Radical Democratic Citizenship Education." *Studies in Philosophy and Education* 28 (3): 269–281. http://dx.doi.org/10.1007/s11217-008-9122-2.

Saddington, Tony. 2000. "The Roots and Branches of Experiential Learning." *NSEE Quarterly* 3 (3): 2–6.

Said, Edward W. 1979. *Orientalism*. New York: Vintage.

Saltmarsh, John. 1996. "Education for Critical Citizenship: John Dewey's Contribution to the Pedagogy of Community Service Learning." *Michigan Journal of Community Service Learning* 3 (1): 13–21.

Saltmarsh, John. 2011a. "Engagement and Epistemology." In *Higher Education and Democracy: Essays on Service-Learning and Civic Engagement*, ed. John Saltmarsh and Edward Zlotkowski, 342–353. Philadelphia, PA: Temple University Press.

Saltmarsh, John. 2011b. "The Civic Promise of Service-learning." In *Higher Education and Democracy: Essays on Service-Learning and Civic Engagement*, ed. John Saltmarsh and Edward Zlotkowski, 28–34. Philadelphia, PA: Temple University Press.

Saltmarsh, John, and Matthew Hartley. 2011a. "Introduction: To Serve a Larger Purpose." In *"To Serve a Larger Purpose": Engagement for Democracy and the Transformation of Higher Education*, ed. John Saltmarsh and Matthew Hartley, 1–13. Philadelphia, PA: Temple University Press.

Saltmarsh, John, and Matthew Hartley. 2011b. "Democratic Engagement." In *"To Serve a Larger Purpose": Engagement for Democracy and the Transformation of Higher Education*, ed. John Saltmarsh and Matthew Hartley, 14–26. Philadelphia, PA: Temple University Press.

Saltmarsh, John, Matthew Hartley, and Patti Clayton. 2009. *Democratic Engagement White Paper*. Boston: New England Resource Center for Higher Education.

Saltmarsh, John, and Edward Zlotkowski. 2011a. "Introduction: Putting into Practice the Civic Purposes of Higher Education." In *Higher Education and Democracy: Essays on Service-Learning and Civic Engagement*, ed. John Saltmarsh and Edward Zlotkowski, 1–8. Philadelphia, PA: Temple University Press.

Saltmarsh, John, and Edward Zlotkowski. 2011b. "Conclusion: Looking Back, Looking Ahead: A Dialogue." In *Higher Education and Democracy: Essays on Service-Learning and Civic Engagement*, ed. John Saltmarsh and Edward Zlotkowski, 354–365. Philadelphia, PA: Temple University Press.

Saltmarsh, John, and Edward Zlotkowski (with Elizabeth Hollander). 2011c. "Indicators of Engagement." In *Higher Education and Democracy: Essays on Service-Learning and Civic Engagement*, ed. John Saltmarsh and Edward Zlotkowski, 285–302. Philadelphia, PA: Temple University Press.

Sandel, Michael J. 2008. *Liberalism and the Limits of Justice*. Cambridge: Cambridge University Press.

Sandmann, Lorilee R. 2008. "Conceptualization of the Scholarship of Engagement in Higher Education: A Strategic Review, 1996–2006." *Journal of Higher Education Outreach and Engagement* 12 (1): 91–104.

Schneider, Carol Geary. 2000. "Educational Missions and Civic Responsibility: Toward the Engaged Academy." In *Civic Responsibility and Higher Education*, ed. Thomas Ehrlich, 98–123. Phoenix, AZ: Oryx Press.

Schön, Donald A. 1995. "The New Scholarship Requires a New Epistemology." *Change* 27 (6): 26–34.

Schugurensky, Daniel. 2006. "The Political Economy of Higher Education in the Time of Global Markets: Whither the Social Responsibility of the University?" In *The University, State, and Market: The Political Economy of Globalization in the Americas*, ed. Robert A. Rhoads and Carlos Alberto Torres, 301–320. Palo Alto, CA: Stanford University Press.

Schwartz-Shea, Peregrine, and Dvora Yanow. 2002. "'Reading' 'Methods' 'Texts': How Research Methods Texts Construct Political Science." *Political Research Quarterly* 55 (2): 457–486.

Scott, David. 2010. *Education, Epistemology and Critical Realism*. London: Routledge.

Seddon, Terri. 2011. "Remaking Civic Formation: Transforming Politics and the Cosmopolitan School." In *Transforming Learning in Schools and Communities: The Remaking of Education for a Cosmopolitan Society*, ed. Jon Nixon, Stewart Ranson, and Bob Lingard, 152–169. London: Continuum.

Sedgwick, Eve Kosofsky. 1990. *Epistemology of the Closet*. Berkeley: University of California Press.

Shaikh, Nermeen. 2007. "Interrogating Charity and the Benevolence of Empire." *Development* 50 (2): 83–89. http://dx.doi.org/10.1057/palgrave.development.1100364.

Shapiro, Harold T. 2005. *A Larger Sense of Purpose: Higher Education and Society*. Princeton, NJ: Princeton University Press.

Sherif, Carolyn Wood. 1987. "Bias in Psychology." In *Feminism and Methodology*, ed. Sandra Harding, 37–56. Bloomington, Indiana: Indiana University Press.

Shiva, Vandana. 1993. *Monocultures of the Mind: Perspectives on Biodiversity and Biotechnology*. London: Zed Books.

Simoni, Jane M. 1996. "Confronting Heterosexism in the Teaching of Psychology." *Teaching of Psychology* 23 (4): 220–226. http://dx.doi.org/10.1207/s15328023top2304_3.

Simpson, Jennifer S. 2003. *I Have Been Waiting: Race and U.S. Higher Education*. Toronto: University of Toronto Press.

Simpson, Jennifer S. 2007. "'Can't We Focus on the Good Stuff?' The Pedagogical Distance between Comfort and Critique." In *Whiteness, Pedagogy, Performance: Dis/placing Race*, ed. Leda M. Cooks and Jennifer S. Simpson, 247–269. Lanham, MD: Lexington Books.

Simpson, Jennifer S. 2008. "'What Do They Think of Us?' The Pedagogical Practices of Cross-Cultural Communication, Misrecognition, and Hope." *Journal of International and Intercultural Communication* 1 (3): 181–201. http://dx.doi.org/10.1080/17513050802101807.

Simpson, Jennifer S. 2010a. "Critical Race Theory and Critical Communication Pedagogy." In *SAGE Handbook of Communication and Instruction*, ed. Deanna L. Fassett and John T. Warren, 361–384. Thousand Oaks, CA: Sage.

Simpson, Jennifer S. 2010b. "'I'm More Afraid of the Four of You than I Am of the Terrorists': Agency, Dissent, and the Challenges of Democratic Hope." *Review of Education, Pedagogy & Cultural Studies* 32 (2): 177–205. http://dx.doi.org/10.1080/10714411003799082.

Simpson, Jennifer S. 2011."Response to Kennerly and to Walker and Hart." Paper presented at the annual meeting of the National Communication Association, New Orleans.

Simpson, Jennifer S. 2014. "Communication Activism Pedagogy: Theoretical Frameworks, Central Concepts, and Challenges." In *Teaching Communication Activism: Communication Pedagogy for Social Justice*, ed. Lawrence R. Frey and David L. Palmer, 77–103. New York: Hampton Press.

Singh, Mala. 2003. "Universities and Society: Whose Terms of Engagement?" In *The Idea of Engagement: Universities in Society*, ed. Svana Bjarnason and Patrick Coldstream, 58–78. London: Association of Commonwealth Universities.

Slaughter, Sheila, and Gary Rhoades. 2004. *Academic Capitalism and the New Economy: Markets, State, and Higher Education*. Baltimore: Johns Hopkins University Press.

Smith, Andrea. 2006. "Heteropatriarchy and the Three Pillars of White Supremacy." In *Color of Violence: The INCITE! Anthology*, ed. Andrea Smith, Beth E. Richie, and Julia Sudbury, 66–73. Boston: South End Press.

Smith, Dorothy E. 1987. "Women's Perspective as a Radical Critique of Sociology." In *Feminism and Methodology*, ed. Sandra Harding, 84–96. Bloomington, Indiana: Indiana University Press.

Smith, Linda Tuhiwai. 2001. *Decolonizing Methodologies: Research and Indigenous Peoples*. London: Zed Books.

Smith, Michael B., Rebecca S. Nowacek, and Jeffrey L. Bernstein. 2010. "Introduction: Ending the Solitude of Citizenship Education." In *Citizenship across the Curriculum*, ed. Michael B. Smith, Rebecca S. Nowacek, and Jeffrey L. Bernstein, 1–12. Bloomington: Indiana University Press.

Sossin, Lorne. 2004. "Public Universities and the Public Interest: Toward a Vision of Governmental Oversight." Paper presented at the Public Universities Seriously Conference, Toronto.

Speck, Bruce W., and Sherry Lee Hoppe. 2004. *Service-Learning: History, Theory, and Issues*. Westport, CT: Praeger.

St Denis, Verna. 2011. "Silencing Aboriginal Curricular Content and Perspectives through Multiculturalism: "There Are Other Children Here."" *Review of Education, Pedagogy & Cultural Studies* 33 (4): 306–317. http://dx.doi.org/10.1080/10714413.2011.597638.

Stanley, Liz, and Sue Wise. 1993. *Breaking Out Again: Feminist Ontology and Epistemology*. New York: Routledg.

Staples, Robert. 2011. "White Power, Black Crime, and Racial Politics." *Black Scholar* 41 (4): 31–41.

Storper, Michael. 2000. "Lived Effects of the Contemporary Economy: Globalization, Inequality, and Consumer Society." *Public Culture* 12 (2): 375–409. http://dx.doi.org/10.1215/08992363-12-2-375.

Strydom, Piet. 2011. *Contemporary Critical Theory and Methodology*. London: Routledge.

Suarez, Alicia E., and Alexandra Balaji. 2007. "Coverage and Representations of Sexuality in Introductory Sociology Textbooks." *Teaching Sociology* 35 (3): 239–254. http://dx.doi.org/10.1177/0092055X0703500303.

Sullivan, Nikki. 2003. *A Critical Introduction to Queer Theory*. New York: New York University Press.

Sutton, Susan Buck. 2011. "Service Learning as Local Learning: The Importance of Context." In *International Service Learning: Conceptual Frameworks and Research*, ed. Robert G. Bringle, Julie A. Hatcher, and Steven G. Jones, 125–144. Sterling, VA: Stylus.

Tatum, Beverly Daniel. 2000. "The Complexity of Identity: 'Who Am I?'" In *Readings for Diversity and Social Justice: An Anthology on Racism, Anti-Semitism, Sexism, Heterosexism, Ableism, and Classism*, ed. Maurieanne Adams, Warren J. Blumenfeld, Rosie Castañeda, Heather W. Hackman, Madeline L. Peters, and Ximena Zúñiga, 9–14. New York: Routledge.

Thobani, Sunera. 2007. *Exalted Subjects: Studies in the Making of Race and Nation in Canada*. Toronto: University of Toronto Press.

Thomas, Nancy. 2005. "Educating for Conscience and Community." In *Higher Education for the Public Good: A Report from the National Leadership Dialogues*. Ann Arbor, MI: National Forum on Higher Education for the Public Good.

Thomas, Nancy L., ed. 2010. *Educating for Deliberative Democracy*. San Francisco: Jossey-Bass.

Thompson, John B. 1990. *Ideology and Modern Culture*. Palo Alto, CA: Stanford University Press.

Torres, Carlos Alberto, and Robert A. Rhoads. 2006. "Introduction: Globalization and Higher Education in the Americas." In *The University, State, and Market: The Political Economy of Globalization in the Americas*, ed.

Robert A. Rhoads and Carlos Alberto Torres, 3–38. Stanford, CA: Stanford University Press.

Tudiver, Neil. 1999. *Universities for Sale: Resisting Corporate Control over Canadian Higher Education*. Toronto: Lorimer.

Tully, James. 2002. "Political Philosophy as a Critical Activity." *Political Theory* 30 (4): 533–555. http://dx.doi.org/10.1177/0090591702304005.

Turk, James. 2000. "What Commercialization Means for Education." In *The Corporate Campus: Commercialization and the Dangers to Canada's Universities and Colleges*, ed. James Turk, 3–13. Toronto: Lorimer.

Turk, James. 2008. *Universities at Risk: How Politics, Special Interests and Corporatization Threaten Academic Integrity*. Toronto: Lorimer.

University of Louisville, Department of Communication. 2012. Accessed 5 Mar. 2012. http://comm.louisville.edu/department/index.php.

University of Waterloo. 2012."Cooperative Education." Accessed 29 Feb. 2012. http://coop.uwaterloo.ca/about/.

University of Waterloo. n.d. "The University Plan," Accessed 4 Sept. 2012. https://uwaterloo.ca/secretariat/university-plan

University of Waterloo. n.d. "Informing the University Plan." Accessed 4 Sept. 2012. https://uwaterloo.ca/secretariat/informing-university.

Varlotta, Lori E. 1997. "Confronting Consensus: Investigating the Philosophies that Have Informed Service-Learning's Communities." *Educational Theory* 47 (4): 453–476. http://dx.doi.org/10.1111/j.1741-5446.1997.00453.x.

Vasey, Dave. 2011. *Opposing "Fortress North America": Tar Sands Development and Indigenous Resistance*. Accessed 10 Aug. 2012. http://newsocialist.org/index.php?option=com_content&view=article&id=513:opposing%1efortres s%1enorth%1eamerica%1etar%1esands%1edevelopment%1eand%1eindige nous%1eresistance&catid=51:analysis&Itemid=98.

Von Mises, Ludwig. 1983. *Nation State and Economy*. New York: New York University Press.

Wachholz, Sandra, and Bob Mullaly. 2001. "The Politics of the Textbook: A Content Analysis of the Coverage and Treatment of Feminist, Radical and Anti-Racist Social Work Scholarship in American Introductory Social Work Textbooks Published between 1988 and 1997." *Journal of Progressive Human Services* 11 (2): 51–76. http://dx.doi.org/10.1300/J059v11n02_04.

Walker, Kandi L., and Joy L. Hart. 2011. *Communication Activism and International Service Learning: A Focus on Health and Well-Being*. Paper presented at the annual meeting of the National Communication Association, New Orleans.

Walzer, Michael. 2006. "Moral Education, Democratic Citizenship." In *To Restore American Democracy*, ed. Robert E. Calvert, 217–230. New York: Rowman & Littlefield.

Wang, Yan, and Golden Jackson. 2005. "Forms and Dimensions of Civic
    Involvement." *Michigan Journal of Community Service Learning* 11 (2): 39–48.
Waters, Johanna, and Rachel Brooks. 2010. "Accidental Achievers?
    International Higher Education, Class Reproduction and Privilege in
    the Experiences of UK Students Overseas." *British Journal of Sociology of
    Education* 31 (2): 217–228. http://dx.doi.org/10.1080/01425690903539164.
Watson, Jack Borden, Jr. 2004. "A Justification of the Civic Engagement
    Model." In *Service-Learning: History, Theory, and Issues*, ed. Bruce W. Speck
    and Sherry Hoppe, 73–83. Westport, CT: Praeger.
Weiten, Wayne, and Doug McCann. 2007. *Psychology: Themes and Variations*.
    Toronto: Thomson Nelson.
West, Cornel. 2001. *From Anna Deveare Smith's film* Twilight. Los Angeles: PBS
    Home Video.
Westheimer, Joel, and Joseph Kahne. 2004. "What Kind of Citizen? The Politics
    of Educating for Democracy." *American Educational Research Journal* 41 (2):
    237–269. http://dx.doi.org/10.3102/00028312041002237.
Wood, Julia T. 1993. "Expanding Conceptual Boundaries: A Critique of
    Research in Interpersonal Communication." In *Transforming Visions: Feminist
    Critiques in Communication Studies*, ed. Sheryl Perlmutter Bowen and Nancy
    Wyatt, 19–49. Cresskill, NJ: Hampton.
Woodhouse, Howard. 2001. "The Market Model of Education and the Threat
    to Canadian Universities." *Encounters on Education* 2: 105–122.
Woodhouse, Howard. 2009. *Selling Out: Academic Freedom and the Corporate
    Market*. Montreal and Kingston: McGill-Queen's University Press.
Young, Allison J., and Michael J. Middleton. 2002. "The Gay Ghetto in the
    Geography of Education." In *Getting Ready for Benjamin: Preparing Teachers
    for Sexual Diversity in the Classroom*, ed. Rita M. Kissen, 91–102. Lanham,
    MD: Rowman & Littlefield.
Young, Iris Marion. 1990. *Justice and the Politics of Difference*. Princeton, NJ:
    Princeton University Press.
Young, Iris Marion. 2000. *Inclusion and Democracy*. Oxford: Oxford University
    Press.
Young, Iris Marion. 2006. "Responsibility and Global Justice: A Social
    Connection Model." *Social Philosophy and Policy* 23 (1): 102–130.
Young, Iris Marion. 2011. *Responsibility for Justice*. Oxford: Oxford University
    Press. http://dx.doi.org/10.1093/acprof:oso/9780195392388.001.0001.
Zamudio, Margaret, Christopher Russell, Francisco Rios, and Jacquelyn L.
    Bridgeman. 2010. *Critical Race Theory Matters: Education and Ideology*. New
    York: Routledge.

Index

administration, university, 136–39, 145
agency, 18, 34–35, 116–17, 210–11,
  218; and democratic practices,
  122, 150; and neoliberalism,
  188–89, 191, 192; and relationship
  to structures, 116–17, 209; faculty
  members', 38, 45, 108–11, 114,
  222–23; students', 45, 63, 108–11,
  163, 205, 210–11, 218, 229
agenda: and civic engagement,
  84–85, 90; and democratic
  societies, 21, 30, 122; in
  educational contexts, 21, 62, 113,
  218; and faculty members, 9, 58,
  63, 89; inevitability of, 88–91
American Association of Colleges
  and Universities, 136–38
autoethnography, 34–35

Black schools, 25–26, 40
Bok, Derek, 140, 144–50, 154, 159,
  235n1

capitalism, 35, 49, 56, 62, 95, 97
charity, 40, 97–99, 103–104, 105, 143
civic engagement, and academic
  neutrality, 86; components of,

77, 83–84, 86; critique of, 84–96;
  definition, 77, 82; frameworks
  for, 70–71, 77; and higher
  education, 68–71, 84–86; history
  of, 83–84; and justice, 88; political
  dimensions, 86, 88, 90, 92; and
  relationship to service learning,
  71. *See also* scholarship of
  engagement; service learning
colonialism, 29–30, 93; in Canada,
  42–43, 225; visibility of, 43
compassion, 75–76, 142–44, 146
competing interests: and higher
  education, 46–47, 52, 53, 57, 145,
  152; and democratic practices,
  61, 93, 111, 125, 170; and the
  scholarship of engagement, 80; and
  service learning, 73, 92, 100, 104
concepts, 193–95; and connection
  with material practices, 113, 123,
  199, 208, 209, 218; and distancing
  from material practices, 8,
  13–14, 16, 71, 93, 111, 129, 146,
  151, 192, 209; and epistemology,
  169–70, 177, 181, 183–84, 193–96;
  and intellectual frameworks,
  9, 54, 71, 114, 124–25, 225; and

and neoliberalism, 189; and
responsibilities of universities,
46–50, 53–54, 145, 207–10; and
scholarship of engagement, 70, 77;
and social contract, 53, 145
social norms: and agency, 116;
and gender and sexuality, 4, 13,
162–63, 167–69, 184, 192; and
civic engagement scholarship, 85;
higher education's engagement
with, 7, 48, 90, 110–11, 208, 227;
and logics of inclusion, 94–95; and
neoliberalism, 37, 190, 192; and
oppression, 118, 158; and pivoting
the centre, 212–13; and textbooks,
179–80, 181, 182
streamlined education, 5–6,
12–13, 166, 170; challenges to,
15; components of, 16; and
dehumanization, 18–19, 134, 200;
and desire for simplification,
13, 18; and epistemology, 16–17,
20, 156, 166, 195; and logic
of inclusion, 30, 93–94; and
neoliberalism, 186, 191, 195;
resistance to, 15–16, 197–98,
207–30; and sexuality, 47; and
the subject, 47, 65, 134, 170, 195;
support for, 37, 129–30, 167,
175, 182
students: agency, broad levels, 135,
205, 210–11; agency, pedagogical,
105–106, 149–150, 218; and
democratic practices, 90–91,
93, 100, 104–105; and ends of
undergraduate education, 7, 50,
53–54, 57, 59–64, 140–41; and
expectations for learning, 12,
17, 19, 110–11, 162–63, 167–71;
and justice, 132–35, 197–200,

223–30; and knowledge, uses of,
7, 11, 45, 106, 213–14; and liberal
educational norms, 11, 127–31,
147–51; location, 105–106, 210–11;
and neoliberalism, 188, 191–92,
193; and service learning, 70–71,
100–101; and understandings of
gender and sexuality, 3–6, 13
subject, the: components of, 18,
219–23; and course content,
17, 115, 123, 129–30, 175; and
critical theory, 61, 63, 124–25;
and dichotomies, 152–53,
156–57; and empathy, 143–44;
and epistemology, 133, 155, 164,
171–73; and faculty members'
constructions of, 81, 139, 168,
171, 198–99, 219–30; and higher
education's social contract, 18,
63, 160–61; and material practice,
112–13, 123, 154, 158, 219–30; and
neoliberalism, 187–88, 190, 192–95;
and ontology, 18; and pedagogical
practices, 219–20, 223–30; and
public life, 123; and social contract,
48; and textbooks, 179–86

tar sands, 43–44, 209
textbooks, 176–86; and democratic
practices, 182; and disciplinary
norms, 178–79; and ideology, 178;
as interested, 178; and knowledge
representation, 177, 178, 181–82,
183–84; as sites of knowing, 167,
179–82; and social norms, 179–80;
and streamlined education, 182
tolerance: and inclusion, 130; and
liberal educational norms, 127,
130, 142, 144, 146; and service
learning, 103–104